Informatik — Fachberichte

Band 189: B. Wolfinger (Hrsg.), Vernetzte und komplexe Informatik-Systeme. Industrieprogramm zur 18. Jahrestagung der GI, Hamburg, Oktober 1988. Proceedings. X, 229 Seiten. 1988.

Band 190: D. Maurer, Relevanzanalyse. VIII, 239 Seiten. 1988.

Band 191: P. Levi, Planen für autonome Montageroboter. XIII, 259 Seiten. 1988.

Band 192: K. Kansy, P. Wißkirchen (Hrsg.), Graphik im Bürobereich. Proceedings, 1988. VIII, 187 Seiten. 1988.

Band 193: W. Gotthard, Datenbanksysteme für Software-Produktionsumgebungen. X, 193 Seiten. 1988.

Band 194: C. Lewerentz, Interaktives Entwerfen großer Programmsysteme. VII, 179 Seiten. 1988.

Band 195: I. S. Bátori, U. Hahn, M. Pinkal, W. Wahlster (Hrsg.), Computerlinguistik und ihre theoretischen Grundlagen. Proceedings. IX, 218 Seiten. 1988.

Band 197: M. Leszak, H. Eggert, Petri-Netz-Methoden und -Werkzeuge. XII, 254 Seiten. 1989.

Band 198: U. Reimer, FRM: Ein Frame-Repräsentationsmodell und seine formale Semantik. VIII, 161 Seiten. 1988.

Band 199: C. Beckstein, Zur Logik der Logik-Programmierung. IX, 246 Seiten. 1988.

Band 200: A. Reinefeld, Spielbaum-Suchverfahren. IX, 191 Seiten. 1989.

Band 201: A. M. Kotz, Triggermechanismen in Datenbanksystemen. VIII, 187 Seiten. 1989.

Band 202: Th. Christaller (Hrsg.), Künstliche Intelligenz. 5. Frühjahrsschule, KIFS-87, Günne, März/April 1987. Proceedings. VII, 403 Seiten, 1989.

Band 203: K. v. Luck (Hrsg.), Künstliche Intelligenz. 7. Frühjahrsschule, KIFS-89, Günne, März 1989. Proceedings. VII, 302 Seiten. 1989.

Band 204: T. Härder (Hrsg.), Datenbanksysteme in Büro, Technik und Wissenschaft. GI/SI-Fachtagung, Zürich, März 1989. Proceedings. XII, 427 Seiten. 1989.

Band 205: P. J. Kühn (Hrsg.), Kommunikation in verteilten Systemen. ITG/GI-Fachtagung, Stuttgart, Februar 1989. Proceedings. XII, 907 Seiten. 1989.

Band 206: P. Horster, H. Isselhorst, Approximative Public-Key-Kryptosysteme. VII, 174 Seiten. 1989.

Band 207: J. Knop (Hrsg.), Organisation der Datenverarbeitung an der Schwelle der 90er Jahre. 8. GI-Fachgespräch, Düsseldorf, März 1989. Proceedings. IX, 276 Seiten. 1989.

Band 208: J. Retti, K. Leidlmair (Hrsg.), 5. Österreichische Artificial-Intelligence-Tagung, Igls/Tirol, März 1989. Proceedings. XI, 452 Seiten. 1989.

Band 209: U. W. Lipeck, Dynamische Integrität von Datenbanken. VIII, 140 Seiten. 1989.

Band 210: K. Drosten, Termersetzungssysteme. IX, 152 Seiten. 1989.

Band 211: H. W. Meuer (Hrsg.), SUPERCOMPUTER '89. Mannheim, Juni 1989. Proceedings, 1989. VIII, 171 Seiten. 1989.

Band 212: W.-M. Lippe (Hrsg.), Software-Entwicklung. Fachtagung, Marburg, Juni 1989. Proceedings. IX, 290 Seiten. 1989.

Band 213: I. Walter, Datenbankgestützte Repräsentation und Extraktion von Episodenbeschreibungen aus Bildfolgen. VIII, 243 Seiten. 1989.

Band 214: W. Görke, H. Sörensen (Hrsg.), Fehlertolerierende Rechensysteme / Fault-Tolerant Computing Systems. 4. Internationale GI/ITG/GMA-Fachtagung, Baden-Baden, September 1989. Proceedings. XI, 390 Seiten. 1989.

Band 215: M. Bidjan-Irani, Qualität und Testbarkeit hochintegrierter Schaltungen. IX, 169 Seiten. 1989.

Band 216: D. Metzing (Hrsg.), GWAI-89. 13th German Workshop on Artificial Intelligence. Eringerfeld, September 1989. Proceedings. XII, 485 Seiten. 1989.

Band 217: M. Zieher, Kopplung von Rechnernetzen. XII, 218 Seiten. 1989.

Band 218: G. Stiege, J. S. Lie (Hrsg.), Messung, Modellierung und Bewertung von Rechensystemen und Netzen. 5. GI/ITG-Fachtagung, Braunschweig, September 1989. Proceedings. IX, 342 Seiten. 1989.

Band 219: H. Burkhardt, K. H. Höhne, B. Neumann (Hrsg.), Mustererkennung 1989. 11. DAGM-Symposium, Hamburg, Oktober 1989. Proceedings. XIX, 575 Seiten. 1989

Band 220: F. Stetter, W. Brauer (Hrsg.), Informatik und Schule 1989: Zukunftsperspektiven der Informatik für Schule und Ausbildung. GI-Fachtagung, München, November 1989. Proceedings. XI, 359 Seiten. 1989.

Band 221: H. Schelhowe (Hrsg.), Frauenwelt – Computerräume. GI-Fachtagung, Bremen, September 1989. Proceedings. XV, 284 Seiten. 1989.

Band 222: M. Paul (Hrsg.), GI – 19. Jahrestagung I. München, Oktober 1989. Proceedings. XVI, 717 Seiten. 1989.

Band 223: M. Paul (Hrsg.), GI – 19. Jahrestagung II. München, Oktober 1989. Proceedings. XVI, 719 Seiten. 1989.

Band 224: U. Voges, Software-Diversität und ihre Modellierung. VIII, 211 Seiten. 1989

Band 225: W. Stoll, Test von OSI-Protokollen. IX, 205 Seiten. 1989.

Band 226: F. Mattern, Verteilte Basisalgorithmen. IX, 285 Seiten. 1989.

Band 227: W. Brauer, C. Freksa (Hrsg.), Wissensbasierte Systeme. 3. Internationaler GI-Kongreß, München, Oktober 1989. Proceedings. X, 544 Seiten. 1989.

Band 228: A. Jaeschke, W. Geiger, B. Page (Hrsg.), Informatik im Umweltschutz. 4. Symposium, Karlsruhe, November 1989. Proceedings. XII, 452 Seiten. 1989.

Band 229: W. Coy, L. Bonsiepen, Erfahrung und Berechnung. Kritik der Expertensystemtechnik. VII, 209 Seiten. 1989.

Band 230: A. Bode, R. Dierstein, M. Göbel, A. Jaeschke (Hrsg.), Visualisierung von Umweltdaten in Supercomputersystemen. Karlsruhe, November 1989. Proceedings. XII, 116 Seiten. 1990.

Band 231: R. Henn, K. Stieger (Hrsg.), PEARL 89 – Workshop über Realzeitsysteme. 10. Fachtagung, Boppard, Dezember 1989. Proceedings. X, 243 Seiten. 1989.

Band 232: R. Loogen, Parallele Implementierung funktionaler Programmiersprachen. IX, 385 Seiten. 1990.

Band 233: S. Jablonski, Datenverwaltung in verteilten Systemen. XIII, 336 Seiten. 1990.

Band 234: A. Pfitzmann, Diensteintegrierende Kommunikationsnetze mit teilnehmerüberprüfbarem Datenschutz. XII, 343 Seiten. 1990.

Band 235: C. Feder, Ausnahmebehandlung in objektorientierten Programmiersprachen. IX, 250 Seiten. 1990.

Band 236: J. Stoll, Fehlertoleranz in verteilten Realzeitsystemen. IX, 200 Seiten. 1990.

Band 237: R. Grebe (Hrsg.), Parallele Datenverarbeitung mit dem Transputer. Aachen, September 1989. Proceedings. VIII, 241 Seiten. 1990.

Band 238: B. Endres-Niggemeyer, T. Hermann, A. Kobsa, D. Rösner (Hrsg.), Interaktion und Kommunikation mit dem Computer. Ulm, März 1989. Proceedings. VIII, 175 Seiten. 1990.

Band 239: K. Kansy, P. Wißkirchen (Hrsg.), Graphik und KI. Königswinter, April 1990. Proceedings. VII, 125 Seiten. 1990.

Informatik-Fachberichte 287

Herausgeber: W. Brauer
im Auftrag der Gesellschaft für Informatik (GI)

Subreihe Künstliche Intelligenz
Mitherausgeber: C. Freksa
in Zusammenarbeit mit dem Fachbereich 1
„Künstliche Intelligenz" der GI

Hermann Kaindl (Hrsg.)

7. Österreichische Artificial-Intelligence-Tagung

Seventh Austrian Conference on Artificial Intelligence

Wien, Austria, 24.-27. September 1991

Proceedings

Springer-Verlag

Berlin Heidelberg New York London Paris
Tokyo Hong Kong Barcelona Budapest

Herausgeber

Hermann Kaindl
Siemens AG Österreich
und
Technische Universität Wien
c/o ÖGAI

Veranstalter / Organizer

Österreichische Gesellschaft für Artificial Intelligence
Austrian Society for Artificial Intelligence
Postfach 177, A-1014 Wien

CR Subject Classification (1991): I.2

ISBN-13: 978-3-540-54567-5   e-ISBN-13: 978-3-642-46752-3
DOI: 10.1007/978-3-642-46752-3

Satz: Reproduktionsfertige Vorlage vom Autor

2133/3140-543210 – Gedruckt auf säurefreiem Papier

Vorwort

Die siebente Österreichische Artificial Intelligence Tagung fand vom 24.–27. September 1991 an der Technischen Universität Wien statt, wo bereits 1987 die dritte Tagung abgehalten worden war. Ein besonderes Merkmal der diesjährigen Tagung ist, daß die Mehrzahl der eingereichten und auch der akzeptierten Beiträge aus dem Ausland stammt. Diese Tagung hat somit einen stark internationalen Charakter, weshalb auch der Tagungsband zweisprachig herausgegeben wurde.

Von 37 eingereichten Beiträgen aus 11 verschiedenen Ländern wurden 16 aufgrund der Gutachten des internationalen Programmkomitees angenommen. (Ein akzeptierter Artikel wurde von den Autoren wieder zurückgezogen.) Die Mitglieder dieses Komitees und die zusätzlichen Gutachter versuchten auch für die akzeptierten Beiträge, konstruktive Kritik anzubringen, sodaß nach den Überarbeitungen für diesen Tagungsband ein hohes Maß an Qualität gewährleistet ist. Die behandelten Themen im Bereich der AI sind weit gestreut, wobei sich aber gewisse Schwerpunkte abzeichnen.

Von den Beiträgen zu den Workshops ist aufgrund der Empfehlung der Veranstalter ein Artikel (von Igor Mozetic und Christian Holzbaur) in diesen Tagungsband zusätzlich aufgenommen worden. Es ist sehr erfreulich, daß auch die beiden eingeladenen Beiträge zur Hauptkonferenz darin zu finden sind.

An dieser Stelle sei den Mitgliedern des Programmkomitees und den zusätzlichen Gutachtern für ihre ausgezeichnete Arbeit und die termingerechte Beurteilung der Beiträge gedankt. Ohne sie wäre es nicht möglich gewesen, eine gerechte Auswahl der Beiträge zu treffen. Zum Erfolg der Tagung haben aber auch jene Mitglieder der ÖGAI maßgeblich beigetragen, die bei der Organisation behilflich waren.

Wien, im September 1991 — Hermann Kaindl

Preface

The Seventh Austrian Conference on Artificial Intelligence took place in September, 1991, at the Technical University of Vienna, the location where already in 1987 the Third Conference was held. A specific feature of this year's conference is that the majority of the submitted as well as the accepted contributions stems from foreign countries. Therefore, this conference has a strong international flavor, and for this reason these proceedings are bilingual.

Out of 37 submitted papers from 11 different countries, 16 have been accepted according to the recommendations of the international program committee. (One of the accepted papers was withdrawn by the authors.) The members of this committee as well as the additional referees tried to give useful reviews also for accepted papers, in order to ensure a high degree of quality for these proceedings after the revisions. The topics of the contributions cover a wide range within AI, but certain tendencies are to be observed.

From the contributions to the workshops, one paper (by Igor Mozetic and Christian Holzbaur) has been included additionally into these proceedings. It is gratifying that both invited speakers have also contributed papers for this collection.

The excellent work of the members of the program committee and the additional referees is acknowledged, and in particular the fact that their refereeing was done in time. Without them it would have been impossible to make a fair selection from the contributions. Moreover, those members of the ÖGAI who helped organizing this conference, considerably contributed to its success.

Vienna, September 1991 — Hermann Kaindl

Tagungsleiter / Conference Chair

Hermann Kaindl   Wien

Programmkomitee / Program Committee

W. Bibel	Darmstadt	J. Diederich	St. Augustin / Davis
G. Görz	Erlangen-Nürnberg	J. Hertzberg	St. Augustin
H. Horacek	Bielefeld	W. Horn	Wien
A. Leitsch	Wien	W. Nejdl	Wien
B. Neumann	Hamburg	J. Retti	Wien
G. Strube	Bochum	R. Trappl	Wien
St. Wrobel	St. Augustin	H. Ziegeler	Wien

Zusätzliche Gutachter / Additional Referees

M. Baaz	B. Becker	O. Dressler	U. Egly
T. Eiter	R. Goebel	H.-W. Güsgen	C. Haider
W. Heinz	C. Holzbaur	A. Haselböck	A. Kohl
C. Kreitz	C. Lischka	J. Matiasek	I. Mozetic
K. Opwis	H. Schreiner	D. Vorberg	G. Weber
H. Wiklicky	G. Widmer		

Workshops

Koordination / Coordination: E. Buchberger (Wien)

Konnektionismus / Connectionism: H. Ziegeler (Wien)
Modellbasiertes Schließen / Model-Based Reasoning: G. Friedrich, F. Lackinger (Wien)
Nicht schon wieder ... / Trading Philosophy for AI? R. Born (Linz)

Inhaltsverzeichnis / Contents

Eingeladene Beiträge / Invited Talks

AI und Hypertext / AI and Hypertext

Natürliche Sprache / Natural Language

Wissensbasierte Systeme / Knowledge-Based Systems

Knowledge-based Generation of Illustrated Documents *

Wolfgang Wahlster, Elisabeth André, Som Bandyopadhyay, Winfried Graf, and Thomas Rist

German Research Center for Artificial Intelligence (DFKI)
Stuhlsatzenhausweg 3, W-6600 Saarbrücken 11, Germany
e-mail: {wahlster, andre, graf, rist}@dfki.uni-sb.de

Abstract

The task of the knowledge-based presentation system WIP is the generation of a variety of multimodal documents from an input consisting of a formal description of the communicative intent of a planned presentation. WIP generates illustrated texts that are customized for the intended audience and situation. We present the architecture of WIP and introduce as its major components the presentation planner, the layout manager, the text generator and the graphics generator. An extended notion of coherence for multimodal documents is introduced that can be used to constrain the presentation planning process. The paper focuses on the coordination of contents planning and layout that is necessary to produce a coherent illustrated text. In particular, we discuss layout revisions after contents planning and the influence of layout constraints on text generation. We show that in WIP the design of a multimodal document is viewed as a non-monotonic planning process that includes various revisions of preliminary results in order to achieve a coherent output with an optimal media mix.

1 Introduction

With increases in the amount and sophistication of information that must be communicated to the users of complex technical systems comes a corresponding need to find new ways to present that information flexibly and efficiently. Intelligent presentation systems are important building blocks for the next generation of user interfaces, because they translate from the narrow output channels provided by most of the current application systems into high-bandwidth communications tailored to the individual user. Since, in many situations, information is only presented efficiently through a particular combination of communication modes, the automatic generation of multimodal presentations is one of the

---

* An extended version of this paper will appear as *WIP: The Coordinated Generation of Multimodal Presentations from a Common Representation* in A. Ortony, J. Slack, and O. Stock (eds.), *Computational Theories of Communication and their Applications*, Berlin: Springer-Verlag, 1991

tasks of such presentation systems. Multimodal interfaces combining, e.g., natural language and graphics take advantage of both the individual strength of each communication mode and the fact that several modes can be employed in parallel, e.g., in the text-picture combinations of illustrated documents.

As the title of this paper indicates, it is an important goal of this research not simply to merge the verbalization results of a natural language generator and the visualization results of a knowledge-based graphics generator, but to carefully coordinate graphics and text in such a way that they complement each other (see also [Wahlster et al. 91]).

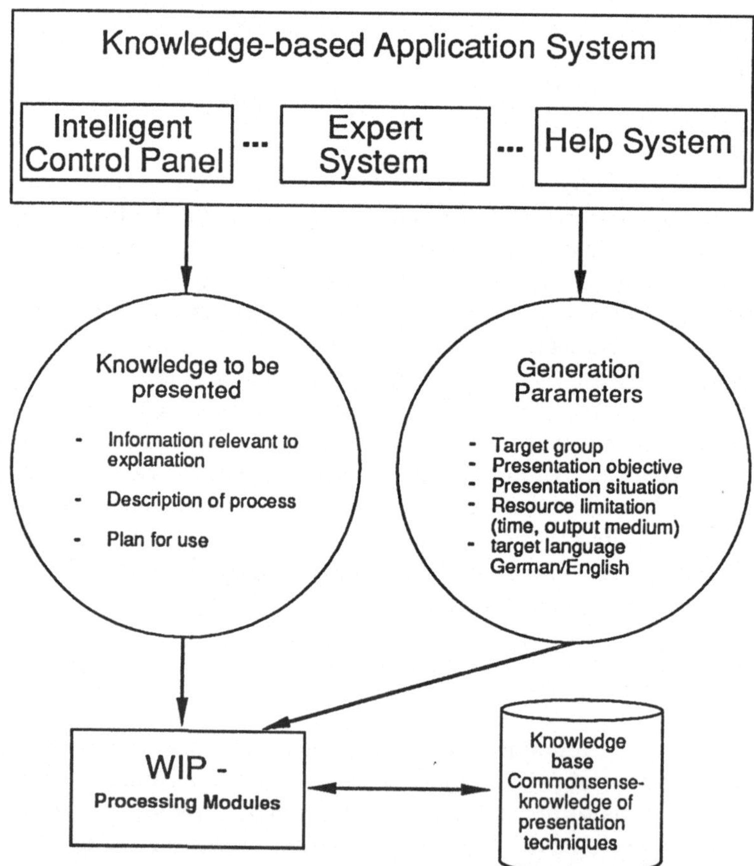

Fig. 1. The Generation Parameters of WIP

1.1 WIP: Knowledge-based Presentation of Information

The task of the knowledge-based presentation system WIP is the generation of a variety of multimodal documents from an input consisting of a formal description of the communicative intent of a planned presentation. The generation process is controlled by a set of generation parameters such as target group, presentation objective, resource limitations, and target language (see Fig. 1).

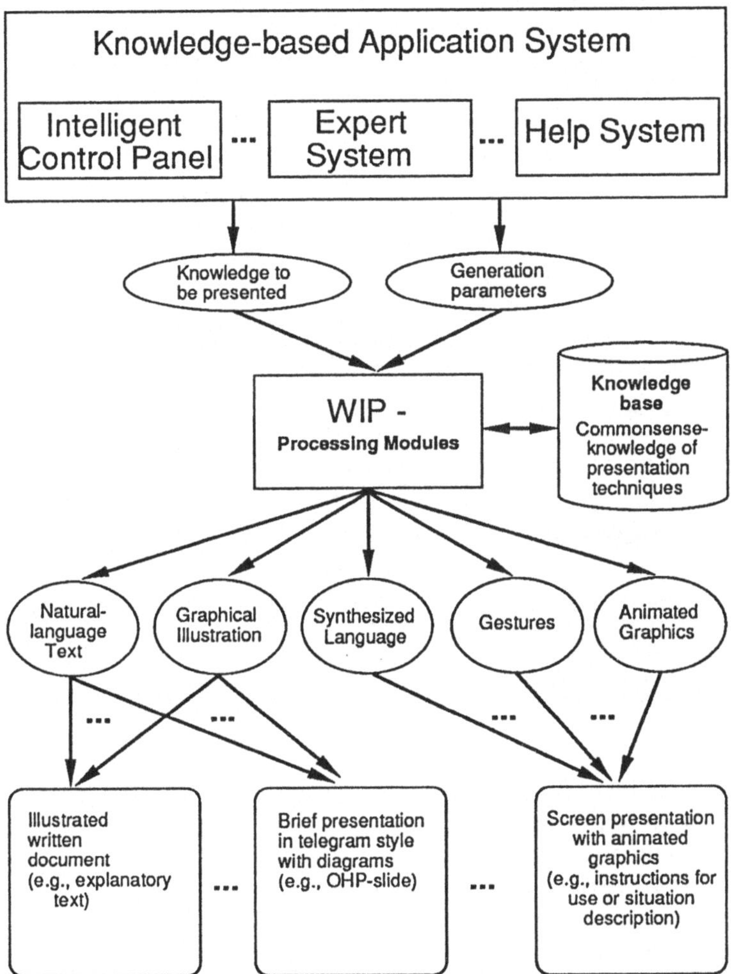

Fig. 2. The Generation of a Variety of Multimodal Presentations

This means that the same information content can be presented in a variety of ways depending on the value combination of these generation parameters. Although WIP is designed as a transportable interface to various knowledge-based application systems, such as intelligent control panels, expert systems, and help systems, which supply the presentation system with the necessary input (see Fig. 2), currently all input for the development and testing of the system is created manually.

One of the basic principles underlying the WIP project is that the generation of the various constituents of a multimodal presentation should be generated from a common representation. This leads to the question of how to divide a given communicative goal into subgoals to be realized by the various mode-specific generators, so that they complement each other. This means that we have to explore computational models of the cognitive decision processes coping with questions such as what should go into text, what should go into graphics, and which kinds of links between the verbal and non-verbal fragments are necessary.

A good example of the use of a WIP system is the generation of user-friendly multimodal instructions for technical devices. As a first domain, we have chosen instructions for the use of espresso-machines. Fig. 3 shows a typical text-picture sequence that may be used to instruct a user in filling the watercontainer of an espresso-machine.

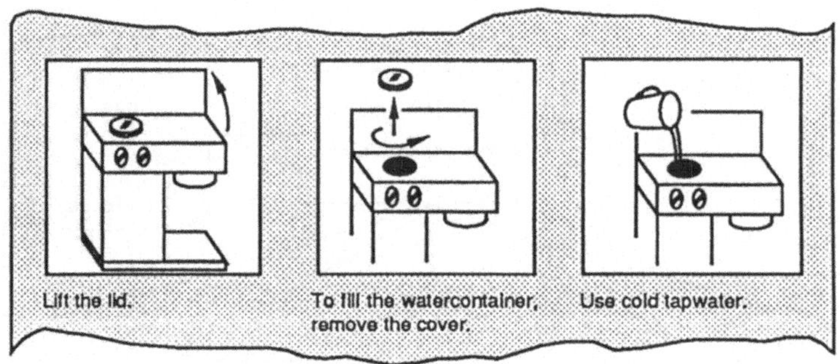

Fig. 3. Multimodal Instructions for the Use of an Espresso-Machine

Currently the technical knowledge to be presented by WIP is encoded in a hybrid knowledge representation language of the KL-ONE family including a terminological and assertional component (see [Nebel 90]). In addition to this propositional representation, which includes the relevant information about the structure, the function, the behavior, and the use of the espresso-machine, WIP has access to an analogical representation of the geometry of the machine in the form of a wire-frame model. This model is used as a basis for the automated design of adequate illustrations.

1.2 Related Research

The automatic design of multimodal presentations has only recently received significant attention in artificial intelligence research. Fig. 4 gives a survey of ongoing projects.

The first group of systems compared in Fig. 4 (XTRA, CUBRICON, AL-Fresco) consists of multimodal dialog systems with an analysis and generation component. XTRA (cf. [Allgayer et al. 89]) provides multimodal access to an

System	Media	Generation of Graphics	Media Coordination	Current Visual Domain	Project Team
XTRA	NL, graphics, pointing	manual	NL and pointing	tax forms	Wahlster et al. (Saarbrücken)
CUBRICON	NL, graphics, pointing	manual	NL and pointing	geographic maps	Shapiro/Neal et al. (Buffalo)
ALFresco	NL, video, pointing	manual	NL and pointing	frescoes	Stock et al. (Trento)
SAGE	NL, graphics	automatic	Not yet	business charts	Roth et al. (CMU)
FN/ANDD	NL, graphics	automatic	Not yet	network diagrams	Marks/Reiter et al. (Harvard)
WIP	NL, graphics	automatic	NL and graphics	espresso machine	Wahlster et al. (Saarbrücken)
COMET	NL, graphics	automatic	NL and graphics	portable radio	Feiner/McKeown et al. (Columbia)

Fig. 4. Current Research on Combining Natural Language, Graphics and Pointing

expert system that assists the user in filling out a tax form. CUBRICON (cf. [Neal&Shapiro 88]) is an intelligent interface to a system for mission planning and situation assessment in a tactical air control domain. ALFresco (cf. [Stock 91]) displays short video sequences about Italian frescoes on a touchscreen and answers questions about details of the videos. In contrast to the first three systems in Fig. 4, the second group currently focuses on the presentation task, although the eventual application environment may also be that of an interactive system.

In the first group of systems, the pointing actions and natural language utterances refer to visual presentations provided by the system builders, whereas the other systems include a component for the generation of graphical displays. All the systems in Fig. 4 *combine* natural language and graphics, but only systems that generate both forms of presentation from a common representation can address the problem of automatic *media choice and coordination*. Although both SAGE and FN/ANDD include graphics design components, they have not yet dealt with the problem of media coordination. SAGE creates multimodal explanations of changes in the results generated by quantitative modeling systems (see [Roth et al. 88]). The ANDD (Automated Network-Diagram Designer) system automatically designs network diagrams from a list of relations and a basic network model, whereas the FN system generates natural language expressions describing certain attributes of a particular object shown in the diagrams (see [Marks&Reiter 90]).

The WIP (see [Wahlster et al. 89]) and COMET (see [Feiner&McKeown 89]) projects share a strong research interest in the coordination of text and graphics. They differ from the rest of the systems in that they deal with physical objects (espresso-machine, radio vs. forms, maps, charts, diagrams) that the user can access directly. For example, in the WIP project we assume that the user is looking at a real espresso-machine and uses the presentations generated by WIP to understand the operation of the machine. Likewise COMET generates directions for the maintenance and repair of a portable radio using text coordinated with 3D graphics. In spite of many similarities, there are major differences between COMET and WIP, e.g., in the systems' architecture. While during one of the final processing steps of COMET the media layout component combines text and graphics fragments produced by media-specific generators, in WIP a layout manager interacts with a presentation planner before text and graphics are generated, so that layout considerations can influence the early stages of the planning process and constrain the media-specific generators.

2 The Architecture of WIP

The architecture of the WIP system guarantees a design process with a large degree of freedom that can be used to tailor the presentation to suit the specific context. During the design process a presentation planner and a layout manager orchestrate the mode-specific generators and the document history handler (see Fig. 5) provides information about intermediate results of the presentation design that is exploited in order to prevent disconcerting or incoherent output. This means that decisions of the language generator may influence graphics generation and that graphical constraints may sometimes force decisions in the language production process.

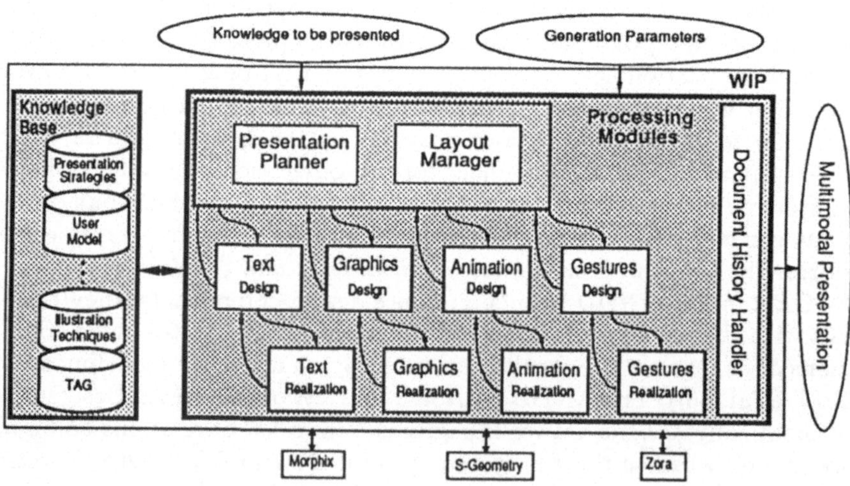

Fig. 5. Architecture of the WIP Project

Fig. 5 shows a sketch of WIP's current architecture used for the generation of illustrated documents. Note that WIP includes two parallel processing cascades for the incremental generation of text and graphics. In WIP, the design of a multimodal document is viewed as a non-monotonic process that includes various revisions of preliminary results, massive replanning or plan repairs, and many negotiations between the corresponding design and realization components in order to achieve a fine-grained and optimal division of work between the selected presentation modes.

2.1 The Presentation Planner

The presentation planner is responsible for contents and mode selection. A basic assumption behind the design of WIP is that not only the generation of text, but also the generation of multimodal documents can be considered as a sequence of communicative acts which aim to achieve certain goals (cf. [André&Rist 90a]). As in textlinguistic studies (cf. [Van Dijk 80] and [Mann&Thompson 88]), we distinguish between *main* (MA) and *subsidiary acts* (SA). Main acts convey the kernel of the message. Subsidiary acts serve to support the main acts. In particular, they ensure that necessary preconditions are satisfied, they enhance the effect of the main act or they resolve ambiguities after anticipating the addressee's understanding processes. Since main and subsidiary acts can, in turn, be composed of main and subsidiary acts, we get a hierarchical act structure. While the root of the hierarchy generally corresponds to a complex communicative act such as describing a process, the leaves are elementary acts, i.e., *speech acts* (cf. [Searle 61]) or *pictorial acts* (cf. [Kjorup 78]).

The structure of a document is, however, not only determined by its act structure, but also by the role acts play in relation to other acts. E.g., one can verbally request an addressee to carry out an action and show with a picture how it should be done. In this example, the act of showing the picture (subsidiary act) is subordinated to the requesting act which conveys the kernel of the message (main act). If the addressee cannot figure out a relation between these acts, the document appears incoherent. Fig. 6 shows a slightly simplified version of the act structure of the instruction sequence in Fig. 3.

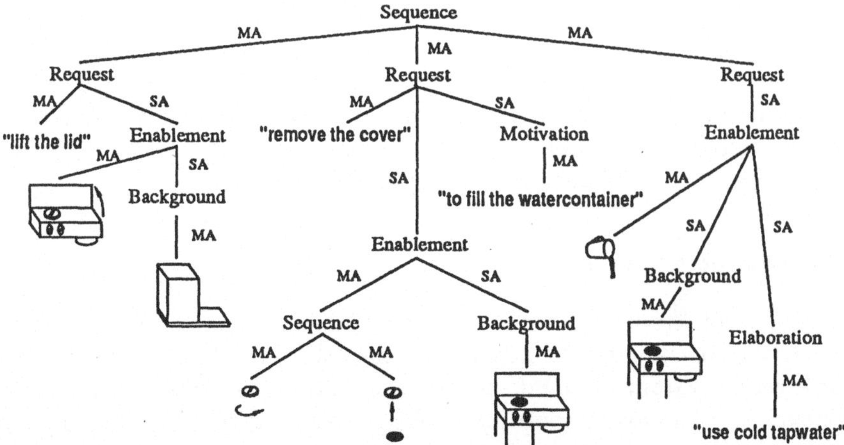

Fig. 6. The Action Structure of the Sample Document

For the automatic synthesis of illustrated documents, we have designed presentation strategies that refer to both text and picture production. To represent the strategies, we follow the approach proposed by Moore and colleagues (cf. [Moore&Paris 89]) to operationalize RST-theory for text planning.

The strategies are represented by a name, a header, an effect, a set of applicability conditions and a specification of main and subsidiary acts. Whereas the header of a strategy indicates which communicative function the corresponding document part is to fill, its effect refers to an intentional goal.[2] The applicability conditions specify when a strategy may be used and put restrictions on the variables to be instantiated. The kernel of the strategies form the main and subsidiary acts. E.g., the strategy below can be used to enable the identification of an object shown in a picture (for further details see [André&Rist 90b]). Whereas graphics should be used to carry out the main act, mode decisions for the subsidiary acts are open.

```
Name:
    Enable-Identification-by-Background
Header:
    (Provide-Background P A ?x ?px ?picture GRAPHICS)
Effect:
    (BMB P A (Identifiable A ?x ?px ?picture))
Applicability Conditions:
    (AND (Bel P (Perceptually-Accessible A ?x))
         (Bel P (Part-of ?x ?z)))
Main Acts:
    (Depict P A (Background ?z) ?pz ?picture)
Subsidiary Acts:
    (Achieve P (BMB P A (Identifiable A ?z ?pz ?picture)) ?mode)
```

For the automatic generation of illustrated documents, the presentation strategies are treated as operators of a planning system (cf. [André&Rist 90a] and [André&Rist 90b]). During the planning process, presentation strategies are selected and instantiated according to the presentation task. After the selection of a strategy, the main and subsidiary acts are carried out unless the corresponding presentation goals are already satisfied. Elementary acts, such as 'Depict' or 'Assert', are performed by the text and graphics generators.

2.2 The Layout Manager

The main task of the layout manager is to convey certain semantic and pragmatic relations specified by the planner by the arrangement of graphic and text fragments received from the mode-specific generators, i.e., to determine the size of the boxes and the exact coordinates for positioning them on the document

---

[2] In [Moore&Paris 89], this distinction between header and effect is not made because the effect of their strategies may be an intentional goal as well as a rhetorical relation.

page. Therefore, we use a grid-based approach as an ordering system for efficiently designing functional (i.e., uniform, coherent, and consistent) layouts (cf. [Müller-Brockmann 81]). This method is also used by Beach for low-level table layout (cf. [Beach 85]) and in the GRID system for automating display layout (cf. [Feiner 88]).

The layout process is carried out in two phases with different levels of detail. In the first phase, a draft version of a high-level page layout is produced. Since at that stage of the process neither the text generator nor the graphics generator has produced any output, the layout manager only has information about the contents, the act structure and the selected mode combination which is available via the document history handler. Thus, the layout manager uses default assumptions to determine a skeletal version of an initial page layout based on uninstantiated text and graphic boxes. As soon as a generator has supplied any output, the corresponding box is instantiated and the incremental process of low-level layout planning can start. Then the layout manager has to position this box on the grid considering design restrictions. As the example below shows, design constraints or visual unbalances in the output presentation can require a total revision of the skeletal layout or in the worst-case even a change of the contents.

A central problem when automatically designing layout is the representation of design-relevant knowledge. According to [Borning&Duisberg 86], constraint networks seem to be a natural formalism to declaratively incorporate aesthetic knowledge into the geometric layout process. Layout constraints can be classified as *semantic*, *geometric* and *topological*, and *temporal*. Semantic constraints essentially correspond to coherence relations, such as sequence and contrast, and can be easily reflected through specific design constraints. They describe perceptual criteria concerning the organization of the boxes, such as the sequential ordering (horizontal or vertical layout), alignment, grouping, symmetry or similarity.

When using constraints to represent layout knowledge, one often wants to prioritize the constraints in those which must be required and others which are preferably held. [3] A powerful way of expressing this layout feature is to organize the constraints in a hierarchy by assigning a preference scale to the constraint network. We distinguish between *obligatory*, *optional* and *default constraints*. The latter state default values, which remain fixed unless the corresponding constraint is removed by a stronger one. Since there are constraints that only have local effects, the constraint hierarchy has to be changed frequently. The constraint solver must therefore be able to add and remove constraints dynamically during runtime.

A typical example of using a constraint hierarchy in geometric layout is the problem of leaving enough white space between two graphic boxes communicating a contrast. The adequate aesthetic criteria can be represented by three constraints of different strength: one obligatory constraint that specifies that the

---

[3] A theory of constraint hierarchies is described in [Borning et al. 89]. An incremental constraint hierarchy solver (cf. also the DeltaBlue algorithm [Freeman-Benson 90]) for WIP has been implemented by Wolfgang Maaß (cf. [Maaß 91]).

distance between the boxes must be greater than zero and a disjunction of two optional constraints that the boxes are preferably aligned side by side or else below each other. To give an example of a typical compound constraint in the syntax of a constraint language, let's have a look at a section of the definition of the 'contrast'-constraint (cf. Fig. 7).

Since the ordering of the constraints in the definition is significant, the stronger constraints should preceed the weaker ones. E.g., according to the definition above, the layout manager will use a horizontal alignment in preference to a vertical one if a contrast-constraint has to be satisfied. For a detailed description of the layout manager see [Graf&Maaß 91].

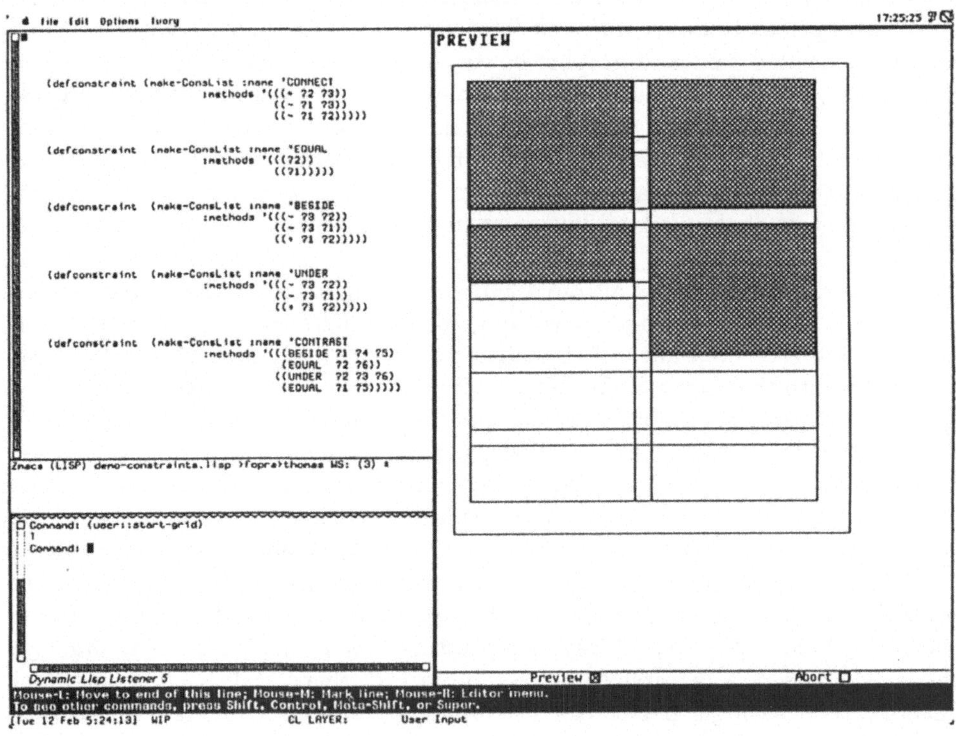

Fig. 7. Constraint definition and a preview showing a grid populated with two contrasting graphic boxes and the corresponding text boxes

2.3 The Text Generator

WIP's text generator is based on the formalism of tree adjoining grammars (TAGs). In particular, lexicalized TAGs with unification are used for the incremental verbalization of logical forms produced by the presentation planner (cf. [Harbusch 90], [Schauder 90]). The grammar is divided into an LD (local dominance) and an LP (linear precedence) part so that the piecewise construction of syntactic constituents is separated from their linearization according to word order rules (cf. [Finkler&Neumann 89]).

The text generator uses a TAG parser in a local anticipation feedback loop (see [Jameson&Wahlster 82]). The generator and parser form a bidirectional system, i.e., both processes are based on the same TAG. By parsing a planned utterance, the generator makes sure that it does not contain unintended structural ambiguities.

Since the TAG-based generator is used in designing illustrated documents, it has to generate not only complete sentences, but also sentence fragments such as NPs, PPs, or VPs, e.g., for figure captions, section headings, picture annotations, or itemized lists. Given that capability and the incrementality of the generation process, it becomes possible to interleave generation with parsing in order to check for ambiguities as soon as possible. Currently, we are exploring different domains of locality for such feedback loops and trying to relate them to resource limitations specified in WIP's generation parameters. One parameter of the generation process in the current implementation is the number of adjoinings allowed in a sentence. This parameter can be used by the presentation planner to control the syntactic complexity of the generated utterances and sentence length. If the number of allowed adjoinings is small, a logical form that can be verbalized as a single complex sentence may lead to a sequence of simple sentences. The leeway created by this parameter can be exploited for mode coordination. For example, constraints set up by the graphics generator or layout manager can force delimitation of sentences, since in a good design, picture breaks should correspond to sentence breaks, and vice versa (see [McKeown&Feiner 90]).

2.4 The Graphics Generator

When generating illustrations of physical objects WIP does not rely on previously authored picture fragments or predefined icons stored in the knowledge base. Rather, we start from a hybrid object representation that includes a wireframe model for each object. Although these wireframe models, along with a specification of physical attributes, such as surface color or transparency, form the basic input of the graphics generator, the design of illustrations is regarded as a knowledge-intensive process that exploits various knowledge sources to achieve a given presentation goal efficiently. E.g., when a picture of an object is requested, we have to determine an appropriate perspective in a context-sensitive way (cf. [Rist&André 90]). In our approach, we distinguish between three basic types of graphical techniques. First, there are techniques to create and manipulate a 3D object configuration that serves as the subject of the picture. E.g., we have developed a technique to spatially separate the parts of an object in order to construct an exploded view. Second, we can choose among several techniques that map the 3D subject onto its depiction. E.g., we can construct either a schematic line drawing or a more realistic looking picture using rendering techniques. The third kind of technique operates on the picture level. E.g., an object depiction may be annotated with a label (see Fig. 8), or picture parts may be colored in order to emphasize them. The task of the graphics designer is then to select and combine these graphical techniques according to the presentation goal. The result is a so-called design plan which can be transformed into executable instructions of the graphics realization component. This component relies on the 3D graphics package S-Geometry and the 2D graphics software of the Symbolics window system.

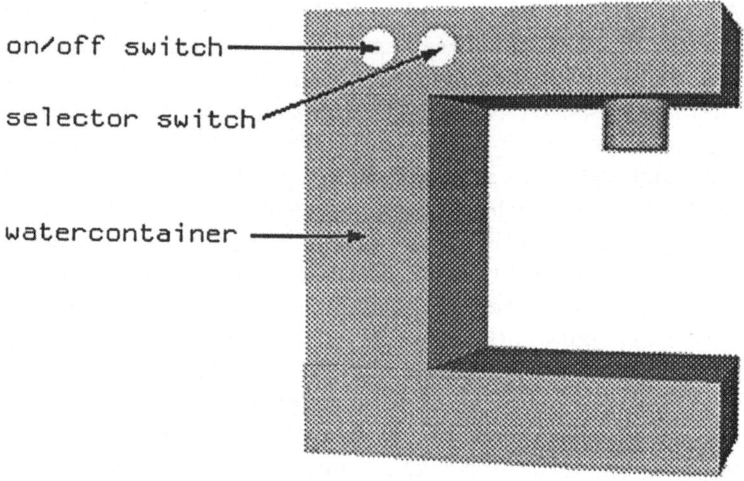

Fig. 8. Rendered Picture with Annotations

2.5 Tailoring Presentations to the Addressee

One advantage of the automated design of multimodal documents over the display of predefined presentations, e.g., in conventional hypermedia systems, is that in a knowledge-based presentation system like WIP the generated document can be tailored to a particular target group and presentation situation. As mentioned in section 1, one of the generation parameters of WIP is information about each individual target group or addressee. If the generated multimodal document is to be informative, understandable and effective in reaching the presentation goal specified in the input, the presentation system has to take into account factors like the addressee's prior knowledge about the domain and his level of expertise, i.e., the system has to exploit a user model (cf. [Wahlster&Kobsa 89]).

The user modeling component of WIP provides the presentation planner with information about the addressee that affects the content and structure of the generated document.

Let's discuss how WIP can use the assumptions about an addressee's domain knowledge contained in the user model to tailor the presentation to each addressee. Suppose that the system's present task is to generate a warning against opening the cover of the watercontainer too early after having used the espresso machine. If the system assumes that the addressee has no detailed knowledge about the preparation of espresso, some motivation should procede the warning itself. In our example, the extreme pressure and high temperature in the watercontainer are the main reasons for the warning. If the system assumes that the addressee does not know the reasons for the extreme pressure and high temperature, it should introduce them before the warning.

In the presentation situation just described, a text like (1) would be communicatively adequate.

(1) *Espresso is coffee prepared in a special machine from finely ground coffee beans, through which steam under high pressure is forced. Because of the extreme pressure and high temperature, you should wait for at least two minutes after switching off the machine before you open the cover of the watercontainer.*

In the opposite case, when the system assumes that the addressee has already used another type of espresso machine, the system can just verbalize a warning like (2). Note that (2) would be pragmatically incoherent (cf. [Bandyopadhyay 90]) for the first type of addressee introduced above, since the reason for the warning would remain unclear to him.

(2) *Wait at least for two minutes after switching off the machine before you open the cover of the watercontainer.*

It is obvious that WIP's user model should not only constrain the text planning, but also guide other processes like media choice, gesture generation (see [Wahlster 91]), and the synthesis of graphics.

3 Conclusions

In this paper, we presented a computational model for the generation of multimodal communications. We showed how the knowledge-based presentation system WIP coordinates graphics and text in such a way that they complement each other in an illustrated document. The basic principles underlying the WIP project are that the generation of all constituents of a multimodal presentation should start from a common representation and that the design of a text-picture sequence can be modeled as a non-monotonic planning process. We showed how WIP's presentation planner and layout manager orchestrate the text and graphics generator during the design process.

Acknowledgements

The development of WIP is an ongoing group effort and has benefited from the contributions of our colleagues Wolfgang Finkler, Karin Harbusch, Jochen

Heinsohn, Bernhard Nebel, Hans-Jürgen Profitlich, and Anne Schauder as well as
our students Andreas Butz, Bernd Herrmann, Antonio Krüger, Daniel Kudenko,
Wolfgang Maaß, Thomas Schiffmann, Georg Schneider, Frank Schneiderlöchner,
Christoph Schommer, Dudung Soetopo, Peter Wazinski, and Detlev Zimmermann.

References

[Allgayer et al. 89] Allgayer, J., Harbusch, K., Kobsa, A., Reddig, C., Reithinger, N.,
and Schmauks, D.: XTRA: A Natural Language Access System to Expert Systems. In: International Journal of Man-Machine Studies Vol. 31 (1989) 161-195

[André&Rist 90a] André, E. and Rist, T.: Towards a Plan-Based Synthesis of Illustrated Documents. In: Proc. of the 9th European Conference on Artificial Intelligence (1990) 25-30

[André&Rist 90b] André, E. and Rist, T.: Synthesizing Illustrated Documents: A Plan-
Based Approach. In: Proc. of InfoJapan 90, Vol. 2 (1990) 163-170

[Bandyopadhyay 90] Bandyopadhyay, S.: Towards an Understanding of Coherence in
Multimodal Discourse. Technical Memo DFKI-TM-90-01, German Research Center for Artificial Intelligence, Saarbrücken Site (1990)

[Beach 85] Beach, R.J.: Setting Tables and Illustrations with Style. Xerox PARC Technical Report CSL-85-3 (1985)

[Borning&Duisberg 86] Borning, A. and Duisberg, A.: Constraint-Based Tools for
Building User Interfaces. ACM Trans. on Graphics 5:6 (1986) 345-374

[Borning et al. 89] Borning, A., Freeman-Benson, B., and Wilson, M.: Constraint Hierarchies. Internal Report, Department of Computer Science and Engineering,
FR- 35, University of Washington, Seattle (1989)

[Feiner 88] Feiner, S.: A Grid-Based Approach to Automating Display Layout. In:
Proc. of the Graphics Interface 88. Palo Alto: Morgan Kaufmann (1988) 192-
197

[Feiner&McKeown 89] Feiner, S. and McKeown, K.: Coordinating Text and Graphics
in Explanation Generation. In: DARPA Speech and Natural Language Workshop
(1989)

[Finkler&Neumann 89] Finkler, W. and Neumann, G.: POPEL-HOW: A Distributed
Parallel Model for Incremental Natural Language Production with Feedback. In:
Proc. of the 11th IJCAI (1989) 1518-1523

[Freeman-Benson et al. 90] Freeman-Benson, B., Maloney, J., and Borning, A.: An Incremental Constraint Solver. Communications of the ACM, Vol. 33, No. 1 (1990)
54-63

[Graf&Maaß 91] Graf, W. and Maaß, W.: Constraint-basierte Verarbeitung graphi-
schen Wissens. To appear in Proc. of the 4th Int. GI-Kongreß Wissensbasierte
Systeme - Verteilte KI. Berlin: Springer-Verlag (1991)

[Harbusch 90] Harbusch, K.: Constraining Tree Adjoining Grammars by Unification.
Proc. of the 13th COLING (1990) 167-172

[Jameson&Wahlster 82] Jameson, A. and Wahlster, W.: User Modelling in Anaphora
Generation: Ellipsis and Definite Description. In: Proc. of the 5th ECAI (1982)
222-227

[Kjorup 78] Kjorup, S.: Pictorial Speech Acts. In: Erkenntnis 12 (1978) 55-71

[Mann&Thompson 88] Mann, W. and Thompson, S.: Rhetorical Structure Theory:
Towards a Functional Theory of Text Organization. In: TEXT, 8(3) (1988)

[Marks&Reiter 90] Marks, J. and Reiter, E.: Avoiding Unwanted Conversational Implicatures in Text and Graphics. In: Proc. of the 8th AAAI (1990) 450-455

[Maaß 91] Maaß, W.: Constraint-basierte Repräsentation von graphischem Wissen am Beispiel des Layout-Managers in WIP. MS thesis, Computer Science Departement, University of Saarbrücken (1991)

[McKeown&Feiner 90] McKeown, K. and Feiner, S.: Interactive Multimedia Explanation for Equipment Maintenance and Repair. In: DARPA Speech and Natural Language Workshop (1990) 42-47

[Moore&Paris 89] Moore, J. and Paris, C.: Planning Text for Advisory Dialogues. In: Proc. of the 27th ACL (1989) 203-211

[Müller-Brockmann 81] Müller-Brockmann, J.: Grid Systems in Graphic Design. Stuttgart: Hatje (1981)

[Neal&Shapiro 88] Neal, J. and Shapiro, S.: Intelligent Multi-Media Interface Technology. In: Proc. of the Workshop on Architectures of Intelligent Interfaces: Elements&Prototypes (1988) 69-91

[Nebel 90] Nebel, B.: Reasoning and Revision in Hybrid Representation Systems. Lecture Notes in AI, Vol. 422, Berlin: Springer-Verlag (1990)

[Rist&André 90] Rist, T. and André, E.: Wissensbasierte Perspektivenwahl für die automatische Erzeugung von 3D-Objektdarstellungen. In: K. Kansy and P. Wißkirchen (eds.). Graphik und KI. IFB 239, Berlin: Springer-Verlag (1990) 48-57

[Roth et al. 88] Roth, S., Mattis, J., and Mesnard, X.: Graphics and Natural Language as Components of Automatic Explanation. In: Proc. of the Workshop on Architectures of Intelligent Interfaces: Elements & Prototypes (1988) 109-128

[Searle 69] Searle, J.: Speech Acts: An Essay in the Philosophy of Language. Cambridge, MA: Cambridge University Press (1969)

[Schauder 90] Schauder, A.: Inkrementelle syntaktische Generierung natürlicher Sprache mit Tree Adjoining Grammars. MS thesis, Computer Science Departement, University of Saarbrücken (1990)

[Stock 91] Stock, O.: Natural Language and Exploration of an Information Space: the ALFresco Interactive System. Technical Report, Istituto per la Ricerca Scientifica e Tecnologica, Trento, Italy (1991)

[Van Dijk 80] van Dijk, T.: Textwissenschaft. München: dtv (1980)

[Wahlster 91] Wahlster, W.: User and Discourse Models for Multimodal Communication. In: J. Sullivan and S. Tyler (eds.). Architectures for Intelligent User Interfaces: Elements and Prototypes. Reading, MA: Addison-Wesley (1991)

[Wahlster&Kobsa 89] Wahlster, W. and Kobsa, A.: User Models in Dialog Systems. In: A. Kobsa and W. Wahlster (eds.). User Models in Dialog Systems. Symbolic Computation Series, Berlin: Springer-Verlag (1989) 4-34

[Wahlster et al. 89] Wahlster, W., André, E., Hecking, M., and Rist, T.: WIP: Knowledge-based Presentation of Information. Report WIP-1, German Research Center for Artificial Intelligence, Saarbrücken (1989)

[Wahlster et al. 91] Wahlster, W., André, E., Graf, W., and Rist, T.: Designing Illustrated Texts: How Language Production Is Influenced by Graphics Generation. In: Proc. of the 5th Conference of the European Chapter of the ACL, Berlin: Springer-Verlag (1991) 8-14

This article was processed using the LaTeX macro package with ICM style

On the Complexity of Clause Condensing

Georg Gottlob

Christian Doppler Laboratory for Expert Systems

Institut für Informationssysteme

Technical University of Vienna, Austria

e-mail: gottlob@vexpert.dbai.tuwien.ac.at

Abstract

This paper deals with complexity issues related to the recognition of redundancy and to the removal of redundant literals from a clause. We first consider *condensing*, a weak type of redundancy elimination. A clause is condensed iff it does not subsume any proper subset of itself. It is often useful (and sometimes necessary) to replace a non-condensed clause C by a condensation, i.e., by a condensed subset of C which is subsumed by C. After studying the complexity of an existing clause condensing algorithm, we show that the problem of testing whether a given clause is condensed is co-NP-complete. Furthermore, we prove that the problems of identifying clause condensations and of testing whether there exists a condensation of a given cardinality are complete for D^P, a complexity class which is likely to properly include both NP and co-NP. We also consider a stronger version of redundancy elimination: a clause C is *strongly condensed* iff it does not contain any proper subset C' such that C implies C'. We show that the problem of testing whether a clause is strongly condensed is undecidable.

1 Introduction

The representation of knowledge in clause-form has become widespread in several areas of Computer Science such as Automated Theorem Proving [4, 16] and other subfields of Artificial Intelligence, Logic Programming [15], and Deductive or Logic Databases [10, 3, 2]. While for obvious reasons, in the context of clause based systems, most of the research still focuses on decidability and completeness issues, other topics such as redundancy detection and redundancy elimination should not be overlooked. These problems become important as soon as one has to deal with large knowledge bases where efficiency of both clause-storage and clause-manipulation is a major concern.

There are several different types of redundancy one may consider in a clause base. To give the reader a brief overview, we first enumerate some types of redundancy that have been studied elsewhere and then explain the kind of redundancy we are interested in. The following list also shows that redundancy in clausal knowledge bases is a rather critical issue since the discovery of several types of redundancy in a knowledge base is undecidable.

- A clause may be redundant because it is a logical consequence of a *set* of other clauses of the knowledge bases. This type of redundancy is in general very hard to detect; the problem is obviously undecidable for general clauses since it is equivalent to a general theorem proving task.

- A clause may be a logical consequence of a *single* other clause present in the knowledge base. Even the detection of this type of redundancy, a restriction of the former type, is undecidable in general; the decidability for Horn clauses is currently an open problem [19, 14]. However, decision procedures have been developed for several particular classes of clauses [14, 13]. Furthermore, the subproblem of testing whether a clause *subsumes* another clause (a strong form of implication) is decidable and has been shown to be NP-complete [1, 6]; subsumption algorithms are studied in [9].

- Sometimes literals of a clause are redundant because they are implied by the other literals of the clause and by the rest of the knowledge base. Consider, for instance, a clause C of the form $\{\neg p(x,y), \neg p(y,x), q(x,y,a)\}$ and assume that another clause D of the form $\{\neg p(x,y), p(y,x)\}$ is also an element of the knowledge base. In rule notation, C is written as $p(x,y) \wedge p(y,x) \Rightarrow q(x,y,a)$ and D is written as $p(x,y) \Rightarrow p(y,x)$. Obviously, we may eliminate either the literal $p(x,y)$ or the literal $p(y,x)$ from C, since by rule D, each of these two literals is implied by the other. It is easy to see that detecting this type of redundancy is again undecidable, because testing whether a literal is redundant in this setting is equivalent to test whether a fact follows from a set of clauses.

The kind of redundancy studied in this paper is a special case of the last redundancy-type described in the above list. We are interested in the following situation: a clause C contains a proper subset C' logically equivalent to C. In this case, C can be replaced by C' independently of the rest of the knowledge base. To our best knowledge, no complexity results have been derived so far concerning this type of redundancy.

Condensing is an important technique for (partially) removing redundancy of this type from a clause. This concept has been introduced by Joyner in [11, 12]. A clause is condensed iff it does not subsume any proper subset of itself. A condensed subset C' of a clause C such that C subsumes C' is called a *condensation* of C.

As an example consider the clause $C = \{p(x,y), p(y,x), p(x,x)\}$ representing the logical formula $\forall x \forall y : p(x,y) \vee p(y,x) \vee p(x,x)$. Clearly, if we apply the substitution $\theta = \{y \leftarrow x\}$ to C the result is equal to $\{p(x,x)\}$. Thus C subsumes its subset $C' = \{p(x,x)\}$. Note that the only proper subset of C' is the empty set, which is clearly not subsumed by C'. Thus C' is a condensation of C.

A algorithm for clause condensing was given by Joyner in his Ph.D. thesis [11]. This algorithm performs as main operations a number of subsumption-tests. In this paper we first derive some complexity results by estimating the number of subsumption-tests done by this algorithm. Since checking for subsumption is NP-complete, it makes sense to ask whether there exists an essentially better way of testing if a clause is condensed. Unfortunately, this question is negatively answered. We show that deciding whether a clause is condensed is co-NP-complete. Furthermore, we show that the problem of *identifying* a condensation of a clause C is complete for D^{P}, a complexity class which – in a subtle sense – is considered to be "harder" than NP and co-NP. We also show that for a clause C and an integer k it is D^{P}-complete to decide whether C has a condensation of cardinality k.

Obviously, if C has a condensation $C' \subset C$ then C is logically equivalent to C'. Note, however, that the converse does not hold. In section 6 we will show by examples that a clause C may have a proper subset C' such that C and C' are logically equivalent, but C does not subsume C'. In particular, there are condensed clauses with this property. A clause where this more general type of redundancy is not present will be referred to as *strongly condensed*. We will show that the question whether a given clause is strongly condensed is undecidable. It follows that the problem of eliminating redundancy of the general type from a clause is algorithmically unsolvable.

The sequel of this paper is structured as follows. In section 2 we introduce the basic concepts and definitions and state some previous results. In section 3 we state some complexity results on Joyner's condensing algorithm. We also show that condensing is a useful technique, especially in presence of large quantities of factual data, since the removal of a linear amount of redundant literals by condensing may result in an exponential speed-up of resolution inference-procedures. Section 4 is dedicated to the complexity study of the problem to decide whether a given clause is condensed. The problems of identifying a condensation of a clause and deciding whether there exists a condensation of a certain cardinality are dealt with in section 5. In section 6 we discuss the notion of strong condensation and prove that testing for strong condensation is undecidable. In section 7 we draw some conclusions and outline further work.

2 Preliminaries and Previous Results

In the following we introduce some basic definitions and notation we use; they largely correspond to those of [4].

Constants will be denoted by lower case letters from the beginning of the alphabet, sometimes with primes or subscripts. Variable symbols are lower case letters from the end of the alphabet, sometimes with primes or subscripts. We also use lower case letters for function and predicate symbols; their distinction will always be clear from the context.

A *term* is either a constant symbol or a variable symbol or an expression of the form $f(t_1, \ldots, t_n)$ where f is an n-place function symbol and the t_i are terms. If p is an n-place predicate symbol and $t_1, \ldots, t_n$ are terms, then $p(t_1, \ldots, t_n)$ is an *atom*. A *literal* is an atom or the negation of an atom. Atoms are positive literals and negated atoms are negative literals.

A *clause* is a finite set of literals. A clause C expresses a formula $\hat{C}$ of predicate logic consisting of the disjunction of the literals in C preceded by a universal quantifier for each variable in C. For instance, the logical formula corresponding to the clause

$$\{\neg p(x, y), \neg p(f(y), g(z)), p(x, z), q(h(x, z), g(a))\}$$

is:

$$\forall x \forall y \forall z : \neg p(x, y) \lor \neg p(f(y), g(z)) \lor p(x, z) \lor q(h(x, z), g(a)).$$

Note that some function or constant symbols in clauses may originate from skolemizations, but this is not of relevance in this paper. In Logic Programming and other fields, clauses are usually written in rule form. The above clause, for instance, can be rewritten as follows:

$$p(x, y) \land p(f(y), g(z)) \Rightarrow p(x, z) \lor q(h(x, z), g(a)).$$

In this paper we will always use the more traditional set notation because the order of the literals in a clause is irrelevant to the concept of condensing and because we find it convenient to apply well-known set theoretic operations and predicates to clauses.

A *Horn clause* is a clause with at most one positive literal. A term, literal, or clause is *ground* if it does not contain any variable symbol.

A *substitution* θ replacing the variables $x_1, \ldots, x_n$ by the terms $t_1, \ldots, t_n$ respectively is written as $\{x_1 \leftarrow t_1, \ldots, x_n \leftarrow t_n\}$. The application of substitutions, their composition, etc., is defined in the standard way (see [4] or [15]). We will also use the concepts of *unifier* and *most general unifier (mgu)* as defined in the standard literature.

We say that a clause C *implies* D and we write $C \Rightarrow D$ iff $\hat{C}$ logically implies $\hat{D}$. Clauses C and D are called *equivalent* iff their corresponding first order formulas $\hat{C}$ and $\hat{D}$ are logically equivalent.

It has been shown by Schmidt-Schauss [19] that the problem whether $C \Rightarrow D$ holds for two clauses C and D is undecidable. We will make use of this undecidability result in section 6.

A clause C *subsumes* a clause D, denoted by $C \triangleright D$, iff there is a substitution θ such that $C\theta \subseteq D$.[1]

Deciding for two clauses C and D whether $C \triangleright D$ is NP-complete [1, 6]. The complexity of standard subsumption algorithms is analyzed in [9]; improved algorithms are presented in [9, 8].

If $C \triangleright D$ and $D \triangleright C$, then we write $C \Leftrightarrow D$.

Note that from $C \triangleright D$ it follows that $C \Rightarrow D$, but the converse is not true in general. The relationship between subsumption and implication is studied in [7].

Clauses C and D are called *variants* if they differ only in the names of their variables, i.e., if there are substitutions θ and σ such that $C\theta = D$ and $D\sigma = C$.

Note that if C and D are variants, then $C \Leftrightarrow D$. However, the converse does not hold in general: Let $C = \{p(x,y), p(x,x)\}$ and $D = \{p(x,y), p(y,y)\}$, then $C \Leftrightarrow D$ but C and D are not variants.

A *condensation* of a clause C is a minimum cardinality subset C' of C such that $C \triangleright C'$. The set of all condensations of C is denoted by $CONDS(C)$. A clause C is *condensed* if $CONDS(C) = \{C\}$.

Examples.

$CONDS(\{p(x,y), p(x,x)\}) = \{\{p(x,x)\}\};$

$CONDS(\{p(x,y), p(a,y)\}) = \{\{p(a,y)\}\};$

$CONDS(\{p(x, f(a)), p(y, f(a)\} = \{\{p(x, f(a)\}, \{p(y, f(a)\}\};$

If $C = \{p(x,y), p(y,z), p(x,z)\}$ then $CONDS(C) = \{C\}$, hence C is condensed.

The *condensing number cond#(C)* of a clause C is the cardinality of a smallest condensation of C. Obviously C is condensed iff $cond\#(C) = |C|$.

The notion of condensing was introduced by Joyner in [12]. It is obvious that any condensation of a clause C is logically equivalent to C. Therefore, in a given set of clauses we can profitably replace any non-condensed clause by a condensation of it. Joyner also shows that a wide class of resolution refutation procedures is compatible with condensing, i.e., these procedures remain complete if each generated resolvent is immediately replaced by a condensation. The use of condensation becomes even *essential* in the design of refutation methods that are decision procedures for large classes of quantificational formulas [12].

Joyner [12] proves the following important result:

---

[1]Note that there are terminological discrepancies concerning subsumption in the standard literature. In [16], for instance, clause implication is termed subsumption, and what we call subsumption here is referred to as θ-subsumption.

Proposition 2.1 *Any two condensations of a clause are variants.*

In [12], Joyner also indicates two methods for obtaining a condensation of a clause C. The first method consists in examining all subsets of C and determining if they are instances of C, i.e., if they are subsumed by C. Of course, this exhaustive method is very inefficient and not advisable for practical use since it requires an exponential number of expensive subsumption tests. However, since the main concern of Joyner's paper is decidability and not efficiency, this method completely fulfills his purposes.

The second method is outlined as follows in [12]: a condensation of C is produced by successively unifying pairs of literals in a clause until no clause which is a variant of a subset of C can be produced. Although this method seems more appealing at the first glance, it unfortunately suffers from subtle problems, as the following example shows.

We exhibit a clause C such that each clause C_{ij} obtained from C by unifying the i-th and the j-th literal, is not a variant of any subset of C. Let $C = \{p(x, y, u), p(y, x, v), p(a, a, a)\}$. We then have:

$$C_{12} = \{p(x, x, u), p(a, a, a)\}$$

$$C_{13} = \{p(a, a, v), p(a, a, a)\}$$

$$C_{23} = \{p(a, a, u), p(a, a, a)\}.$$

Clearly, none of these C_{ij} is a variant of any subset of C. If the second condensing method were correct, this would mean that C is condensed. However, this is not the case since $CONDS(C) = \{\{p(a, a, a)\}\} \neq C$.

It is easy to see that one possibility of correcting the algorithm is to simultaneously unify suitable *subsets* of literals of C (and not just *pairs*) until the resulting clause is a variant of a subset of C and cannot be further reduced. For example, if the three literals of clause C in the above example are simultaneously unified, we immediately get the condensation.

However, also this method is rather expensive since it will in general invoke an exponential number of variant-tests. To see this, it suffices to consider clauses of the form $B_n = \{\neg q(x_1, x_2), \neg q(x_2, x_3) \ldots \neg q(x_{n-1}, x_n), q(x_n, x_1)\}$. Note also that no efficient algorithm is known today for testing whether two clauses are variants since this problem is isomorphism-complete.

A better condensing algorithm has been given in Joyner's thesis [11]. In the next section we show that this algorithm performs only a polynomial number of "critical" subsumption tests.

3 Joyner's Condensing Algorithm

The algorithm essentially consists of a single rewriting rule whose iterated application reduces a given clause C to a condensation. The method is based on the principle of successively unifying pairs of literals of a clause until a condensation is obtained. Our representation of the algorithm differs slightly (but not substantially) from the one given in [11]. The condensing algorithm uses as subroutine a function-procedure $subs(C_1, C_2)$ which returns a substitution σ such that $C_1\sigma \subseteq C_2$ in case clause C_1 subsumes C_2 and the special symbol $\perp$ otherwise. This subroutine can be implemented by using standard subsumption algorithms [4, 20] or by using some more sophisticated algorithms such as the ones described in [9, 8].

The condensing algorithm is as follows:

Algorithm CONDENSE
INPUT: a clause C;
OUTPUT: a condensation of C;
BEGIN
$D := C$
  WHILE there exist unifiable literals L_i and L_j in D
           with mgu θ such that $subs(D\theta, D) = \sigma \neq \perp$
   DO $D := D\theta\sigma$;
RETURN D;
END.

This algorithm does not specify which pair of literals L_i, L_j should be chosen if there are several such pairs meeting the loop-condition. Indeed, this choice is completely irrelevant. In Joyner's original version of the algorithm, the lexicographically first literals meeting this condition are chosen.

A detailed complexity analysis of the CONDENSE algorithm would depend on the particular choice of the subsumption-algorithm used for the subroutine *subs*. We did not commit ourselves to a particular subsumption algorithm, nor did Joyner, hence we cannot derive exact complexity bounds. Instead, we remark that the algorithm has polynomial runtime except for the work performed inside the *subs* subroutine (recall that subsumption-testing is NP-complete). It thus makes sense to estimate how often this subroutine is called by CONDENSE. The following theorem gives an upper bound on the number of such calls.

Theorem 3.1 *The CONDENSE algorithm applied to an input clause C performs in the worst case $O(|C|^3)$ calls to the subs procedure.*

PROOF. Let $|C|=n$. There are not more than n evaluations of the while-condition. At the k-th evaluation of the while-condition, D has at most $|C| + 1 - k$ literals, hence there are at most $\binom{|C|+1-k}{2}$ pairs $\{L_i, L_j\}$ of literals for which the algorithm tries to find a mgu. Each such unification attempt can give raise to at most one call of *subs*. Note that for each unifiable pair $\{L_i, L_j\}$ under consideration, it is sufficient to find not more than *one* mgu θ, because if $subs(D\theta, D) = \perp$, then $subs(D\lambda, D) = \perp$ for each other mgu λ of $\{L_i, L_j\}$. The total number of *subs*-calls is thus bounded by:

$$\sum_{k=1}^{n} \binom{n+1-k}{2} = \sum_{k=1}^{n} \binom{k}{2} = \binom{n+1}{3} = O(n^3).$$

We now show that $O(n^3)$ is an attainable bound. Let us assume w.l.o.g. that the algorithm uses lexicographic preference whenever it has to choose a literal from a clause. Let $n = 2m + 1$ be an odd integer. Consider the following (generic) clause:

$$C_n = \{p(x_1), \ldots, p(x_m), q(y_1), \ldots, q(y_m), r(x_1, \ldots, x_m)\}.$$

Note that the literals in this clause are lexicographically ordered, thus the algorithm will always proceed from left to right. Obviously, all $q(y_i)$ will be lumped by unification to one single literal. However, at the very beginning of the computation, and after each unification of some $q(y_i)$ with some $q(y_j)$, the algorithm unifies each $p(x_i)$ with each $p(x_j)$, $i \neq j$, and performs a subsumption test. There are thus not less than $m * \binom{m}{2} = O(m^3) = O(n^3)$ subsumption tests. $\square$

CONDENSE has thus a noticeably smaller worst case complexity in terms of subsumption calls than the two algorithms described in the previous section, since these algorithms involve $O(2^n)$ critical operations (subsumption tests or variant tests) for clauses of size n in the worst case.

Nevertheless, condensing is a relatively expensive technique: the CONDENSE algorithms involve several subsumption tests – and subsumption testing is known to be NP-complete. In the next section we will even show that condensing itself is NP-hard and thus a polynomial condensing algorithm is not likely to exist. Hence it is more than legitimate to ask what can be gained by condensing and whether we should use this technique at all.

While it has been shown that the use of condensing is necessary in certain very special resolution strategies in order to make them decision procedures for relevant classes of theories [12], it turns out that condensing can be most profitable even with standard resolution techniques. Indeed, the presence of non-condensed clauses in a knowledge base may have detrimental effects to the efficiency of any resolution-based inference procedure. It is easy to find examples, where a non-condensed clause with a linear number of redundant literals is responsible for an exponential explosion of the number of generated resolvents.

As a rather trivial example, consider a knowledge base KB consisting of a Horn clause

$$C : \{\neg p(x_1), \neg p(x_2), \dots, \neg p(x_n), \neg p(a), q(a)\},$$

in rule notation:

$$C : p(x_1) \wedge p(x_2) \wedge \dots \wedge p(x_n) \wedge p(a) \Rightarrow q(a),$$

and of ground unit clauses (facts) $\{p(a_i)\}$ for $1 \leq i \leq m$.

Assume that we want to test whether $q(a)$ is a logical consequence of KB (it obviously isn't). For this purpose, we add the goal $\neg q(a)$ to KB and try to refute it by resolution. If we use general (unrestricted) resolution, then more than m^n resolvents will be generated before the procedure halts with negative exit. On the other hand, if C is replaced by its condensation $p(a) \Rightarrow q(a)$, then the procedure halts with the same result after having generated only m resolvents. Analogously, if we use Logic Programming (SLD-resolution [15] or Prolog [5]) to solve the above problem, then the runtime of the program changes from exponential to polynomial, if we replace C by its condensation.

4 The Complexity of Condensing

The CONDENSE algorithm heavily relies on subsumption tests. Unfortunately, all known subsumption algorithms have exponential worst-case complexity. Moreover, deciding whether a clause subsumes another clause is NP-complete. Therefore, the question whether it is possible to design a better condensing algorithm with guaranteed polynomial runtime naturally arises. In this section we will show that this is not possible unless P=NP. We will prove that the problem of deciding whether a given clause is condensed is co-NP-complete.

Theorem 4.1 *Deciding whether a clause is condensed is co-NP-complete. The problem remains co-NP-complete even if restricted to positive clauses with no function symbols and with at most binary predicate symbols.*

PROOF. Membership in co-NP is easy to see by showing that the complement of our problem is in NP. A nondeterministic polynomial method for showing that a clause C is not condensed is as follows: guess a proper subset C' of C and guess a substitution θ such that $C\theta \subseteq C'$. Checking $C\theta \subseteq C'$ obviously can be done in polynomial time.

In order to show that the problem is co-NP-hard, we will polynomially transform the complement of the well-known CLIQUE problem to it. An instance of the CLIQUE problem is described by two parameters, a graph G without loops and a positive integer k, and by the question whether G contains a clique of size k. CLIQUE is known to be NP-complete ([6]). To each instance $I = < G, k >$ of CLIQUE we construct a clause $C_{G,k}$ such that I has a negative answer iff $C_{G,k}$ is condensed.

$C_{G,k}$ consists of the union of two components :

$$C_{G,k} = GR_G \cup CL_k$$

where GR_G, the "graph component", encodes the graph G, CL_k, the "clique component" encodes a generic clique of size k.

Assume that the vertex set of G is $\{c_1, \ldots, c_n\}$. The two components of $C_{G,k}$ are defined as follows:

The graph component GR_G contains a a pair of literals $g(c_i, c_j)$ and $g(c_j, c_i)$ for each edge $\{c_i, c_j\} \in G$. The symbols $c_1 \ldots c_n$ are interpreted as constant symbols in $C_{G,k}$.

The clique component CL_k consists of the following set of literals: $\{g(x_i, x_j) | 1 \leq i, j \leq k \text{ and } i \neq j\}$ where all x_i are variable symbols.

We now show that $C_{G,k}$ is condensed iff G has no clique of size k.

Observe that if $C_{G,k}$ is not condensed, then, in order to get a condensation, the entire clique component CL_k must disappear. In other terms, $C_{G,k}$ is not condensed if and only if there exists a substitution θ such that $CL_k\theta \subseteq GR_G$. Indeed, since, as easily seen, the component CL_k is itself condensed, any useful substitution for producing a condensation must unify literals of CL_k with literals of GR_G. Furthermore, *all* variables of CL_k must be transformed to constants by θ, for otherwise $C_{G,k}\theta$ would contain at least one literal of the form $g(x, c)$ where x is a variable and c is a constant and thus $C_{G,k}\theta$ would not be a subset of $C_{G,k}$.

It is easy to see that there exists a substitution θ such that $CL_k\theta \subseteq GR_G$ iff G contains a clique of size k. The "if"- direction is evident. To see the "only-if"-direction of this claim, notice that θ cannot replace two distinct variables by the same constant since G is loop-free, hence $CL_k\theta$ is a clique of size k.

The transformation from $< G, k >$ to $C_{G,k}$ can easily be done in polynomial time, hence the problem of testing whether a clause is condensed is NP-hard and thus NP-complete. Note that clause $C_{G,k}$ is positive, has no function symbols and only binary predicate symbols. The second part of the theorem follows immediately. $\square$

The following corollaries are immediate consequences of theorem 4.1.

Corollary 4.2 *If $P{\neq}NP$ then there exists no polynomial condensing algorithm.*

Corollary 4.3 *Let C be a clause of cardinality n. Deciding whether $\text{cond}\#(C) = n$ is co-NP-complete.*

An interesting question is whether this NP-completeness result can be generalized to the following decision problem: given a clause C and a positive integer $k \leq |C|$, does it hold that $cond\#(C) = k$? This problem is dealt-with in the next section.

5 D^P-complete Problems

In this section we provide evidence that identifying a condensation of a clause is – in a very subtle sense – harder than just solving an NP-complete (or a co-NP-complete) decision problem.

A closer look at the CONDENSE algorithm reveals that if the input clause C is not condensed, then the algorithm performs always at least one subsumption test with positive exit and at least one subsumption test with negative exit. In other words, the algorithm involves both, the positive solution of an NP-complete problem (subsumption) and the positive solution of a co-NP-complete problem (non-subsumption).

More generally, the problem of deciding whether a clause $C' \subset C$ is a condensation of C can be formulated as the conjunction of an NP-complete problem and a co-NP-complete problem: C' is a condensation of C iff C subsumes C' (NP-complete) and C' is condensed (co-NP-complete). From this representation it does not follow that the problem is in NP, nor can we conclude that it lies in co-NP. It is thus natural to ask whether this problem belongs to either one of these classes. We will show that this is not the case (unless P=NP) by proving that our problem is D^P-complete.

The complexity class D^P was introduced by Papadimitriou and Yannakakis in [18] and further studied in [17]. A problem is in D^P if it can be represented as the conjunction of a problem in NP and a problem in co-NP. Obviously, NP $\cup$ co-NP $\subseteq D^P \subseteq$ PSPACE. A problem is D^P-complete if any other problem of D^P can be polynomially transformed to it. D^P-complete problems are thus the "hardest" problems in D^P. A simple example for a D^P-complete problem is SAT-UNSAT, i.e., given a pair of propositional clause-sets C_1, C_2, decide whether it holds that C_1 is satisfiable and C_2 is unsatisfiable [18]. It is easy to see that, unless NP=co-NP, a D^P-complete problem is neither in NP nor in co-NP.

Why should a D^P-complete problem be considered a harder problem than any NP-complete or co-NP-complete problem ? From a purely deterministic worst-case standpoint, there is probably no reason to do so. Indeed, the best known deterministic algorithms for solving NP-complete or co-NP-complete problems run in single-exponential time, and the same holds for D^P. However, if an NP problem instance is positively solvable, then there is a short proof for it which can be found in polynomial time by a nondeterministic "guess-and-check" algorithm. The same holds for negatively solvable instances of co-NP problems. On the other hand, unless NP=co-NP, neither the positive nor the negative instances of a D^P-complete problem allow short proofs in general. In this sense D^P can be considered harder as NP or co-NP.

The next theorem can thus be interpreted as follows: in general we need exponential space for writing down a (polynomially checkable) proof for the fact that a clause C' is or is not a condensation of a clause C.

Theorem 5.1 *Deciding whether a clause C' is a condensation of a clause C is D^P-complete*

PROOF. Membership in D^P has already been shown. In order to prove D^P-hardness, we will show that SAT-UNSAT can be polynomially transformed into our problem. To show this it suffices to show a) that there exists a polynomial transformation from SAT to our problem, b) that there exists a transformation from UNSAT (the complement of SAT) to our problem, and c) that two instances of our problem can be polynomially transformed to a single instance.

a) Since CLIQUE is NP-complete, any instance of SAT can be transformed in polynomial time to an equivalent instance $I =< G, k >$ of CLIQUE. In the proof of Theorem 4.1 we have shown that $< G, k >$ is positively solvable iff $C_{G,k}$ is not condensed. Furthermore, it immediately follows from the proof of Theorem 4.1 that $C_{G,k}$ is not condensed iff $CONDS(C_{G,k}) = \{GR_G\}$. Thus, I is positively solvable iff GR_G is a condensation of $C_{G,k}$. This shows that SAT is polynomially transformable to our problem.

b) UNSAT is obviously polynomially transformable into NO-CLIQUE, the complement of CLIQUE. An instance $I =< G, k >$ of NO-CLIQUE in turn, by the proof of theorem 4.1 is positively solvable iff the clause $C_{G,k}$ is condensed, or equivalently, iff $C_{G,k}$ is a condensation of $C_{G,k}$. This shows that UNSAT is polynomially transformable to our problem.

c) Let $< C, C' >$ and $< D, D' >$ be two instances of our problem. Consider clauses D_* and D'_* resulting from D and D' by uniformly replacing each predicate and variable symbol by a new distinct symbol not occurring in $C \cup C'$. Obviously, D'_* is a condensation of D_* iff D' is a condensation of D. Furthermore, it is easy to see that $C' \cup D'_*$ is a condensation of $C \cup C' \cup D_* \cup D'_*$ iff C' is a condensation of C and D' is a condensation of D. $\square$

A similar theorem holds for the identification of the condensation number $cond\#(C)$ of a clause C.

Theorem 5.2 *It is* D^P*-complete to decide for a clause C and for an integer k, $1 \leq k \leq |C|$, whether* $cond\#(C) = k$.

PROOF. First notice that the problem is effectively in D^P, since $cond\#(C) = k$ can be formulated as a conjunction of the following problems: 1.) there exists a subset $C' \subseteq C$ with $|C'| = k$ and $C \triangleright C'$ (this problem is in NP) and 2.) For no subset $C' \subset C$ with $|C'| < k$ does $C \triangleright C'$ (this problem is in co-NP).

For showing that it is D^P-hard, we transform a well-known D^P-complete problem, the EXACT CLIQUE problem [18] to it. An instance $I =< G, m >$ of EXACT CLIQUE consists of a graph $G = (V, E)$ and an integer m (with $1 \leq m \leq |V|$); the answer to I is "yes" iff the largest clique of G has size exactly m.

Let $I =< G, k >$ be an instance of EXACT CLIQUE. Assume G consists of n vertices. Let the clauses $C^*_{G,k}$, for $1 < k \leq n$ be defined in the same way as $C_{G,k}$ in the proof of Theorem 4.1 but with a renaming of variables and predicate symbols in such a way that for $i \neq j$ $C^*_{G,i}$ and $C^*_{G,j}$ are disjoint in both variables and predicate symbols. Now let

$$C^*_G = \bigcup_{1 < k \leq n} C^*_{G,k}.$$

If G has a clique of size m, it clearly also has cliques of size i for $1 < i < m$. Thus, if the maximal clique of G is of size m, then for $1 < k \leq m$, $C^*_{G,k}$ is not condensed, and its unique condensation is GR^k_G, the graph component of $C^*_{G,k}$ (see also proof of Theorem 5.1). Furthermore, if the maximal clique of G is of size m, then $C^*_{G,k}$ is condensed for $k > m$. Since C^*_G is the union of $n - 1$ completely unrelated clauses $C^*_{G,k}$, the condensation of C^*_G is equal to the union of the condensations of the $C^*_{G,k}$. It follows, that G contains a clique of size k iff

$$cond\#(C^*_G) = \sum_{k=2}^{m} |GR^k_G| + \sum_{k=m+1}^{n} |C^*_{G,k}| .$$

Our transformation is complete. It is easy to see that this transformation can be done in polynomial time. $\Box$[2]

6   A Stronger Notion of Condensing

Condensing is not the only type of redundancy elimination one may conceive when a clause C is given. Another – rather trivial – method is tautology elimination. Obviously, if a clause is tautological, then the entire clause can be safely dropped from its environment. It is well-known that a clause is a tautology iff it contains a pair $L_1, \neg L_1$ of complementary literals, hence tautology recognition is easy. A more sophisticated method of redundancy elimination, *strong condensing*, will be studied in what follows.

Condensing relies on the concept of subsumption. If C subsumes a subset C', then we can replace C by C', since C and C' are equivalent clauses. The same principle remains valid if instead of subsumption the more general concept of *clause implication* is used. Indeed, if $C \Rightarrow C'$ with $C' \subset C$ then $C \equiv C'$. Based on this observation, we introduce some new concepts.

A clause C is *strongly condensed* if C does not contain any proper subset C' such that $C \Rightarrow C'$. Since every subset of C implies C, C is strongly condensed iff it does not contain any subset logically equivalent to it. A *strong condensation* of C is a minimum cardinality subset of C implied by C (i.e., a minimum cardinality subset of C equivalent to C). Obviously, every strong condensation of C is itself strongly condensed. Furthermore, if a clause is strongly condensed, then it is also condensed. However, there are condensed clauses, that are not strongly condensed.

Examples.   The clause
$$\{\neg p(x), \neg p(a), p(f(x)), p(f(f(a)))\}$$
is condensed, but not strongly condensed. Its unique strong condensation is $\{\neg p(a), p(f(f(a)))\}$. The clause
$$\{\neg p(x, y), \neg p(y, z), p(x, z), \neg p(u, v), \neg p(v, w), \neg p(w, w'), p(u, w')\}$$
is condensed but not strongly condensed. A strong condensation is:
$$\{\neg p(u, v), \neg p(v, w), \neg p(w, w'), p(u, w')\}.$$

Note that, unlike condensations, strong condensations of a clause are not necessarily variants.

Example.   Consider the clause
$$C = \{\neg p(u, v, w), \neg p(x, y, z), p(y, z', u)\}.$$

C is condensed, but has two strong condensations C' and C'':
$$C' = \{\neg p(u, v, w), p(y, z', u)\}$$
$$C'' = \{\neg p(x, y, z), p(y, z', u)\}.$$
Clearly, C' and D' are not variants of each other.

---

[2]Note that this proof (with slight modifications) could also have been used to prove Theorem 5.1. We preferred, however, to prove that theorem in a different way, involving less complicated constructions.

In order to characterize the strong condensations of a clause, we introduce the concept of self-resolvent.

A clause D is a *self-resolvent* of a clause C if one of the following conditions holds:

- D is a variant of C

- D is a resolvent of two self-resolvents of C.

$C^{@}$ denotes the set of all self-resolvents of C.

The following proposition which links clause implication to subsumption has been shown in [7].

Proposition 6.1 *Let C be an arbitrary clause and D a nontautological clause. $C \Rightarrow D$ iff there is a $C^* \in C^{@}$ such that $C^* \rhd D$.*

Thus the strong condensations of a clause C are the minimum-cardinality subsets of C that are instances of self-resolvents of C.

Obviously, a clause C has non-trivial self-resolvents only if C is recursive, i.e., only if C contains at least one pair of literals L_1, $\neg L_2$ such that L_1 and L_2 are unifiable. It follows that the concepts of condensation and strong condensation coincide on nonrecursive clauses.

Unfortunately, for general clauses there is an unsurmountable gap between condensation and strong condensation. We will show that the question whether a clause is strongly condensed is undecidable. For proving this, we make use of an important result by Schmidt-Schauss concerning clause implication:

Proposition 6.2 *(Schmidt-Schauss [19])   For general clauses C and D, the question whether C implies D is undecidable.*

The next theorem, where we show that testing whether a clause C is strongly condensed is undecidable, consists in a strengthening of Proposition 6.2. We show that the proposition remains valid, even if D is a proper subset of C.

Theorem 6.1 *The question whether a clause C is strongly condensed is undecidable.*

PROOF. Let us first note that the problem "$C \Rightarrow D$" remains undecidable even if we assume that both clauses C and D are non-tautological. This follows trivially from the fact that $C \Rightarrow D$ is decidable as soon as C or D is a tautology. Indeed, if C is a tautology, then $C \Rightarrow D$ iff D is a tautology. On the other hand, if D is a tautology, then $C \Rightarrow D$ is always true.

Let us therefore consider a pair of non-tautological clauses C and D and show that we can reduce the decision problem $C \Rightarrow D$ to a finite number of tests for strong condensation.

Let $D^{\bullet}$ denote the ground clause obtained from D by uniformly replacing each variable of D by a new distinct constant not occurring in $C \cup D$. It is easy to see that $C \Rightarrow D$ iff $C \Rightarrow D^{\bullet}$.

We show that $C \Rightarrow D^{\bullet}$ iff for each nonempty subset C' of C, $C' \cup D^{\bullet}$ is not strongly condensed (our theorem follows immediately).

If: We first show that each strong condensation of $E = C \cup D^{\bullet}$ must contain $D^{\bullet}$ as subset. Let E' be a strong condensation of E. E' is logically implied by E and hence, by Proposition 6.1, E' is an instance of some $E^* \in E^{@}$. Now observe that each clause in $E^{@}$ contains $D^{\bullet}$ as subset. Indeed, since the literals of $D^{\bullet}$ are all ground, they cannot disappear during self-resolution: assume E_1 and E_2 are self-resolvents of E containing both $D^{\bullet}$, and assume E_1 and E_2 resolve upon literals $L_1 \in E_1$ and $L_2 \in E_2$ of opposite sign; then any resolvent $(E_1\theta - L_1\theta) \cup (E_2\theta - L_2\theta)$ obviously contains $D^{\bullet}$ as subset. Thus $D^{\bullet} \subseteq E^*$ and hence $D^{\bullet} \subseteq E'$.

Now assume that for each nonempty subset of C' of C, $C' \cup D^{\bullet}$ is not strongly condensed. Then, in particular E is not strongly condensed. Since $D^{\bullet}$ is contained in each strong condensation of E, and since each superset of $D^{\bullet}$ in E is not strongly condensed, $D^{\bullet}$ is necessarily the only strong condensation of E. It follows that E is logically equivalent to $D^{\bullet}$, thus $E = (C \vee D^{\bullet}) \Leftrightarrow D^{\bullet}$, hence $C \Rightarrow D^{\bullet}$.

Only if: Assume $C \Rightarrow D^{\bullet}$. Let $C' \subseteq C$ with $C' \neq \emptyset$. Obviously $C' \Rightarrow C$ and thus $C' \Rightarrow D^{\bullet}$. It follows that $C' \cup D^{\bullet}$ is logically equivalent to its proper subset $D^{\bullet}$ and hence $C' \cup D^{\bullet}$ is not strongly condensed. $\square$

7   Conclusions and Further Research

From our results it follows that condensing is an expensive but rather useful technique. Joyner's CONDENSE algorithm uses $O(n^3)$ subsumption tests in the worst case for an input-clause with n literals. It thus appears worthwhile to look for improvements of this algorithm. Indeed, it is possible to derive a condensing algorithm which uses only $O(n)$ subsumption tests in the worst case and 0 such tests in the best case. Such an algorithm will be described in a forthcoming paper.

Given our undecidability result, we cannot recommend to attempt to transform a general clausal knowledge base into an equivalent one whose clauses are all strongly condensed. This may be feasible and useful only for restricted clause-classes. In particular, it would be interesting to see if strong condensation is decidable on Horn clauses. The topic deserves further research.

Acknowledgment.

The author is grateful to Th. Eiter and Ch. Fermüller for their valuable comments on an earlier version of this paper.

References

[1] L.D. Baxter. The NP-completeness of subsumption. unpublished manuscript, 1977.

[2] S. Ceri, G.Gottlob, and L Tanca. What you always wanted to know about datalog (and never dared to ask). *IEEE Transactions on Knowledge and Data Engineering*, 1(1), March 1989.

[3] S. Ceri, G. Gottlob, and L. Tanca. *Logic Programming and Databases*. Surveys in Computer Science. Springer Verlag, 1990.

[4] C.L. Chang and R.C.T. Lee. *Symbolic Logic and Mechanical Theorem Proving*. Academic Press, 1973.

[5] W.F. Clocksin and C.S. Mellish. *Programming in Prolog*. Springer Berlin/Heidelberg/New York, 1981.

[6] M. Garey and D.S. Johnson. *Computers and Intractability – A Guide to NP-Completeness*. W.H.Freeman, New York, 1979.

[7] G. Gottlob. Subsumption and implication. *Information Processing Letters*, 24:109–111, January 1987.

[8] G. Gottlob and A. Leitsch. Fast subsumption algorithms. In *Proceedings of the EUROCAL 85 Conference on Computer Algebra*, Lecture Notes in Computer Science. Springer Verlag, 1985.

[9] G. Gottlob and A. Leitsch. On the efficiency of subsumption algorithms. *Journal of the ACM*, 32(2):280–295, April 1985.

[10] H.Gallaire and J.Minker, editors. *Logic and Databases*. Plenum Press, New York, 1978.

[11] W.H. Joyner. *Automatic Theorem Proving and the Decision Problem*. PhD thesis, Harvard University, May 1973.

[12] W.H. Joyner. Resolution strategies as decision procedures. *Journal of the ACM*, 23(1):398–417, July 1976.

[13] A. Leitsch. Implication algorithms for classes of Horn clauses. *in: Informatik+Oekonomie, Berlin*, 1988.

[14] A. Leitsch and G. Gottlob. Deciding Horn clause implication problems by ordered semantic resolution. In F. Gardin, editor, *Computational Intelligence II, Proceedings of the International Symposium, Milan, Italy, 25-27 Sept. 1989*. North Holland, Amsterdam, 1989.

[15] J.W. Lloyd. *Foundations of Logic Programming*. Springer Verlag, Berlin, 1984, 1987.

[16] D. Loveland. *Automated Theorem Proving: A Logical Basis*. North Holland, Amsterdam, 1978.

[17] C.H. Papadimitriou and D.Wolfe. The complexity of facets resolved. *J. Comput. System Sci.*, 37:2–13, 1988.

[18] C.H. Papadimitriou and M.Yannakakis. The complexity of facets (and some facets of complexity). *J. Comput. System Sci.*, 28:244–259, 1984.

[19] M. Schmidt-Schauss. Implication of clauses is undecidable. *Theoretical Computer Science*, 59:287–296, 1988.

[20] R.B. Stillman. The concept of weak substitution in theorem proving. *Journal of the ACM*, 20(4):648–667, October 1973.

HESDE - A Hypertext based Expert-System debugging Tool

Craig Boyle, John Schuette
Department of Computer Science
Texas A&M University
College Station,
Texas 77843-3112
USA
internet: craig@cssun.tamu.edu

Abstract

The task of debugging Expert Systems is notoriously difficult. The HESDE (Hypertext Expert-System Debugging Environment) provides a flexible way to capture, and allow browsing of, an expert systems execution trace. HESDE operates in a rule-based environment, hence the objects of interest are the rule, facts and agenda. During a consultation the interaction between these objects is stored and *automatically transformed* into Hypertext network. After consultation, debugging is facilitated by allowing the user to browse the network.

Experimentation has shown HESDE to be superior to KEE for debugging certain tasks. Future work will allow authoring (dynamic modification of the network during execution) and extension to non-rule based paradigms.

Introduction

Expert Systems have made the transition from research prototype to commercially viable tools[1]. Consequently the motivation to produce reliable, high performance, expert systems at low cost is high. Unfortunately the complex heuristic nature of expert systems means that expert systems are difficult to debug.

The hypothesis of this study is that a hypertext based debugging tool is more productive than one traditional tool, the graphical execution trace (one of several traditional debugging paradigms). In this context, the definition of a "productive" system is one that:

- is easy to learn and use,
- is fast to use,
- helps the knowledge engineer "understand" the expert system, and
- is relatively insensitive to changes in the particulars of the expert system's execution.

This definition of productivity is motivated by several factors. As with traditional programs, expert systems evolve over a potentially long lifetime. Over this lifetime, personnel not involved with the original development of the project will eventually be used to maintain the system. Their debugging tools should make it relatively easy for the new knowledge engineer to grasp the processing of the system. Furthermore,

Depending on the tool, such a change may make the debugging task harder for the knowledge engineer; it would be helpful if the debugging tool presents the knowledge engineer with a familiar landscape regardless of changes in the nature of the consultation's progress.

This paper describes the design, implementation and evaluation of HESDE. A fuller explanation can be found in [2]

Hypertext as a debugging tool

Hypertext [3] provides us with a non-linear means of organizing information. Traditionally Hypertext has been used to represent textual and graphical data in a network. Users may browse this network by selecting links between data.

We note that the structure of a Hypertext document is *semantically similar* to that of an expert system execution trace. A rule based expert system operates using recognize-act cycle over a number of rules and facts. Rules are semantically linked through the dynamics of an expert system's execution. Rules and facts are linked as condition-instantiations and action-results. It is thus possible and appropriate to represent an expert system's execution trace in terms of Hypertext nodes and links.

The Hypertext Expert-System Debugging Environment

HESDE (Hypertext Expert-System Debugging Environment) currently complements the CLIPS[4] expert system shell. HESDE passively records the execution of CLIPS, noting rule firings, fact instantiations and their inter-relationships. After the execution of CLIPS HESDE presents a browsable version of the execution environment to the user. HESDE is transparent to the CLIPS user. Figure 1 shows the HESDE environment. CLIPS acts as normal to the user, concurrent with CLIPS's execution, a network is created. Once CLIPS' execution is complete the user may browse the network. The following sections will explain the functionality, structure and use of the network.

The HESDE network

The following table summarizes the nodes and links found in a HESDE network. All nodes have links to the RLN, FLN, and ALN; these links are not included here.

Node type	Displays	Link targets
RIN	rule instance	master rule
		previous rule instance
		subsequent rule instance
		rule agenda
		antecedent facts
RMN	rule prototype	rule instance
RLN	list of rules	master rules
FIN	fact instance	previous fact instance
		subsequent fact instance
		asserting rule instance
FLN	list of facts	fact instances
AIN	rules on agenda	rule instances
ALN	list of agendas	agenda instances

Table 1. Node types and functions.

The node types defined for the HESDE correspond to the basic objects in an expert system: the rules, facts, and agendas. The above list of node types is sufficient because these are the only types of objects in CLIPS and this HESDE is based on CLIPS.. One possibility mentioned in the future work session is the adaptation of the HESDE design to other expert system tools such as KEE. New node types and relationships may have to be introduced to represent new features supported by the new tool.

Each of the objects in table 1 results in the creation of a node. Figure 2 illustrates the connection between the Rule List node and rule master nodes. Note that the agenda list and facts list can both be reached by clicking on the ALN and FLN icons. In the following figures the "clickable" objects are boxed. These boxes are the hypertext links.

Figure 3 shows a typical Rule Master Node (RMN). The RMN displays the CLIPS rule in full textual format and allows movement to either the agenda list, fact list or rule list. The Rule Instance Node (RIN) permits the user view a particular instance of the RMN. The RIN is essential to differentiate among several uses of a node on different cycles. Figure 4 shows a RIN which is an instance of the RMN in Figure 3. If the user wishes to examine the state of the agenda on cycle 23, which is when the RIN was created, he can do so by clicking on the agenda button. If the user wishes to look at succeeding or preceding uses (instances) of the rule, he/she clicks either the "<-instance" or "instance->" buttons.

Similar nodes are created for the agenda and facts, allowing an in depth, cycle by cycle view of the execution network. See [2] for further detail.

Implementation

HESDE was implemented on a Macintosh II using LightSpeed C and is fully demonstratable. Prototypes were based on Hypercard [6], but this approach proved too inflexible because of external function memory limitations.

Testing

To show the usefulness of HESDE, it was compared with a popular conventional tool. For comparison, we chose KEE[5] which uses a graphical overview as the principal means of viewing a network. For experimentation, six users were assigned to KEE and HESDE respectively. They were asked to simulate the debugging of a pre-defined expert system by performing a set of typical tasks.

The task list was compiled based on the kinds of information a debugging knowledge engineer might need. For instance, tasks 1, 4, 8, and 11 correspond to Gilbert's [7] justification answers. Tasks 6 and 10 are related to his antecedence answer type. The other tasks deal with the basic programming concepts; tasks 2 and 9 relate to control of rule firing; tasks 3, 5, and 7 just correspond to the knowledge engineer's examining the text of a rule.

For eight of the eleven tasks, HESDE proved to be statistically significantly better in terms of speed and accuracy. There was no significant difference in incidental learning between the subject groups.

Conclusion

HESDE provides a robust and flexible hypertext-based environment for viewing and debugging an expert system's rule base. Testing has shown that HESDE outperforms at least one commercial expert system's debugging environment. We believe that HESDE will best be used as a complement to other debugging tools rather than a replacement.

Future Work

Much could be done to enhance HESDE. Areas under consideration include:

- Dynamic Operation,
    - ability to invoke HESDE during, rather than after a consultation

    - ability to modify execution environment from HESDE

- Extension to other paradigms and environments

References

1. Waterman, D. *A Guide to Expert Systems.* Addison-Wesley, Reading, Mass., 1986.

2. Schuette, J.F., *Hypertext as a Debugging Tools for Knowledge based Systems,* Master's thesis, Department of Computer Science, Texas A&M University, College Station, Texas, 1990.

3. Conklin, J. *Hypertext: An introduction and survey.* IEEE Computer, September 1987, 17-41.2.

4. Artificial Intelligence Section, Johnson Space Center. *CLIPS Reference Manual.* NASA, 1988.

5. IntelliCorp, Inc. *IntelliCorp KEE Software Development System Rulesystem3 Reference Manual.* IntelliCorp, Inc., 1987.

6. Apple Computer, Inc. *HyperCard User's Guide.* Apple Computer, Inc, Cupertino, CA, 1987.

7. Gilbert, G. *Question and answer types.* Research and Development in Expert Systems IV; Moralee, D., ed, 1987.

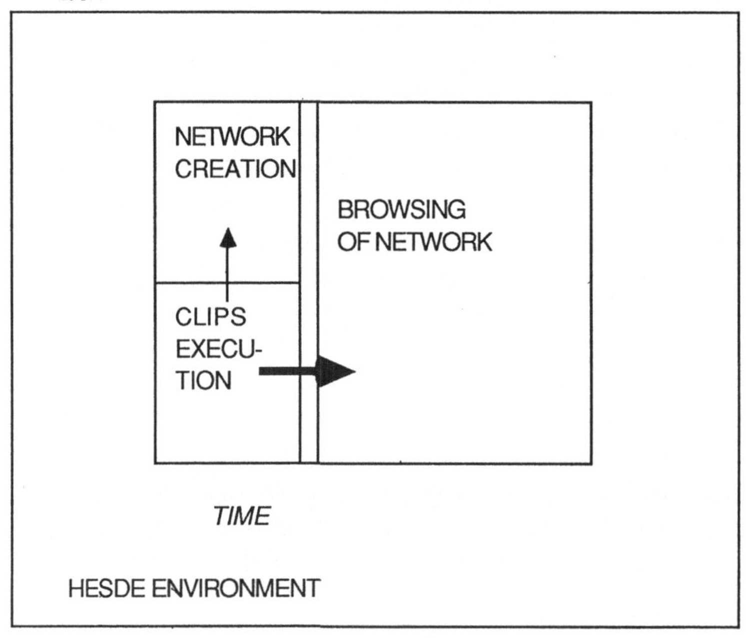

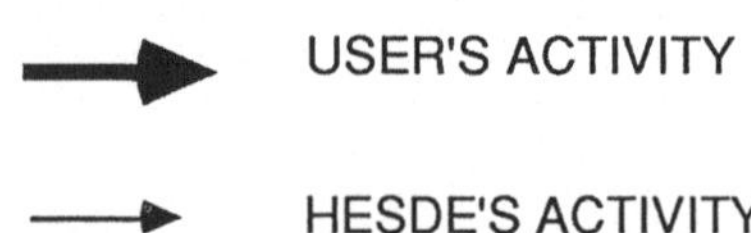

FIGURE 1. HESDE Environment

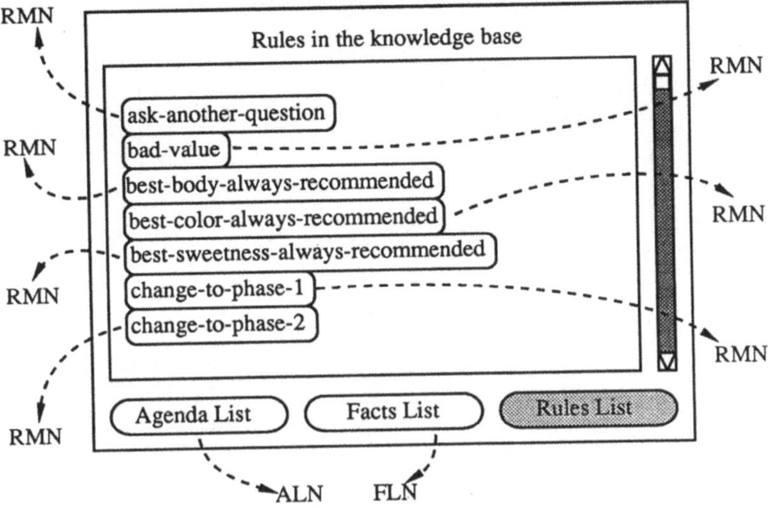

Figure 2: RLN (Rule List Node)

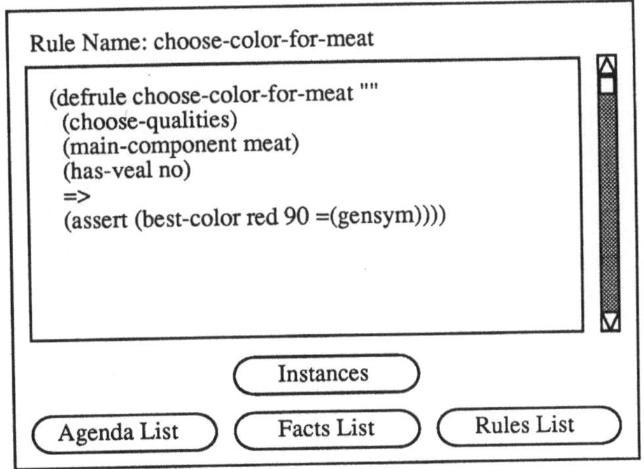

Figure 3 A RMN. (Rule Master Node)

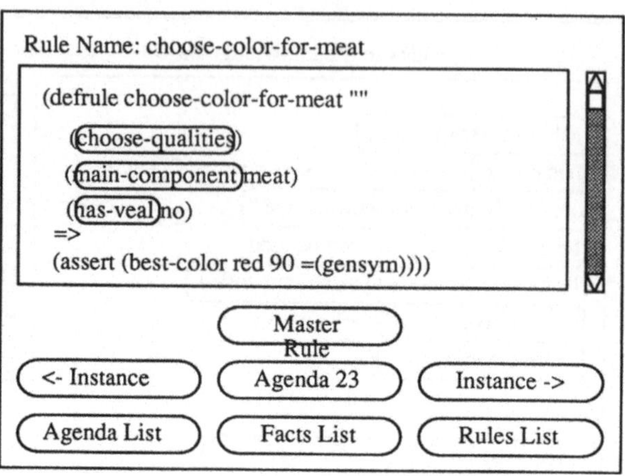

Figure 4: A RIN (Rule Instance Node)

A MODEL OF TASK-ORIENTED COMMUNICATION
BASED ON PRINCIPLES OF
RATIONAL ACTION AND INTERACTION

HELMUT HORACEK

Universität Bielefeld
Fakultät für Linguistik und Literaturwissenschaft
Postfach 8640, D-4800 Bielefeld 1, Deutschland

ABSTRACT

This paper presents a simple rule-based approach to express the rational behind physical actions and communicative acts by formally reconstructing the behavior of the agents involved on the basis of their mental states. The model of rational action and interaction is grounded on four principles comprising the concepts of mental initiative, physical activity, purposeful selection, and cooperation, which are expressed as inference rules. It is shown how the adequacy of a communicative act for achieving a certain task-oriented goal can be derived by deductive and abductive use of these rules, given a suitable environment in terms of the competence and the propositional attitudes of the agents involved. Finally, the potential of extending this basic model is sketched out.

1. INTRODUCTION

In the field of artificial intelligence several attempts have been undertaken to explain and formally reconstruct the behavior of rational interaction, which has been done from various backgrounds leading to, in particular, speech act theory (e.g., [9]), and methods based on mental states comprising mutual knowledge and intentions (e.g., [4]). As for the impact on practical use in implemented systems, most approaches can roughly be considered to fall into either of two highly diverse clusters: mechanisms applied in implemented (dialog) systems are usually characterized by some simplifying implicit assumptions (HAM-ANS [6], for instance, implicitly expects user utterances to be questions unless an explicit expectation dictates the contrary), and they frequently provide some facilities for subdialogs based on the exploitation of expectations about possible sequences of speech acts and a simple analysis of their contents. In addition, some approaches concentrate on certain aspects of the intentions underlying dialog contributions, like ARGOT [1, 2] does in tracking plans, and WISBER [7] does in meaningfully relating real world actions to portions of knowledge which serve as a prerequisite for performing the envisioned actions in reality. However, the fact that these mechanisms are, to some extent, based on somehow compiled and/or specialized knowledge makes generalizations and extentions in these systems a tough task.

These conceptual shortcuts are overcome in (mostly theoretical) models with a well-defined semantics (e.g., [10]) which, as an unfortunate compensation, usually suffer from notorious inefficiency (as, for instance, the ambitious system KAMP [3] does). In addition, they sometimes include strict assumptions which are important for making the formal theory work but, in the long run, these assumptions seem to be unrealistic when facing real world situations which they should be applicable to. For instance, the theory expanded in [4] requires agents to accept the ´inevitables´ as desirable, and to adopt only achievable goals, which, in general, does not look to be necessarily the case in the view of the imperfectness of information agents usually suffer from.

By aiming at a certain degree of integration, we adopt results from theoretical approaches (e.g., the concepts underlying speech acts can be explained more deeply in terms of mental states of agents, as [4] proposes), but we express them in a rule-based mechanism (which is much easier to handle than, e.g., the formal semantics defined in [4]) to make the associated reasoning potential realistically applicable to practical systems. However, we have to admit that we still make some implicit assumptions (which we feel to be necessary in task-oriented man-machine communication) - for instance, assuming the agents´ sincerity throughout all phases of reasoning.

Thus, our aim is to come up with a practical (i.e., simple and efficiently realizable) mechanism that relates propositional attitudes to real world actions and communicative acts. We do this by motivating what we consider to be essential properties of communicative situations and feasible restrictions for expressing them in a formal model with reasonable effort. We focus on essential properties by adopting adequate simplifications, and we obtain feasible restrictions by specifying necessary assumptions. Based on these prerequisites we introduce a basic version of our model, which is grounded on clearly identified fundamental principles of rational behavior (expressed as inference rules). Then we show how the adequacy of a communicative act for achieving a certain task-oriented goal can be derived by deductive and abductive use of these rules, given a suitable environment in terms of the competence and the propositional attitudes of the agents involved. Finally, we discuss extentions that become relevant when relaxing the simplifications introduced.

2. THE MODEL OF ACTION AND INTERACTION

Apart from keeping it as simple as possible, a major aim in producing the basic version of our model is to focus on the relations between action and interaction. For that purpose we adopt a very simplistic view of actions in and of themselves: a transition between two states is considered as a *simple* action irrespective of the complexity of the changes involved. Hence, what is usually seen as a sequence of more elementary actions is interpreted as a single and primitive action here. Moreover, we rely on the idealization that an agent´s beliefs concerning the suitability of actions to achieve state changes are <u>entirely</u> *consistent* with the laws of the physical world and its present state - thus, agents are assumed to be omnipotent in that respect. Consequently, they never make mistakes by selecting inappropriate actions, and the performance of an action <u>always</u> leads to the successful achievement of the results envisioned.

In addition to these simplifications, we adopt some useful <u>assumptions</u> (and, we believe, necessary ones for task-oriented man-machine communication). A central assumption, which we feel to be a fundamental prerequisite in a cooperative environment, is concerned with the attitude of agents towards each other: we assume agents to be always *sincere*. A further assumption is that a state change cannot occur by itself or by the occurrence of events which are outside the scope of influence of the agents involved (this is some kind of *closed world* assumption). Because of the simplifications introduced above, also those kind of actions are excluded from causing an envisioned change which occur accidentally rather than intentionally (or as the result of a mistake). Thus, waiting can never be an adequate action to achieve a state change - some kind of activity has to be performed by one of the agents considered. Finally, we assume agents <u>never</u> to be *lazy* or *tired* or having some other reason (for instance a goal of higher priority) which inhibits them performing a desired action, i.e., once agents are willing and capable to perform an action, they will do it.

As a consequence of these assumptions and simplifications, a state change envisioned always needs the actual occurrence of an action which, in turn, must be the consequence of its agent´s intention. This leads to the fundamental distinction between some <u>mental initiative</u> (which is based on a certain desire of an agent), that manifests itself in the <u>selection</u> of an appropriate action, which, in turn, leads to the performance of some <u>physical activity</u> that results in the envisioned change in the real world. However, if the environment considered comprises more than a single agent, exhibiting <u>cooperativity</u> is a prerequisite for achieving success by combined forces, which raises the necessity of communication among the agents involved. Consequently, we formulate four basic principles by which we express the cornerstones of our model of rational action and interaction: the principles of **mental initiative, physical activity, purposeful selection**, and **cooperation** (see Figure 1).The effect of cooperativity is to adopt goals of other agents which results in taking some burden of labour from another agent if this appears to be convenient. Notice that merely sharing the other agent´s want is not sufficient - this could be interpreted as some kind of solidarity. In the basic version presented here, we neglect problems of conflict resolution in case several actions or, respectively, agents are considered adequate in a selection task.

In order to formalize these principles we use similar primitives and techniques as those applied in the dialog control component developed for the WISBER system [5, 8]. However, in this simple version presented here, we omit time intervals which are associated with actions and states in that approach. Consequently, actions, states, and agents are the only sorts needed here. An action is expressed as a state transition, which is formalized by *enables* (s_1, a) and *has-effect* (a, s_2), where a is an action that is enabled by state s_1 and, if it actually occurs, results in state s_2. Propositional attitudes are represented as modal operators expressing wants *(W)* and beliefs *(B)* of an agent. Hence, $W(a, x)$ expresses that, depending on the sort x belongs to, agent a wants a state (x) to be achieved, or an action (x) to occur. $B(a, x)$ expresses that agent a believes in the truth of proposition x. In addition, we use the general terms *Do* (a, x) for agent´s a performing of action x and *Express* (a, b, x) for agent´s a performing of a speech act with agent b as its addressee and proposition x as its content. Moreover, *Can-Do* (a, x) is introduced to express that the prerequisites of performing action x for agent a are fulfilled. The meaning associated with this term comprises an agent´s general *capability* to perform this kind of action and the concrete *possibility* (or *opportunity*) to do this in the actual situation (this distinction has been introduced in [8]).

---

1. The principle of **mental initiative**:

This principle applies if a desire to achieve a goal occurs. By virtue of the <u>assumption</u> about *state changes*, some action suitable for resulting in the envisioned goal state must be undertaken (not necessarily by the same agent), which is the force provided by the rule associated.

(1) $\forall$ a, st: (**W** (a, st) & $\rightarrow$ **W** (a, $\exists$ act: (has-effect (act, st) &
               B (a, $\neg$ st) & ps   enables (ps, act) & $\exists$ x: Do (x, act))))

        <u>If</u> agent *a* has a want to achieve state *st*,
           and he/she believes that this state does not (yet) hold in the present state *ps*,
        <u>then</u> a want is derived which entails some agent *x* to do an action *act* that, once it occurs,
           is supposed to result in the envisioned state (and is applicable in the present state *ps*).

---

2. The principle of **physical activity**:

This principle applies if an agent wants a certain action to occur. If an appropriate environment is present, the force behind the rule associated is that the action will be performed due to the <u>assumption</u> about the agents' *willingness*.

(2) $\forall$ a, act: (**W** (a, Do (a, act)) & $\rightarrow$ Do (a, act))
                Can-Do (a, act)

        <u>If</u> agent *a* has a want to perform action *act*, and he/she can also do it,
        <u>then</u> it can be derived that this agent really will perform action *act*.

---

3. The principle of **purposeful selection**:

This principle applies if a variable in the propositional content of an agent's want needs an adequate substitute. The force behind the rule associated is that a potential substitute is also chosen (<u>disregarding</u> problems of *conflict resolution*).

(3a) $\forall$ a, st: (**B** (a, has-effect (act, st)) & $\rightarrow$ x = act)))   (selecting actions according
              W (a, $\exists$ x: (has-effect (x, st)   to suitable state transitions)

        <u>If</u> agent *a* has a want that some yet unspecified action *x* should be found which results
           in state *st*, and he/she believes that there is an action *act* which actually does so,
        <u>then</u> it can be derived that (agent *a* wants that) the unspecified action to be instantiated to *act*.

(3b) $\forall$ a, act: (**W** (a, $\exists$ x: (Do (x, act) & $\rightarrow$ **W** (a, Do (b, act)))))))   (selecting agents according
              B (a, $\exists$ b: (Can-Do (b, act))   to their assumed competence)

        <u>If</u> agent *a* has a want that some yet unspecified agent *x* should perform action *act*,
           and he/she believes that there is an agent *b* who can really perform that action,
        <u>then</u> it can be derived that agent *a* wants the other (agent *b*) to perform action *act*.

---

4. The principle of **cooperation**:

This principle applies if an agent has recognized a want of another. Thus, a desire to perform a suitable action in favor of the other agent (if given the opportunity) is created, which is the force behind the rule associated (due to the <u>assumption</u> of *cooperation*).

(4) $\forall$ a, b, st: (**B** (b, **W** (a, st)) & $\rightarrow$ **W** (b, Do (b, act))))
               B (b, $\exists$ act: (has-effect (act, st) &
                    Can-Do (b, act))

        <u>If</u> agent *b* believes that agent *a* has a want to achieve some state *st*, and he/she also believes
           that there is an action *act* which results in state *st* and which agent *b* is able to perform,
        <u>then</u> it can be derived that agent *b* wants to perform action *act*.

Figure 1: Four principles of rational action and interaction

(5)	$\forall$ a, b, prop: (Express (a, b, prop) $\rightarrow$ **B** (b, prop))	The effect of a speech act is that its addressee believes its content (according to the <u>sincerity</u> assumption)
(6)	$\forall$ a, b, prop: Can-Do (a, Express (a, b, prop))	All agents involved are capable of performing speech acts

Figure 2: Definitions associated with speech acts

The principles are formulated as inference rules (see Figure 1) which, once the premise is proved, the conclusion can be derived by virtue of the meaning associated with the respective rule (i.e., the principles are taken as axioms for our purposes). Thus, reasoning in our environment is primarily considered as causal chaining; the apparent temporal relations between the propositional attitudes derived can be re-expressed in terms of causal dependencies. Apart from the usual deductive use, also assumption-based and abductive applications may be beneficial in a reasoning process. Finally, we introduce a definition of the <u>effect of speech acts</u> on the mental state of the addressee, which is a straightforward derivation of the sincerity assumption (see definition (5) in Figure 2). In addition, agents are unconditionally assumed to be capable of performing speech acts (see definition (6) in Figure 2).

3. AN EXAMPLE

The urgency of performing some action (which, frequently, may also include interaction) arises whenever an agent encounters a difference between the global situation currently present and some goal state he/she wants to become true. In a short example we demonstrate how the principles introduced can be applied to derive the speech act of requesting another agent to perform an action from the want to envision the resulting state (see Figure 4 for the sequence of inference steps involved), and to derive the performance of this action by the other agent from the recognition of this speech act (all under the assumption that ´everything goes well´ - which corresponds to the assumptions the basic version of our model includes). The necessary <u>environment</u> is defined by the assertions (7) to (9c) in Figure 3. In addition, this inference process relies on a **meta-principle of reasoning** (10) which is used for finding goal substitutions to justify abductive inferencing in addition to deductive inferencing licensed by classical logic: whenever agent a wants to achieve G and believes that F implies G, then agent a wants to achieve F.

(10) $\mathbf{W}$ (a, G) & $\mathbf{B}$ (a, F $\rightarrow$ G) $\rightarrow$ $\mathbf{W}$ (a, F)

As for the recognition of this speech act, straightforward (i.e., deductive) application of (5) and of principles (3) and (2) (in that order) results in the derivation of act_1 being performed by a_2.

4. EXTENDABILITY

The simple version of the model introduced is adequate to include speech acts and the performance of other actions without much degree of variety. Though we certainly think that it is important to cope also with, for instance, the effect of mistakes in a realistic model, we believe that their exclusion is a well justified simpli-fication for coming up with a basic model. Thus, the consideration of all problems concerned with creation and maintenance of plans, the occurrence of associated deviations and mistakes is deferred to more elabo-rate versions of the basic model.

Being just a basis for demonstrating reasoning about interaction, this mechanism provides several hooks so that it can be expanded to be able to cope with more complex environments:

- Assertions containing the predicate *Can-Do* need not necessarily be available in the appropriate form the knowledge base whenever there is a need for (as this has been the case in the example presented). Hence, reasoning also has to do with acquiring the *opportunity* for a certain agent to perform an envisioned action (which is what the consultation dialogs in [7] are all about - relating a real world goal to the information missing for performing an action to achieve that goal - see [5, 8]).

(7)	$\mathbf{W}$ (a_1, st_1)	agent a_1 wants to achieve state st_1
(8)	$\mathbf{B}$ (a_1, $\neg$ st_1)	which he/she believes currently not to hold, and
(9a)	Can-Do (a_2, act_1)	agent a_2 has the capability and opportunity to do,
(9b)	has-effect (act_1, st_1)	action act_1, which results in (the envisioned) state st_1
(9c)	enables (ps, act_1)	and is applicable to the present state *ps*.

Figure 3: A simple environment for demonstrating the cooperation of two agents

(11)	$W\,(a_1,\ \exists\ act\!:\ (has\text{-}effect\ (act,\ st_1)$ $\&\ \exists\ x\!:\ Do\ (x,\ act)))$	is obtained by substituting assumptions (7) and (8) in the premise of principle (1), thus deriving its conclusion where the entities a_1 and st_1 are substituted for a and for st.
(12)	$W\,(a_1,\ \exists\ x\!:\ Do\ (x,\ act_1))$	is then derived by applying principle (3a) and assertion (9b); then only the second term of conjunction (11) needs to be treated further, and act_1 is substituted for act.
(13)	$W\,(a_1,\ Do\ (a_2,\ act_1))$	obtained by applying principle (3b) and assertion (9a), so that a_2 is substituted for x.
(14)	$W\,(a_1,\ W\,(a_2,\ Do\ (a_2,\ act_1)))$	results then by applying principle (2) abductively ($G = Do\ (a_2,\ act_1)$), ($F \rightarrow G$) = principle (2)); the first term in the resulting conjunction in the scope of the want is identical to (9a), so that only the second term needs further elaboration.
(15)	$W\,(a_1,\ B\,(a_2,\ W\,(a_1,\ act_1)))$	is obtained again by applying abduction, this time to principle (4): ($G = W\,(a_2,\ Do\ (a_2,\ act_1))$); again, the first term in the resulting conjunction in the scope of the want can be proved immediately (by putting (9a) in the scope of belief) leaving only the second term.
(16)	$W\,(a_1,\ Express\ (a_1,\ a_2,\ W\,(a_1,\ act_1)))$	results by means of the third abductive inference, applied to (5): ($G = B\,(a_2,\ W\,(a_1,\ act_1))$).
(17)	$Express\ (a_1,\ a_2,\ W\,(a_1,\ act_1)))$	finally, principle (2) is applied to the speech act, which is possible assuming that a_1 is able to perform speech acts - according to (6).

Figure 4: Deriving the performance of a request from a want to achieve a certain goal

- There is not always a simple action available that converts the current state of the world into a desired one (as expressed in the simplifying formalization of principle 1). Therefore, in a more realistic environment, tracking of *plans* has to be done instead, much in the way demonstrated by ARGOT [1, 2].

- Finally, there is not always a single solution for selecting appropriate agents or action according to principle (3); thus, a suitable control mechanism is required that can explore several alternatives if needed. Moreover, the presence of conflicting goals will introduce further complications.

As a consequence of these extentions, a straightforward rule application (be it deductively or abductively) will hardly be sufficient anymore. Assumption-based reasoning will provide adequate means to cover the more complex situations arising. Thus, assumptions made in the course of the reasoning process may become topics of a communication, which is typical for (problem-oriented) real world conversations.

REFERENCES

[1] Allen J., Frisch A., Litman D.: *ARGOT: The Rochester Dialogue System*. In <u>AAAI-82</u>, pp. 66-70, Pittsburgh, 1982.

[2] Allen J.: *Argot: A System Overview*. In <u>Computational Linguistics</u>, N. Cercone (ed.), pp. 97-109, Oxford Pergamon Press, 1983.

[3] Appelt D.: *Planning English Sentences*. Cambridge University Press, 1985.

[4] Cohen P., Levesque H.: *Speech Acts and Rationality*. In <u>ACL-85</u>, pp. 49-60, 1985.

[5] Gerlach M., Horacek H.: *Dialog Control in a Natural Language System*. In <u>EACL-89</u>, Somers H., McGee M. (eds), pp. 27-34, Manchester, 1989.

[6] Hoeppner W. et al.: *Beyond Domain-Independence: Experience with the Development of a German Language Access System to Highly Diverse Background Systems*. In <u>IJCAI-83</u>, Vol. 1, pp. 588-594, Karlsruhe, 1983.

[7] Horacek H. et al.: *From Meaning to Meaning A Walk Through WISBER´s Semantic-Pragmatic Processing*. In <u>GWAI-88</u>, Hoeppner W. (ed.), Springer Publ., Geseke, pp. 118-129, 1988.

[8] Horacek H., Gerlach M.: *Goal-Oriented Dialog Control*. In <u>ECAI-90</u>, Aiello L. (ed), pp. 357-362, Stockholm, 1990.

[9] Searle J., Vanderveken: *Foundations of Illocutionary Logic*. Cambridge University Press, 1989.

[10] Werner E.: *Toward a Theory of Communication and Cooperation for Multiagent Planning*. In <u>Theoretical Aspects of Reasoning About Knowledge, Proceedings of the 1988 Conference</u>, Morgan Kaufman Publishers, pp. 129-143, 1988.

VIE-*DU* — Dialogue by Unification*

Ernst Buchberger, Elizabeth Garner, Wolfgang Heinz
Johannes Matiasek, Bernhard Pfahringer

Austrian Research Institute for Artificial Intelligence
Schottengasse 3, A-1010 Vienna

Email: ernst@ai-vie.uucp

Abstract

The paper presents an overview of VIE-*DU*[1], a natural language system for advisory dialogues in German. Based on the fact that good linguistic coverage forms a necessary prerequisite for a consultation system, considerable emphasis has been placed on developing a principled and sound grammatical component. This task has been guided by three criteria, namely generality, declarativeness and easy implementability. In order to achieve these goals we have chosen attribute-value-structures (AVSs), augmented with types and constraints, as our basic representational formalism, combining these structures by unification. VIE-*DU* thus presents a unified approach to the treatment of syntax, semantics and pragmatics. The underlying grammatical theory combines ideas from the Government and Binding tradition with HPSG and situation semantics. With regard to discourse, we have developed a framework for representing speech acts within situation semantics as a means of determining user intentions, and are making use of the 'persistent goals' of Cohen & Levesque (1990) to provide a principled theory for mixed initiative dialogue. The knowledge base of the system allows for the specification of defaults, dealing with possible contradictions and a mechanism for explicitly blocking inheritance of defaults for atypical cases. Its formal semantics is close to the AVSs that form the basis of the grammar, thus contributing to the general idea of uniform representation.

1   Introduction

VIE-*DU* is a natural language system for advisory dialogues currently being developed at the Austrian Research Institute for AI. The project aims at examining possibilities of natural language interaction transcending the abilities of current natural language information systems. Whereas the latter (e.g. database interfaces) represent a qualitative leap in man-machine-communication, they usually lack the background knowledge necessary for deriving the user's intentions and for interpreting the information in the database, factors which restrict the system's ability to cope with natural dialogue. Thus, the user is still forced to a certain amount of formalization of her query, if she wants to get the desired results.

VIE-*DU* is an attempt towards better man-machine interaction. Its area of application is advisory dialogues in the field of public funding for housing improvements, but the construction of the system is modular, in order to be applicable in different domains.

The system's knowledge base contains various knowledge sources including a model of the user's intentions and knowledge, as well as domain and dialogue knowledge. An inference component

---

*This research has been sponsored by the Austrian *Fonds zur Förderung der wissenschaftlichen Forschung*, Grant No. P7986-PHY.

[1]VIE-*DU* stands for VIEnnese system for Dialogue by means of Unification. Alternatively, you may imagine that the completed system will speak "wie du (und ich)" (German for "like you (and me)"), a goal that definitely will not be attained, but acts as a sort of utopian guideline.

acts on this knowledge base in order to interpret the user's utterances. A parser translates user utterances into the internal representation, and a generator produces utterances. Both components make use of the same grammar, based on a unification formalism. Aspects of syntax and semantics (not only at sentence, but also at text level) are both given appropriate consideration.

Methodologically, a central aspect of the project is the integration of modern theories of syntax, semantics, pragmatics and knowledge representation within a unification-based approach. We will therefore concentrate in this paper on representational issues within VIE-$\mathcal{DU}$, in particular the grammar and the knowledge base.

2 The Grammar

A basic prerequisite for dealing with consulting situations is good linguistic coverage. Therefore we place considerable emphasis on developing a principled and sound grammatical component for German. The design of this linguistic component is guided by the following criteria:

1. *Generality:* General linguistic principles should be expressible

2. *Declarativeness:* The grammar should be neutral with regard to parsing and generation

3. *Implementability:* The grammar should be easily implementable

In addition, the guiding principles of the grammar should conform to the approach taken for the system as a whole.

In the sections which follow we provide example sentences from a consultation dialogue in our domain which illustrate the importance of the contributions of each of the subcomponents of the grammar to advisory dialogues.

2.1 Grammar and Implementation

We have decided to base the grammar formalism on attribute-value-structures (AVSs; for an overview cf. Johnson (1988) and Shieber (1986)). This choice contributes to the criterion of *Declarativeness* due to its neutrality with regard to parsing and generation. Grammar formalisms that use AVSs and that have influenced our work are those of HPSG (Pollard & Sag (1987)) and Fenstad et al. (1987).

In order to fulfil the criterion of *Implementability* we have developed a unification formalism for feature descriptions (Matiasek (1989)), which has the ability to cope with disjunction and negation (cf. Smolka (1989), Eisele & Dörre (1990)).

Furthermore, feature structures are typed and constraints may be attached to types. This gives us the possibility to formulate grammatical constraints in a concise and principled way (criterion of *Generality*).

The use of Generative Grammar, HPSG and situation semantics as a theoretical basis for the linguistic component of our system fits in well with our overall approach: general rules, formulated as constraints, give partial information that is combined to reach a fully interpreted structure.

2.2 Syntax

The syntactic component of the grammar is constructed within the framework of Generative Grammar, in particular the Government-Binding (GB) approach (Chomsky (1981), Chomsky (1986)). The general principles are represented as attribute-value constraints in an HPSG style notation.

To illustrate the workings of the syntactic component we refer to an analysis of Case assignment of German that has been developed in Heinz & Matiasek (1991). Here, general principles of Case such as the distinction between structural and inherent Case and the separation between syntactic Case indices and their morphological representation, have been realized in the grammar formalism.

Examples like (1) show case variation of 'subjects' between nominative and accusative case in German.

(1)   a) Der Installateur baut eine Dusche ein.
        the plumber$_{nom}$ builds a shower in
        'The plumber is installing a shower'

     b) Ich lasse den Installateur eine Dusche einbauen.
        I let the plumber$_{acc}$ a shower build in
        'I'm having the plumber install a shower'

We give a lexical entry for *einbauen* in (2) that assigns two structural Case indices to the arguments, external and internal.

(2)
$$
\begin{bmatrix}
\text{PHON} & \textit{einbauen} \\[4pt]
\text{SYN} & \begin{bmatrix}
\text{HEAD} & [\ \text{CAT}\ \ \mathbf{V}\ ] \\[4pt]
\text{ARGS} & \begin{bmatrix}
\text{LIST} & \langle\ \boxed{1}\ ,\ \boxed{2}\ \rangle \\[4pt]
\text{STRUCT} & \begin{bmatrix}
\text{LIST} & \langle\ \boxed{1}\ ,\ \boxed{2}\ \rangle \\
\text{EXT} & \boxed{1} \\
\text{INT} & \boxed{2}
\end{bmatrix}
\end{bmatrix}
\end{bmatrix}
\end{bmatrix}
$$

The assignment of the morphological cases is now given by general principles. The internal argument of a verb receives accusative case, the external argument has to receive case from outside. In our example (1a) the tensed environment assigns nominative, whereas in (1b) accusative case is assigned to *the plumber* via *lassen*.

A general rule to this effect (the assignment of case to internal arguments by different heads) is given by (3).

(3) **Structural M-Case: Internal**

$$
\begin{bmatrix}
\text{SYN} & \left\{
\begin{array}{l}
\begin{bmatrix}
\text{HEAD}\,|\,\text{CAT} & \mathbf{V} \\
\text{ARGS}\,|\,\text{STRUCT}\,|\,\text{INT} & [\ \text{SYN}\,|\,\text{LOC}\,|\,\text{HEAD}\,|\,\text{CASE}\ \ \mathbf{4}\ ]
\end{bmatrix} \\[10pt]
\begin{bmatrix}
\text{HEAD}\,|\,\text{CAT} & \mathbf{N} \\
\text{ARGS}\,|\,\text{STRUCT}\,|\,\text{INT} & [\ \text{SYN}\,|\,\text{LOC}\,|\,\text{HEAD}\,|\,\text{CASE}\ \ \mathbf{2}\ ]
\end{bmatrix} \\[10pt]
[\ \text{ARGS}\,|\,\text{STRUCT}\,|\,\text{INT}\ \ *\ ]
\end{array}
\right\}
\end{bmatrix}
$$

Thus, Case assignment can be treated in a cognitively adequate and principled way while preserving the benefits of the unification approach for implementation.

For the treatment of noun phrases we adopt a DP-analysis. In the classical approach, the noun, and thus the main feature-bearing element of the NP, is taken as the head. Theoretical (determiners as non-maximal projections in specifier position) as well as empirical considerations, however, have led to a splitting of the noun phrase into an NP with the noun as head, and a DP with the determiner element (D) as head, which takes the NP as complement (cf. Abney (1986), Haider (1988)). One nice consequence of this splitting is that phrases other than NPs can be used as complements of the determiner, e.g. APs (*die Alten* 'the old'), PPs (*der von draußen* 'the one from outside') and clauses (*der, der kommt* 'the one coming'). The adoption of a DP-analysis also facilitates the semantic interpretation.

Other syntactic phenomena (such as verb-second) are to be treated in a similar fashion—analyzing them within the GB-framework and implementing them as attribute-value structures.

2.3   Semantics

In order to allow for the integration of contextual features, we have adopted a semantic theory in which context is accorded greater emphasis, namely situation semantics as developed by Barwise and Perry (Barwise & Perry (1983), Barwise (1987), Barwise (1989), Cooper et al. (1990)).

To implement this theoretical approach, we represent the basic *infons* of situation theory (e.g.(4)) with AVSs such as (5).

$$(4) \qquad\qquad \langle\!\langle INSTALL, x, y; 1 \rangle\!\rangle$$

$$(5) \qquad \left[\text{SEM} \left[\begin{array}{ll} \text{REL} & INSTALL \\ \text{ARGS} & \langle\, \boxed{1}\,,\, \boxed{2}\,\rangle \\ \text{POL} & 1 \\ \text{ROLES} & \left[\begin{array}{ll} \text{IAGENT} & \boxed{1} \\ \text{IPATIENT} & \boxed{2} \end{array} \right] \end{array} \right] \right]$$

In the situation semantics framework, thematic roles can be identified with complex indeterminates within thematic situation-types as indicated in (4). This enables a coupling of syntactic and semantic arguments via their thematic roles. As a result, general constraints on the relation beween the syntactic and semantic representation (by way of AVSs) can be expressed.

Other semantic phenomena (e.g. quantification employing Generalized Quantifiers) are covered similarly by a situation semantics treatment with an implementation in AVSs. We have also developed a framework for the treatment of non-singular terms, i.e. plurals and groups, using this same approach (Heinz & Matiasek (1990)).

2.4   Dialogue Structure and Pragmatics

The dialogue component of VIE-$\mathcal{DU}$ is concerned with determining user intentions as well as building a dialogue structure to assist in dialogue control and reference resolution. We aim at a uniform approach to these goals, similar to that employed in WISBER (Sprenger & Gerlach (1988)). Our approach differs from WISBER, however, in its use of situation semantics, which allows us to accord a greater position to the role of context in the interpretation of utterances, as well as to develop a finer-grained approach to semantics. Moreover, we are attempting to develop a principled coverage of a wide range of discourse situations in VIE-$\mathcal{DU}$ including utterances usually ignored by dialogue systems on the basis of their being uncooperative.

2.4.1   Deriving Intentions from Utterances

Intentions are derived in VIE-$\mathcal{DU}$ by means of a theory of speech acts. Following Allen & Perrault (1980) and Sprenger & Gerlach (1988), speech acts are seen as containing information about the cognitive state of the user, including her beliefs and goals. Determining the illocutionary force of an utterance allows this information to be interpreted and added to the user model, providing the system with the means of determining an appropriate response to it.

Our approach to speech acts seeks to reformulate them in the traditional planning framework of preconditions, actions and effects. A speech act is an action (the utterance) which occurs in a particular discourse environment (which includes the preconditions) and which extends the discourse situation (by the effects). Implementing this within a situation semantics framework involves the use of conditional constraints as introduced in Barwise (1989), Chapter 5. For example the conditional constraint (6) is a constraint relativised to some background condition B. If we have a background situation of this type, the constraint holds. B represents the preconditions and E the effects of the speech act contained in the user model. A refers to the action of the utterance. (For a more detailed description of representing speech acts in situation semantics cf. Garner & Heinz (1991)).

$$(6) \qquad\qquad A \Rightarrow E \mid B$$

Various linguistic devices, including performative verbs, modal verbs, word order, as well as a series of cue words, (e.g. 'please' used to signal a request) allow us to deduce information about the content of B and E. Such devices carry, however, different degrees of information. Performative verbs are maximally specified. The use of a performative verb such as *behaupten*, 'assert', for example, as in:

(7) Mein Nachbar behauptet, daß der Einbau einer Zentralheizung gefördert wird.
  'My neighbour asserts that central heating installation is subsidised.'

enables us to infer two preconditions: first that the agent of the verb (my neighbour) believes that central heating installation is subsidised (a belief associated with the lexical entry of *behaupten*, given in (8)); second, that the speaker of the utterance believes that the agent made this assertion (a general precondition of all declarative utterances shown in (9)).

$$(8) \qquad \langle\!\langle e \models \langle\!\langle \dot{t}; \mathrm{Assert}, \dot{ag}, \dot{theme} \rangle\!\rangle \Rightarrow B_1 \models \langle\!\langle \dot{t}; \mathrm{Bel}, \dot{ag}, \dot{theme} \rangle\!\rangle \rangle\!\rangle$$

$$(9) \qquad B_2 \models \langle\!\langle \dot{t}_\phi; \mathrm{Bel}, \dot{sp}, e \rangle\!\rangle$$

The effect (E) of the utterance is to raise B_1 and B_2 to the status of mutual beliefs of the speaker and the addressee as in (10). This can also be regarded as the purpose of the utterance.

$$(10) \qquad ds \models \langle\!\langle \dot{t}_\phi + \delta; \mathrm{MutBel}, \dot{sp}, \dot{add}, B_1 \wedge B_2 \rangle\!\rangle$$

Two different types of imperative utterances occur in VIE-$\mathcal{DU}$. The first type includes orders, such as 'Open the door' and represent a goal of the speaker. The second type usually falls under the rubric of 'advisory imperatives' and is used to communicate a suggestion of the speaker relative to a specified situation. (11b) is an example:

(11) a) User: *Wie muß ich vorgehen, um die Förderung zu erhalten?*
  'What do I have to do to get a subsidy?'

  b) System: *Besorgen Sie sich ein Antragsformular X-1798-J-9252.*
  'Obtain a copy of the application form X-1798-J-9252.'

Situation semantics allows us to capture the similarity between these two uses of imperatives. For example, we can represent imperatives as relations restricted to actions occuring in situation-types in which the agent of the action is anchored to the addressee and the time of the action is restricted to the future, as in (12):

$$(12) \qquad \langle\!\langle s \mid s \models \langle\!\langle \dot{t}_{fut}; \mathrm{Rel}_{act}, \dot{ag}_{add} \rangle\!\rangle \rangle\!\rangle$$

At the same time our framework for speech acts allows us to distinguish between the two types of imperatives on the basis of the different background conditions in which they occur. In a context (discourse situation) such as (11) where on the basis of (11a) it is mutually believed before the utterance of the imperative that the user has a goal that the system inform her how to get a subsidy, then the imperative sentence represents a situation-type which will meet this goal of the user. In a discourse situation where there exist no mutually believed current goals the situation-type will be anchored inside a goal such as (13):

$$(13) \qquad ds \models \langle\!\langle \dot{t}_\phi; \mathrm{Goal}, \dot{sp}, (s \models \langle\!\langle \dot{t}_\phi + \delta; \mathrm{Obtain}, \dot{add}, form\ \mathrm{X}\text{-}1798\text{-}J\text{-}9252 \rangle\!\rangle) \rangle\!\rangle$$

A significant problem in NL systems using explicit speech act recognition is how to account for indirect speech acts such as the following:

(14) a) *Can you open the door?* - used as a request that the addressee open the door

  b) *Do you know what the time is?* - used as a request that the addressee inform the speaker of the time

In VIE-$\mathcal{DU}$ we are also able to deal with such examples by means of conditional constraints, e.g. to deal with utterances such as (14b) we need a constraint such as the following:

$$(15) \quad \begin{array}{c} \mathrm{Goal}, \dot{sp}, (s_1 \models \langle\!\langle \mathrm{Inform}, \dot{add}, \dot{sp}, [\dot{pol} \mid (s_2 \models \langle\!\langle \mathrm{Know}, \dot{add}, e, \dot{pol} \rangle\!\rangle)] \rangle\!\rangle) \\ \Rightarrow \\ \mathrm{Goal}, \dot{sp}, (s_3 \models \langle\!\langle \mathrm{Inform}, \dot{add}, \dot{sp}, [\dot{x} \mid e] \rangle\!\rangle) \end{array}$$

where $\dot{x}$ is a parameter within e. This constraint applies, for example, relative to a background that the addressee does not believe the speaker has a goal to know if e is true.

2.4.2 Dialogue Control

Dialogue control in natural language dialogue systems is usually guided by the principle of cooperativity. This is reflected in our system by the following basic rule:

$$(16) \quad
\begin{aligned}
ds \models \langle\!\langle \text{Bel}, a\dot{d}d, (s_1 \models \langle\!\langle \text{Goal}, \dot{s}p, [\dot{s}_2 \mid (\dot{s}_2 \models \langle\!\langle \dot{A}^n, a\dot{d}d, x_2...x_n \rangle\!\rangle)]\rangle\!\rangle)\rangle\!\rangle \Rightarrow \\
ds \models \langle\!\langle \text{Goal}, a\dot{d}d, [\dot{s}_2 \mid (\dot{s}_2 \models \langle\!\langle \dot{A}^n, a\dot{d}d, x_2...x_n \rangle\!\rangle)]\rangle\!\rangle
\end{aligned}$$

This states that if the addressee believes that the speaker has a goal that the addressee perform an action then it will become the goal of the addressee to perform that action. Grosz & Sidner (1990) have dubbed this the *master-slave assumption*.

In fact, however, natural language consulting systems are characterised by their display of mixed initiative, which dramatically increases the range of possible behaviour exhibited by the user. Consider, for example, a typical query within our domain:

(17) *Wie hoch ist Ihr Haushaltsnettoeinkommen?*
     What is your total household income?

An utterance such as (17) contains two types of information:

- information about the communicative act (i.e. the fact that the utterance expresses a goal of the system that the user carry out an **inform** action)

- information about the content of the **inform** (e.g. the value of the missing parameter).

The user may respond, or fail to respond to either of these pieces of information. In the simplest scenario the user understands that the system wants the user to carry out an **inform** act, understands what information the system requires and is willing to provide the information. This is in fact the situation decribed by (16). However, there exist a variety of other possibilities:

1. The user may misunderstand the illocutionary force of the utterance (and subsequently respond inappropriately to the utterance)

2. The user may misunderstand the information the system requires (and hence provide the wrong information).

3. The user may reject the goal of the system (perhaps because the goal of the system conflicts with the user's own goal, cf. 'I would rather not tell you that.')

4. The user may be undecided about whether to carry out the goal (in which case she may launch a subdialogue sequence to discover information that will enable her to make this decision, e.g. asking for the reason behind the system's goal).

5. The user may require a further piece of information in order to carry out the goal (e.g. the clarification of a concept in the system's question).

6. The user may be unable to carry out the **inform** act due to not knowing the necessary piece of information (cf. 'I don't know').

In order to account for these possibilities we need to augment the framework for dialogue control given in (16). We achieve this by taking over the notion of *persistent goal* from Cohen & Levesque (1990).

Persistent goals (hereafter p-goals) are goals for which the agent possesses a degree of commitment. A p-goal is a goal that an agent will maintain until:

1. The agent believes the goal has been achieved

2. The agent believes the goal is impossible

3. A background condition, q (which we will use to refer to goals superordinate to the original p-goal) no longer holds.

The utterance of (17) entails a p-goal θ such that:

$$(18) \qquad \theta = \langle\!\langle \text{Informref}, a\dot{d}d, \dot{sp}, \dot{v} \rangle\!\rangle$$

where $\dot{v}$ is the user's household income. The effect of the felicitous utterance entails that:

$$(19) \qquad \langle\!\langle \text{MutBel}, a\dot{d}d, \dot{sp}, (s \models \langle\!\langle \text{Goal}, \dot{sp}, \theta \rangle\!\rangle)) \rangle\!\rangle$$

The above-listed responses to (17) affect the status of the p-goal and the mutual belief in various ways. In the event that the user misunderstands either the illocutionary force of the utterance, or its propositional content (situations (1) and (2) above) then the speaker must drop her belief that (19), maintaining, however, the p-goal. Since the p-goal has not been successfully communicated to the addressee, it will remain the guiding force behind the system's next action, (perhaps an attempt to reformulate the query). In the event that the user refuses to adopt the p-goal (situation (3)) then the system either drops the p-goal on the grounds that it is impossible or attempts to convince the user. A consulting system requires however a degree of cooperativity from the user to be successful.

In the event that the user requests further information from the system (situations (4) and (5)) again the p-goal remains intact. However, in this situation the system's belief has not been contradicted, and the system may assume that the user understands the system's p-goal (even though in the event of a clarification sequence the content of the belief about the system's goal may contain variables which are anchored in the system's belief). As a result the system will expect a further response from the user upon completion of the subdialogue. Finally, if the user is unable to answer the query (situation 6) the system will again drop the p-goal on the grounds of impossibility.

P-goals may be embedded in other p-goals. For example, a p-goal of the system that a user inform the system of the size of her appartment will be embedded in a p-goal to know the size of the user's appartment. The superordinate p-goals in fact play the role of q in the description for p-goals given above. If a superordinate p-goal is dropped then so are all the sub-goals dependent on it.

The subdialogues and the embedded p-goals enable us to construct a dialogue structure, which can be used in reference resolution. (Grosz & Sidner (1986))

3 Knowledge Representation

The knowledge base of the system is based on VIE-KL (Trost & Pfahringer (1988)), a representation language in the KL-ONE (Brachman & Schmolze (1985)) tradition of languages, consisting of a T-Box for the representation of conceptual knowledge and an A-Box for assertions. A classifier and a realizer support inferences for planning and problem solving. VIE-KL is used for representing domain-specific knowledge as well as discourse knowledge, the user model and the actual user interaction. It is well suited for the task since its formal semantics is close to the AVSs that form the basis of the grammar, and the hierarchical structure of the A-Box is suitable for the representation of discourse. Our ultimate goal is the integration of feature logics and terminological reasoning (as proposed e.g. by Smolka (1989)), thus equipping AVSs with more definitional expressiveness.

A major enhancement of VIE-KL is the integration of defaults (Pfahringer (1989)). Currently, there are two trends in AI concerning defaults (cf. Etherington (1987)): one using formal models of inheritance networks, the other starting from classical logic and augmenting it towards default logics that admit a uniform representation of defaults and strictly valid assertions. Recently, a third, intermediate approach has been taken: a number of dialects of the KL-ONE family of languages provide an opportunity for the user to represent and process certain default assertions. Examples are the P(rototype)-Box (Eschenbach (1988)), the possibility to specify default values for number and type of role fillers in SB-ONE (Kobsa (1989)) and the D(efault)-Box of LOOM (MacGregor & Bates (1987)).

We propose augmenting the T-Box language with a single "typically-implies"-link with the following meaning: if C1 is linked to C2 via the typically-implies-link, the inference that instances of C1 are also instances of C2 is drawn automatically, unless specific information about the instance contradicts (skeptical inheritance as defined by Horty et al. (1990)).

Furthermore, based on the automatic inheritance of defaults, the need for excluding the inheritance of defaults for atypic cases arises naturally. It is possible to integrate these properties into the concept definition, thus blocking the inheritance automatically. Making information explicit in this way excludes the possibility of leaving the decision open. We therefore propose a second primitive, "not-a-typical", which corresponds to the "notApplicable"-clauses in default logic.

The defaults of the T-Box have to be administrated at the assertional level. Here we follow the work of Ginsberg (1986) on multi-valued logic. Ginsberg bases his work on the assumption of backward chaining, thus avoiding the problem of update. Since A-Boxes usually adopt forward chaining or an intelligent coupling of the two methods, the problem of update arises. Our work in this area goes towards the development of a sort of non-monotonic truth maintenance system.

To perceive the usefulness of explicit representation of defaults, consider the following situation occuring during a consultation: in order to be eligible for a subsidy, the applicant's income must not exceed a certain threshold. Valid proof of income is provided either by the applicant's last pay slip or by the previous year's tax declaration, depending on whether the applicant is an employee, or a freelance worker. Now if the applicant asks how she is supposed to prove her income, the system could start a (possibly confusing) dialogue to find out exactly what kind of proof is applicable or just jump to a *default* conclusion and tell the applicant to enclose her last pay slip. In the event that the default value was the wrong choice, the applicant will in any case launch a complaint and tell the system. If the system has more knowledge about the applicant (e.g. that she is a freelance writer), then the system could choose the correct advice automatically, since the wrong default value is overridden by definitions given for this special sub-class of applicants. This retraction of (wrong) default assumptions can of course occur later in the consultation session too, if newly acquired facts contradict defaults. Such a retraction may necessitate a clarification dialogue, e.g. 'I see you do freelance work. Sorry for having misinformed you, but you will have to enclose your tax declaration.' If the representation used for modelling the domain knowledge allows for such explicit handling of defaults, these capabilities need not be hard-wired into the pragmatic component of the system.

The frame-based default management proposed by Padgham (1988) shows some similarities to our approach. Padgham's system allows her to specify definitions and defaults separately, using so-called *type cores* and *type defaults*. For each type, the core and default are linked by what we would call "typically-implies" links. Interestingly, this system does not provide for "not-a-typical" links, the standard "disjoint" links (applicable to both type cores and type defaults) seem to suffice. This may be due to the more restrictive representation schema found in such inheritance networks which do not allow for structured objects as slot-fillers.

To sum up, we propose the specification of defaults ("typically-implies"), a mechanism for dealing with possible contradictions ("skeptical inheritance") and a declarative control by means of special annotations ("not-a-typical"). The main task is the development of a formal semantics and of techniques for efficient implementation.

The above-mentioned augmentations of VIE-KL form the basis for adequate user modelling and a correct analysis of user utterances based on defaults. This knowledge about defaults will enable the system to react in an adequate way, so that the text planning component will structure its contributions in a way to provide the user with the optimal amount of information, by explaining relevant facts and clarifying misunderstandings, yet avoiding possibly irritating the user with redundant information.

4 Concluding Remarks

We have presented an overview of VIE-$\mathcal{DU}$, a natural language system for advisory dialogues in German. Central to the system is the integration of modern theories of syntax, semantics, and knowledge representation within a unification-based framework:

Using attribute-value-structures as a notational device, ideas from the Government-Binding approach are combined with HPSG and situation semantics. The dialogue component makes use of a version of speech act theory and takes over the concept 'persistent goal' from Cohen & Levesque (1990) as a means of accounting for the characteristics of mixed initiative dialogue. The knowledge base augments VIE-KL, a KL-ONE-like language, with features for dealing with defaults. Research on the project is still ongoing. Available results include novel approaches to the representation of Case in German, the treatment of plural forms and speech acts. Example sentences from a consultation dialogue in the domain of public funding for housing improvements demonstrate the importance of each of the subcomponents for advisory dialogues.

References

Abney, S. (1986) 'Functional Elements and Licensing', paper presented at the 1986 GLOW Colloquium at Girona, *GLOW Newsletter* **16**, 11-13

Allen, J.F. and C.R. Perrault (1980) 'Analyzing Intention in Utterances', in *Artificial Intelligence* **15**, 143-178.

Barwise, J. (1987) 'Recent Developments in Situation Semantics', in M. Nagao, ed., *Language and Artificial Intelligence: Proceedings of an International Symposium on Language and Artificial Intelligence* (Kyoto, Japan, March 1986). North-Holland, Amsterdam

Barwise, J. (1989) *The Situation in Logic*, CSLI Lecture Notes 17, CSLI, Stanford

Barwise, J. and J. Perry (1983) *Situations and Attitudes*, MIT Press, Cambridge, Mass.

Brachman, R.J. and J.G. Schmolze (1985) 'An Overview of the KL-ONE Knowledge Representation System', *Cognitive Science* **9**, 171-217

Chomsky, N. (1981) *Lectures on Government and Binding*, Foris, Dordrecht

Chomsky, N. (1986) *Knowledge of Language: Its Nature, Origin and Use*, Praeger, New York

Cohen, P.R. and H.J. Levesque (1990) 'Persistence, Intention and Commitment', in P.R. Cohen, J. Morgan and M.E. Pollack (eds.) *Intentions in Communication*, MIT Press, Cambridge, Mass.

Cooper, R., K. Mukai and J. Perry, eds. (1990) *Situation Theory and its Applications*, Vol. 1, CSLI Lecture Notes 22, CSLI, Stanford

Eisele, A. and J. Dörre (1990) 'Feature Logic with Disjunctive Unification', in *Proceedings of the 13th COLING* **2**, Helsinki,100-105

Eschenbach, C. (1988) 'Über Ansätze zur Darstellung von Konzepten und Prototypen', LILOG-Report 34, IBM-Germany, Stuttgart

Etherington, D.W. (1987) 'A Semantics for Default Logic', in *Proceedings of the 10th International Joint Conference on Artificial Intelligence (IJCAI-87)*, Morgan Kaufman, Los Altos, CA

Fenstad, J.E., P.-K. Halvorsen, T. Langholm and J. van Benthem (1987) *Situations, Language and Logic*, Reidel, Dordrecht

Garner E. and W. Heinz (1991) 'On the Representation of Speech Acts in Situation Semantics', in *Proceedings of the 15th German Workshop on Artificial Intelligence*, Springer, Berlin

Ginsberg, M. (1986) 'Multi-Valued Logics', in *Proceedings of the Fifth National Conference on Artificial Intelligence (AAAI-86)*, Morgan Kaufman, Los Altos, CA

Grosz, B.J. and C.L. Sidner (1986) 'Attention, Intention, and the Structure of Discourse', *Computational Linguistics* 12, 175-204

Grosz, B.J. and C.L. Sidner (1990) 'Plans for Discourse', in P.R. Cohen, J. Morgan and M.E. Pollack (eds.) *Intentions in Communication*, MIT Press, Cambridge, Mass.

Haider, H. (1988) 'Die Struktur der deutschen Nominalphrase', *Zeitschrift für Sprachwissenschaft* 7, 32-59

Heinz, W. and J. Matiasek (1991) 'Case-Assignment in a Computational Grammar for German', to appear in *Proceedings der 3.Fachtagung der Sektion Computerlinguistik der DGfS*, Osnabrück, also available as Technical Report TR-91-5, Austrian Research Institute for Artificial Intelligence, Vienna

Heinz, W. and J. Matiasek (1990) 'A Framework for Treating Non-Singular Terms in a Natural Language Consulting System', to appear in *Proceedings of the Workshop "Semantisch-Pragmatische Verarbeitung von Pluralen und Quantoren in NLP", Eringerfeld (Sept. 1990)*, also available as Technical Report TR-90-15, Austrian Research Institute for Artificial Intelligence, Vienna

Horty, J.F., Thomason, R.H., and Touretzky, D.S. (1990) 'A Skeptical Theory of Inheritance in Nonmonotonic Semantic Networks', *Artificial Intelligence* 42

Johnson M. (1988) *Attribute–Value Logic and the Theory of Grammar*, CSLI Lecture Notes 16, CSLI, Stanford

Kobsa, A. (1989) 'The SB-ONE Knowledge Representation Workbench', Workshop on Formal Aspects of Semantic Networks, Catalina Island

Matiasek, J. (1989) 'FUN - Ein erweiterter Feature-Unifikations-Formalismus', Ms. Austrian Research Institute for Artificial Intelligence, Vienna

MacGregor, R. and Bates, R. (1987) 'The LOOM Knowledge Representation Language', TR ISI/RS-87-188, Information Sciences Institute, University of Southern California, Marina del Rey, CA

Padgham, L. (1988) 'A Model and Representation for Type Information and Its Use in Reasoning with Defaults', in *Proceedings of the Seventh National Conference on Artificial Intelligence (AAAI-88)*, Morgan Kaufmann, San Mateo, CA

Pfahringer, B. (1989) 'Integrating Definitions and Defaults', Technical Report TR-89-8, Austrian Research Institute for Artificial Intelligence, Vienna

Pollard, C. and I. Sag (1987) *Information-Based Syntax and Semantics, Vol. 1: Fundamentals*, CSLI Lecture Notes 13, CSLI, Stanford

Shieber, S. (1986) *An Introduction to Unification-Based Approaches to Grammar*, CSLI Lecture Notes 4, CSLI, Stanford

Smolka, G. (1989) *A Feature Logic with Subsorts*, LILOG-Report 33, IBM-Germany, Stuttgart

Sprenger, M. and M. Gerlach (1988) 'Expectations and Propositional Attitudes - Pragmatic Issues in WISBER', in *Proceedings of the ICSC-88*, Hong Kong, 327-334

Trost, H. and B. Pfahringer (1988) 'VIE-KL: An Experiment in Hybrid Knowledge Representation', Technical Report TR-88-8, Austrian Research Institute for Artificial Intelligence, Vienna

Eine deklarative Beschreibung von Linkstilgungslücken in koordinierten Strukturen des Deutschen

Rudolf Hunze
ZFE IS INF 23
Siemens AG, München
email: hunze@ztivax.uucp

Zusammenfassung

In diesem Papier schlage ich eine Methode vor, um linguistisch motivierte Vorkommensbeschränkungen von Linkstilgungslücken mit Hilfe von Features bzw. Featuregleichungen in deklarativer Weise innerhalb der Grammatik selbst zu beschreiben. Die Methode ist unabhängig von der Verarbeitung der Grammatik und erlaubt sowohl die Analyse als auch die Generierung von Koordinationsellipsen mit derselben Grammatik. Die grundlegende Idee besteht darin, von einer koordinationsfreien Grammatik auszugehen und diese durch Einführung neuer Regeln unter weitgehend uniformer Modifikation der alten Grammatikregeln zu einer Grammatik zu erweitern, welche die Behandlung von Koordinationsphänomenen gestattet. Die neuen Regeln enthalten dabei auch leere Expansionen, welche die Koordinationsellipsen realisieren. Die Kontrolle der leeren Expansionen erfolgt durch eine gewisse Parallelität der Phrasenstruktur der verschiedenen Konjunkte, wobei die Phrasenstruktur und die Parallelitätsbedingungen durch Features bzw. Featuregleichungen der erweiterten Grammatik beschrieben werden. Die angegebene Beschreibung ist zwar auf das Deutsche zugeschnitten, die Methode ist aber prinzipiell auch für das Englische anwendbar.

1 Typen von Koordinationsellipsen im Deutschen

In diesem Papier betrachte ich

(1) $X_1, X_2, \ldots X_{n-1}$, koord X_n

als die allgemeine Form einer Koordination.[1] Hierbei ist koord eine Konjunktion und X eine syntaktische Kategorie. $X_1, X_2, \ldots X_{n-1}$ heißen die nicht-letzten und $X_2, \ldots X_n$ die nicht-ersten Konjunkte. Im Deutschen können die Tilgungsphänomene koordinierter Strukturen in drei Gruppen eingeteilt werden.[2]

- Linkstilgung in nicht-letzten Konjunkten

- Gapping des finiten Verbs und eventuell weiterer Konstituenten in nicht-ersten Konjunkten

- Subjektlücken bei Verberst- oder Verbzweitstellung (SGF-Koordination) [Hoe83]

Die Kombination von Linkstilgung und Gapping ist auch möglich. In koordinierten Strukturen mit drei und mehr Konjunkten können sogar beide Tilgungsarten gleichzeitig in einem Konjunkt vorkommen. SGF-Koordination ist eine Spezialität des Deutschen, die es im Englischen nicht gibt. Ferner ist im Englischen nur eine eingeschränkte (als right node raising) bezeichnete Art von Linkstilgung möglich.

---

[1] Die zweiteiligen Konjunktionen wie *sowohl.. als auch, entweder.. oder* usw. werden ähnlich behandelt.
[2] siehe z.B. [Tru88], der auch für das Englische viele Beispiele gibt.

1.1 Linkstilgung

Linkstilgung kann im Gegensatz zu den anderen Tilgungsarten bereits auf NP-Ebene entstehen.[3]

(2) *der rote [] und der grüne [Ball von Peter]*

(3) *eine lange [1] und eine kurze [1Reise] in eine nahe [2] und in eine ferne [2Stadt]*

(4) *Weißt Du, ob Peter einen Ball [] und Karl ein Fahrrad [bestellt hat]?*

(5) *Peter hat einen roten [] und Karl hat einen grünen [Ball bestellt].*

(6) *Peter bestellt [] ,aber Karl bezahlt [den Ball].*

(7) *Peter sah die weißen [] und die braunen [] und Karl sah die schwarzen [Pferde].*

(3) zeigt, daß Linkstilgungslücken(Lt-Lücken) innerhalb der Phrasenstruktur rekursiv eingebettet sein können. (4) bis (7) sind Beispiele von Linkstilgung auf der S-Ebene. (5) zeigt, daß Linkstilgung im Deutschen im Gegensatz zum Englischen nicht auf eine einzelne Konstituente beschränkt ist. (7) ist ein Beispiel dafür, daß sogar koordinierte NPs Lt-Lücken enthalten können. Die charakteristische syntaktische Beschränkung bei Linkstilgung ist die Eigenschaft der Rechtsperipherie. Diese besagt, daß eine Lt-Lücke stets am rechten Rand eines Konjunktes auftritt. Deshalb ist (8) ungrammatisch.[4]

(8) *∗ der rote [] aus Hamburg und der grüne [Ball] aus Paris*

1.2 Gapping

Der klassische Fall ist die Tilgung des finiten Verbs im zweiten Konjunkt (9). Es können aber auch noch weitere Konstituenten getilgt werden, z.B. ein Partizip (10) oder das Subjekt (11).

(9) *Peter {bestellte} einen Ball und Karl {} ein Fahrrad.*

(10) *Peter {hat} einen Ball {bestellt} und Karl {} ein Fahrrad {}.*

(11) *Morgens {trifft der Vater} den Chef und abends {} den Sohn.*

(12) *Wer {hat} rote [] und wer {} grüne [Bälle bestellt]?*

(13) *Wer {hat} rote [], wer {} gelbe [] und wer {} grüne [Bälle bestellt]?*

In (12) und (13) treten Gapping und Linkstilgung gemeinsam auf, bei (13) sogar gleichzeitig im mittleren Konjunkt.

1.3 SGF-Koordination

Hierbei handelt es sich um die alleinige Tilgung des Subjekts im zweiten Konjunkt, sofern das Verb in erster oder zweiter Position steht.

(14) *In den Wald ging der Jäger und schoß den Hasen.*

Eine Erklärung für diese Art von Tilgung bereitet allen Theorien Probleme.[5] Nach Höhle schließt SGF-Koordination Linkstilgung und Gapping aus.

---

[3]Hinweis zur Schreibweise: [] kennzeichnet die Position, wo Material getilgt wurde.

[4]Fälle wie *die roten Bälle aus Hamburg und der blaue aus Rom* werden hier nicht behandelt, da sie nicht zur Linkstilgung, sondern zum N-Gapping zählen.

[5]siehe [Wun88], [Tru88].

2 Ausgangspunkt: eine Grammatik ohne Koordination

Der von unserer Gruppe benutzte Formalismus zur Beschreibung linguistischen Wissens heißt
TUG (Trace Unification Grammar, [Blo91]) und kann im Prinzip als Erweiterung von PATR-II[6]
angesehen werden.Er erlaubt neben dem kontextfreien Teil die Spezifizierung von Gleichungen
auf beiden Seiten einer Grammatikregel. Die Gleichungen beziehen sich dabei auf Attribute der
zugehörigen syntaktischen Kategorien. So bedeutet in der Regel

cat1 $\longrightarrow$ cat2 cat3
    cat1:feat1 = cat2:feat1

daß der Wert von Feature feat1 von Kategorie cat1 mit dem Wert des gleichnamigen Features
von Kategorie cat2 unifiziert wird. Die Features können hierarchisch angeordnet sein, woraus sich
Zugriffspfade auf die Werte der Features ergeben können. So bedeutet

cat1 $\longrightarrow$ cat2 cat3
    cat1:feat1:feat2 = cat2:feat3:feat4

daß der Wert des Features feat2 von Feature feat1 von Kategorie cat1 mit dem Wert des Features
feat4 von Feature feat3 von Kategorie cat2 unifiziert wird.
Der Grammatikformalismus gestattet ferner die Verarbeitung von disjunktiv spezifizierten Glei-
chungsmengen, wie sie in Abschnitt 8 vorkommen.

3 Eine kleine Beispielgrammatik

Nachfolgend verwende ich zur Illustration auf eine kleine Beispielgrammatik[7]. Die Größe der
Grammatik spielt bei den Überlegungen keine Rolle, sofern es sich um eine Grammatik handelt,
die nur unäre Expansionen und binäre Expansionen zuläßt.[8]

lexikalische Kategorien:	det, n, adj, card (Kardinalzahlen), p
nichtlexikalische Kategorien:	np, n1, pp
unäre Grammatikregeln:	n1 $\rightarrow$ n, al $\rightarrow$ adj, np $\rightarrow$ n1 (die nicht maximale n-Projektion)
binäre Grammatikregeln:	n1 $\rightarrow$ det n1, n1 $\rightarrow$ al n1, n1 $\rightarrow$ card n1,
	n1 $\rightarrow$ n1 pp, pp $\rightarrow$ p np

Die oben angegebenen Regeln sind natürlich durch Featuregleichungen augmentiert. Diese sind
aber für die nachfolgenden Überlegungen ohne Belang, sodaß lediglich der kontextfreie Teil der
Regeln angeführt worden ist.

4 Wie kann die koordinationsfreie Grammatik erweitert werden?

Ein naheliegender Gedanke besteht in der Angabe von Metaregeln [Sed85]

(15) X $\rightarrow$ X koord X

---

[6]siehe z.B. [Shi84]

[7]Es handelt sich dabei um ein Fragment der in unserer Gruppe benutzten NP-Grammatik. Die syntaktische
Beschreibung von Lt-Lücken ändert sich zwar auch auf Satzebene nicht, aber es kommt bei Verbzweitstellung zu
einer Überlagerung von Verbbewegung und Lt-Lücken (5-7), die noch einer weiteren Klärung bedarf.

[8]Die Methode kann auch auf Grammatiken mit ternären Expansionen ausgedehnt werden.

wobei X eine beliebige syntaktische Kategorie ist. Leider zeigen die in Abschnitt 1 angeführten Beispiele jedoch, daß Koordination nicht als uniformes Phänomen betrachtet werden kann. Zunächst ist nicht klar, ob überhaupt alle syntaktischen Kategorien, insbesondere die von nicht maximalen Projektionen, koordinierbar sind. Es nutzt auch nichts, (15) auf bestimmte Kategorien zu beschränken, wenn man bedenkt, daß Linkstilgung schon auf der NP-Ebene, Gapping jedoch erst auf der S-Ebene möglich ist. Dennoch besteht eine gewisse Gleichartigkeit bei der Beschreibung von Koordinationsphänomenen, allerdings erst auf der Regelebene und nicht schon auf der Ebene der syntaktischen Kategorien. In der Erweiterung der Beispielgrammatik ist dies dadurch realisiert, daß alle Grammatikregeln um einen gemeinsamen Teil erweitert werden, wobei einige Regeln noch zusätzliche Erweiterungen erfahren.

5 Eine Formulierung von empirischen Bedingungen für Linkstilgung

Eine Reihe notwendiger Bedingungen für Linkstilgung kann in den folgenden 5 Bedingungen zusammengefaßt werden. Die grundlegende Idee besteht dabei darin, daß aus der Phrasenstruktur des ersten Konjunkts Bedingungen für die verbleibenden Konjunkte abgeleitet werden können, sofern das erste Konjunkt eine Lt-Lücke enthält. Die Bedingungen lauten im einzelnen:

(16) Wenn das erste Konjunkt keine Lt-Lücke enthält, dann enthalten die anderen Konjunkte ebenfalls keine Lt-Lücke. In diesem Fall sind die Konjunkte syntaktisch unabhängig von einander.

(17) Wenn das erste Konjunkt eine Lt-Lücke enthält, dann enthalten alle anderen nicht-letzten Konjunkte die gleiche Lt-Lücke in der gleichen Position ihrer Phrasenstruktur (strukturelle Parallelität). In der Phrasenstruktur des letzten Konjunkts erscheint an der entsprechenden Position dagegen der Füller für die Lt-Lücke.

(18) Erscheint in einem Konjunkt eine Lt-Lücke, so bedeutet dies, daß der Input für dieses Konjunkt zu Ende ist und das nächste Wort im noch verbleibenden Input bereits zum nächsten Konjunkt gehört. Dies ist gerade die Eigenschaft der Rechtsperipherie.(siehe (8))

(19) Eine Lt-Lücke erbt alle syntaktische Information von ihrem Füller. Dies ergibt sich daraus, daß sie phoneti ch identisch mit ihrem Füller sein muß . Im Unterschied zu Lt-Lücken müssen Gapping-Lücken nicht phonetisch identisch mit ihrem Füller sein, wie das Beispiel *Peter {liest} das Buch und die Eltern {} die Zeitung* zeigt.

(20) Lt-Lücken etablieren keine referentielle Identität mit ihrem Füller. (siehe (2), wo es sich um verschiedene Bälle handelt.) Dies ist für die semantische Interpretation von Bedeutung.

6 Leere Expansionen

Zur Beschreibung von Linkstilgungslücken erlaube ich in der Grammatik leere Expansionen der Form X → []. In der angeführten Beispielgrammatik beschränken sich diese Expansionen auf die Regel n1 → [], mit deren Hilfe die Struktur von *der rote und der grüne Ball* beschrieben wird. Man sieht jedoch sofort, daß diese Expansion zu unrestriktiv ist, denn sie erlaubt auch[9] die ungrammatische Struktur *der und der Ball* .[10] Ich begegne dieser Übergenerierung von Lücken durch Einführung eines zweiwertigen Features 'ldglic' (left-deletion-gap-licensed) , welches in den Regeln, die das Vorhandensein einer Lt-Lücke erlauben, mit 'yes' instantiert wird.[11]

---

[9]wegen der Regel n1 → det n1

[10]Ein Beispiel wie *dieser und jener Ball* wird nicht als Linkstilgung, sondern als Artikelkoordination aufgefasst.

[11]Die auf beiden Seiten der Regel vorkommende Kategorie n1 wird in einem Fall durch den Index ' annotiert.

n1 $\longrightarrow$ det n1'
                  n1':ldglic = no.

n1 $\longrightarrow$ a1 n1'
                  n1':ldglic = yes.

n1 $\longrightarrow$ []
                  n1:ldglic = yes.

7 Die Kodierung der Phrasenstruktur als Merkmal der grammatischen Kategorien

In der Erweiterungsgrammatik wird für jede Kategorie das neue Feature 'tree' zur Beschreibung der Phrasenstruktur eingeführt. 'tree' ist selbst ein komplexes Merkmal und besitzt folgende Attribute:

syncat	die syntaktische Kategorie von tree

ldg	ein Merkmal mit Wert $-$ falls tree keine Lt-Lücke enthält
	                                       $+$ falls tree eine Lt-Lücke enthält und lexikalisches Material
	                                  $++$ falls tree leer ist

daughters	eine Liste der Bäume der Töchter von syncat
sem	die dem tree beigefügte semantische Struktur
synf	die Menge der syntaktischen Merkmale (wegen (19) sind die syntaktischen Merkmale von Füller und Lücke zu identifizieren)

8 Eine Beschreibung der Eigenschaft 'Rechtsperipherie' mittels der Phrasenstruktur

Jede unäre Grammatikregel M $\rightarrow$ L wird um dieselbe Disjunktion von Gleichungen erweitert, die nachfolgend mit constraints_on_ld_gaps(M,L) bezeichnet wird. Es handelt sich dabei um folgende Gleichungsmenge:[12]

constraints_on_ld_gaps(M,L) steht für
    M:tree:ldg = $-$, L:tree:ldg = $-$ oder
    M:tree:ldg = $+$, L:tree:ldg = $+$ oder
    M:tree:ldg = $++$.

Die Bedeutung dieser Disjunktion besteht darin, daß entweder die Bäume von Mutter und Tochter beide lückenfrei sind oder beide eine Lücke und lexikalisches Material enthalten oder der Mutterbaum leer ist. Es ist bei Anwendung der Regel M $\rightarrow$ L nicht möglich, daß der Tochterbaun leer ist. Dies hätte nämlich zur Folge, daß auch der Mutterbaum leer wäre, so daß man nicht mehr zwischen einer L-Lt-Lücke und einer M-Lt-Lücke unterscheiden kann. Bei der Anwendung unärer Regeln können daher überhaupt keine neuen Lt-Lücken entstehen. Im Falle binärer Regeln M $\rightarrow$ L R ist dies nicht so. Jede binäre Regel wird um die Alternative constraints_on_ld_gaps(M,L,R) erweitert.

constraints_on_ld_gaps(M,L,R) steht für
    M:tree:ldg = $-$,   L:tree:ldg = $-$,   R:tree:ldg = $-$ oder
    M:tree:ldg = $+$,   L:tree:ldg = $-$,   R:tree:ldg = $+$ oder
    M:tree:ldg = $+$,   L:tree:ldg = $-$,   R:tree:ldg = $++$, R:ldgdglic = yes   oder
    M:tree:ldg = $+$,   L:tree:ldg = $+$,   R:tree:ldg = $++$, R:ldgdglic = yes   oder
    M:tree:ldg = $++$.

---

[12]Gleichungsmengen können mit symbolischen Namen bezeichnet werden.

Die erste Zeile bedeutet, daß mit einer lückenfreien Mutter auch die beiden Töchter lückenfrei sind. Zeile zwei bis vier spezifizieren die möglichen Fallunterscheidungen für den Fall, daß die Mutter eine Lücke enthält. Zunächst einmal kann die linke Tochter lückenfrei sein. Dann muß die Lücke irgendwo im Baum der rechten Tochter sein (R:tree:ldg = +) oder die rechte Tochter selbst ist schon die Lücke (R:tree:ldg = ++). Das geht aber nur, wenn die Lücke auch durch die Grammatikregel erlaubt wurde (R:ldgdglic = yes). Es kann aber auch sein, daß schon die linke Tochter eine Lücke enthält (L:tree:ldg = +). Dann muß wegen (18) das Konjunkt bereits am Ende sein d.h. die rechte Tochter eine Lt-Lücke sein. Der zunächst theoretisch mögliche Fall

M:tree:ldg = +, L:tree:ldg = +, R:tree:ldg = +

scheidet aus, denn er widerspricht der Eigenschaft (18). Auch der Fall

M:tree:ldg = +, L:tree:ldg = ++ , R:tree:ldg = ?

kann ausgeschlossen werden, denn (18) verlangt, daß R leer ist (R:tree:ldg = ++), wenn L eine Lt-Lücke enthält. Hieraus folgt, daß M leer ist, was der Annahme widerspricht, daß M lexikalisches Material enthält. Schließlich stellt M:tree:ldg = ++ wie im unären Fall die Abbruchbedingung für die weitere Regelanwendung dar.

9 Parallele Strukturen

Bisher ist noch nichts über die Parallelität der Phrasenstruktur der Konjunkte gesagt worden, die diesen durch die Existenz einer Lt-Lücke auferlegt wird. Dies ist in der Tat eine Frage, deren Beantwortung von den empirischen Bedingungen der untersuchten Sprache abhängt. Man könnte die Parallelität etwa durch folgende Definition zu erfassen suchen:

Definition: (parallele syntaktische Bäume)
Zwei syntaktische Bäume tree1 und tree2 sind parallel, gdw. i),ii) und iii) gelten:
    i)   tree1:syncat = tree2:syncat
    ii) die Anzahl der Töchter von tree1 ist gleich der Anzahl der Töchter von tree2
    iii) Ist D1 die n-te Tochter von tree1 und D2 die n-te Tochter von tree2,
          dann sind D1 und D2 parallel (n beliebig)

Diese Definition beschreibt die Daten aber nicht richtig.

(21) *Peter bestellt [] ,aber Peters freigiebiger Vater bezahlt [den Ball].*

Hier sind die Bäume von *Peter* und *Peters freigiebiger Vater* nicht parallel. Eine Abschwächung der obigen Definition scheint die Daten richtig zu beschreiben. Parallelität wird hierbei nur von solchen Teilbäumen verlangt, die Lücken enthalten.

Definition: (ldg-parallele syntaktische Bäume)
Zwei syntaktische Bäume tree1 und tree2 sind ldg-parallel, gdw. i),ii) und iii) gelten:
    i)   tree1:syncat = tree2:syncat
    ii) Ist tree1:ldg oder tree2:ldg in {+,++}, so ist tree1:ldg=tree2:ldg und
          die Anzahl der Töchter von tree1 ist gleich der Anzahl der Töchter von tree2
    iii) Ist D1 die n-te Tochter von tree1, D2 die n-te Tochter von tree2 mit D1:ldg
          in {+,++} oder D2:ldg in {+,++}, so folgt D1:ldg=D2:ldg und
          D1 ist ldg-parallel zu D2. (n beliebig)

10 Die Kodierung von Parallelitätsbedingungen in der erweiterten Grammatik

Um die Bäume von verschiedenen Konjunkte miteinander vergleichen zu können, wird jede syntaktische Kategorie um die Merkmale treeI und treeO erweitert. Dabei sind treeI und treeO vom Typ 'tree'. Obwohl die nachstehende Kodierung der Parallelitätsbedingungen vollständig deklarativ ist, so erlaubt sie doch eine prozedurale Interpretation. Diese geht davon aus, daß jedes Konjunkt einen Vergleichsbaum treeI besitzt, der bei der Verarbeitung dieses Konjunktes in bestimmter Weise berücksichtigt werden muß . Das Konjunkt baut dann einen eigenen Baum treeO auf, den es an das nächste Konjunkt als dessen treeI weitergibt. Das erste Konjunkt hat dabei einen unspezifizierten Vergleichsbaum. Die Grammatikregeln werden nun wie oben um eine neue Gleichungsmenge erweitert, die mit parallel_ld_gaps(M,L) (unärer Fall) bzw. parallel_ld_gaps(M,L,R) (binärer Fall) abgekürzt wird. Die mögliche Verteilung der Lücken im Baum folgt dabei den in constraints_on_ld_gaps gemachten Angaben.[13] [14]

parallel_ld_gaps(M,L)	steht für		
M:treeI:ldg = −,	L:treeI:ldg = −,		
M:treeO:ldg = −,	L:treeO:ldg = −		oder
M:treeI:ldg = +,	L:treeI:ldg = +,		
M:treeO:ldg = +,	L:treeO:ldg = +,	M:last_conj = no,	
M:treeI:daughters= '[L:treeI]			oder
M:treeI:ldg = +,	L:treeI:ldg = +,		
M:treeO:ldg = −,	L:treeO:ldg = −,	M:last_conj = yes,	
M:treeI:daughters = '[L:treeI]			oder
M:treeI:ldg = ++,	M:last_conj = yes,		
M:treeO:ldg = −,			
L:treeI:ldg = −,			
fill_ld_gap(M).			

Wenn der Vergleichsbaum keine Lücke enthält, darf der Baum des Konjunktes auch keine Lücke enthalten. Das ist die Bedingung (16).[15] Enthält der Vergleichsbaum eine Lücke, so muß man ihn hinabsteigen, um die Parallelität zu gewährleisten. Dies wird durch die Bedingung M:treeI:daughters= '[L:treeI] ausgedrückt. (Gemäß der letzten Definition über die Parallelität fehlt dieser Abstieg im Fall lückenfreier Bäume). Je nachdem, ob man sich im letzten Konjunkt befindet oder nicht, muß im neuen Baum eine parallele Lücke erzeugt werden oder die Lücke muß gefüllt werden. Das ist gerade die Bedingung (17). Das Füllen der Lücke im letzten Konjunkt erfolgt, wenn der Vergleichsbaum selbst schon die Lücke ist. Dies bedeutet, daß nun jede Grammatikregel angewendet werden darf, deren linke Seite mit der syntaktischen Kategorie der Lücke zusammenfällt. Das Ergebnis der Regelanwendung muß nun noch mit der Lücke unifiziert werden. All dies geschieht durch fill_ld_gap(M).[16] Das schrittweise Weiterreichen des Vergleichsbaums sorgt dafür, daß der Füller auch die mittleren Konjunkte erreicht. Im binären Fall sieht constraints_on_ld_gaps wie folgt aus:

parallel_ld_gaps(M,L,R)	steht für		
M:treeI:ldg = −,	L:treeI:ldg = −,	R:treeI:ldg = − ,	
M:treeO:ldg = −,	L:treeO:ldg = −,	R:treeO:ldg = −	oder
M:last_conj = no,			
M:treeI:ldg = +,	L:treeI:ldg = −,	R:treeI:ldg = +,	
M:treeO:ldg = +,	L:treeO:ldg = −,	R:treeO:ldg = + ,	
M:treeI:daughters = '[L:treeI,R:treeI]			oder

M:last_conj = no,
M:treeI:ldg = +,
M:treeO:ldg = +,
M:treeI:daughters = '[L:treeI,R:treeI]

L:treeI:ldg = −,
L:treeO:ldg = −,

R:treeI:ldg = ++,
R:treeO:ldg = ++,

oder

M:last_conj = no,
M:treeI:ldg = +,
M:treeO:ldg = +,
M:treeI:daughters = '[L:treeI,R:treeI]

L:treeI:ldg = +,
L:treeO:ldg = +,

R:treeI:ldg = ++,
R:treeO:ldg = ++,

oder

M:last_conj = yes,
M:treeI:ldg = +,
M:treeO:ldg = −,
M:treeI:daughters = '[L:treeI,R:treeI]

L:treeI:ldg = −,
L:treeO:ldg = −,

R:treeI:ldg = +,
R:treeO:ldg = − ,

oder

M:last_conj = yes,
M:treeI:ldg = +,
M:treeO:ldg = −,
M:treeI:daughters = '[L:treeI,R:treeI]

L:treeI:ldg = −,
L:treeO:ldg = −,

R:treeI:ldg = ++,
R:treeO:ldg = −,

oder

M:last_conj = yes,
M:treeI:ldg = +,
M:treeO:ldg = −,
M:treeI:daughters = '[L:treeI,R:treeI]

L:treeI:ldg = +,
L:treeO:ldg = −,

R:treeI:ldg = ++,
R:treeO:ldg = −,

oder

M:treeI:ldg = ++, M:last_conj = yes,
M:treeO:ldg = −,
L:treeI:ldg = −,
R:treeI:ldg = −,
fill_ld_gap(M).

Beim rekursiven Abstieg innerhalb der Phrasenstruktur ist zu beachten, daß diese in einem nicht-letzten Konjunkt stoppt, sobald eine Lt-Lücke entdeckt wurde, also eine Ebene früher als im letzten Konjunkt. Es gibt daher keinen Fall M:treeI:ldg = ++, M:last_conj = no. Vielmehr wird durch Anwendung der Fälle M:treeI:ldg = +, L:treeI:ldg = -, R:treeI:ldg = ++, M:last_conj = no bzw. M:treeI:ldg = +, L:treeI:ldg = +, R:treeI:ldg = ++, M:last_conj = no in Verbindung mit der Regel R → [] die aus einem früheren Konjunkt stammende Lücke übernommen. Die leere Expansion ist dabei um die Gleichungsmenge make_ld_gap[17] erweitert, welche für den Transport von syntaktischer und semantischer Information durch die Lücke sorgt.

11 Regeln für koordinierte Strukturen

Schließlich müssen noch Regeln für koordinierte Strukturen angegeben werden. Als Beispiel gebe ich die Regel für die Koordinierung von NPs an und benutze die Expansionen np → npR[18] koord np' , npR → np, npR' , npR → np. Bei der Formulierung der Parallelitätsbedingungen ist zu beachten, daß die koordinierte NP nun selbst als Teil einer koordinierten Struktur auftreten kann (siehe (7)). Zum Beispiel kann die koordinierte NP selbst mit einer Lücke enden (7), wenn sie als nicht-letztes Konjunkt einer koordinierten Phrase auftritt. (7) zeigt auch, daß die Parallelität innerhalb koordinierter Strukturen auf den Baum eines einzelnen Konjunktes beschränkt werden muß .

---

[17]Aus Platzgründen verzichte ich hier auf die genaue Angabe der Bedingungen.
[18]npR ist eine neue Kategorie, welche gemäß (1) die nicht-letzten Konjunkte erfaßt.

12   Zusammenfassung: die erweiterte Grammatik

Nach Einführung der Merkmale ldglic,last_conj,treeI und treeO für alle Kategorien ergibt sich folgendes Bild:

neue lexikalische Kategorien: koord
neue nicht lexikalische Kategorien: npR
neue Grammatikregeln:
np $\longrightarrow$ npR koord np
      $\langle$ gewisse Gleichungen zur Verteilung der Lücken $\rangle$
npR $\longrightarrow$ np npR
      $\langle$ gewisse Gleichungen zur Verteilung der Lücken $\rangle$
npR $\longrightarrow$ np
      $\langle$ gewisse Gleichungen zur Verteilung der Lücken $\rangle$
n1 $\longrightarrow$ []
      n1:ldglic = yes,
      make_ld_gap.

Erweiterung der alten Grammatikregeln: Jede unäre Regel hat die Form
M $\longrightarrow$ L
      $\langle$ Gleichungen für die Regelanwendung im nicht koordinierten Fall $\rangle$
      parallel_ld_gaps(M,L).
n1 $\longrightarrow$ a1 n1'
      $\langle$ Gleichungen für die Regelanwendung im nicht koordinierten Fall $\rangle$
      n1':ldglic = yes,
      parallel_ld_gaps(n1,a1,n1').
Alle anderen binären Regeln haben die Form
M $\longrightarrow$ L R
      $\langle$ Gleichungen für die Regelanwendung im nicht koordinierten Fall $\rangle$
      R:ldglic = no,
      parallel_ld_gaps(M,L,R).

Die Beispielgrammatik verarbeitet folgende Formen, wenn man noch zusätzliche Regeln für die Koordinierung von PPs aufnimmt:

der rote,der gelbe und der grüne Ball
ein blaues Quadrat,ein rotes und ein grünes Dreieck und ein gelber Kreis
zwei rote und vier gelbe teure Bälle aus Rom
die roten und die gelben Bälle aus Rom und aus Wien
die Menschen in den reichen und den armen Ländern
die jungen und die alten Menschen in den reichen und den armen Ländern
die jungen und die alten Menschen in den reichen und in den armen Ländern
Plantagenbesitzer mit hohem und Feldarbeiter mit niedrigem Lebensstandard

13   Das Lexikon

Da eine lexikalische Kategorie L ein Blatt im Phrasenstrukturbaum darstellt, kann für sie nicht gelten: L:treeI:ldg = + . Für L gilt stattdessen L:treeI:ldg in $\{-,++\}$. Für solche lexikalische Kategorien, die nicht Lt-Luecken sein können[19], gilt sogar L:treeI:ldg = −.

---

[19]In der Beispielgrammatik sind dies alle.

14 Wieviele Lt-Lücken braucht man?

Ich plädiere in diesem Abschnitt dafür, Lt-Lücken nur dann in der grammatischen Beschreibung anzunehmen, wenn dies aus syntaktischen Gründen zwingend erforderlich ist. Dies gilt für die in Abschnitt 1 beschriebenen Beispiele, bei denen es sich um Fälle von 'non constituent coordination' handelt. Die nachstehenden Beispiele können dagegen auch ohne die Annahme von Lt-Lücken analysiert werden und zwar (22) als Artikel-Koordination, (23) als ap-Koordination, (24) als p-Koordination und (25) und (26) als n1-Koordination.

(22) *dieser und jener Ball*

(23) *die vielen roten und blauen Blumen*

(24) *in und um Ulm*

(25) *der Ausschank und der Verkauf von Alkohol an Jugendliche*

(26) *der König und der Ministerpräsident von Norwegen*

Nimmt man z.B. für (26) die eindeutige(!) Phrasenstruktur Phr1

```
np(
   n1(
      n1(
         n1(det(der),n1(n(König))),
         koord(und),
         n1(det(der),n1(n(Ministerpräsident)))),
      pp(p(von),np(n1(n(Norwegen))))))
```

an, so wird die Entscheidung, ob sich das Attribut *von Norwegen* auch auf *König* bezieht, in die Ebene der semantisch-pragmatischen Analyse verlagert. Analysiert man aber diejenige Bedeutungsvariante, bei der sich das Attribut *von Norwegen* auch auf *König* bezieht unter Annahme einer Lt-Lücke, so erhält man für die andere Bedeutungsvariante, bei der sich das Attribut *von Norwegen* nicht auf *König* bezieht, eine andere Phrasenstruktur, m.a.W. unterschiedlichen semantischen Interpretationen entsprechen dann unterschiedliche Phrasenstrukturen. Die syntaktische Analyse liefert hier immer zwei Lesarten, selbst wenn die Interpretation aus semantisch-pragmatischen Gründen eindeutig sein sollte. Demgegenüber hat die Phrasenstruktur Phr1 den Vorzug, sich semantisch vage zu verhalten. Ein weiterer Nachteil, ein Beispiel wie (25) durch die Annahme von Lt-Lücken zu analysieren, besteht darin, daß die Anzahl der pp-Lücken a priori nicht bekannt ist. Dies führt auf das technische Problem der unendlichen Rekursion bei der Expansion n1 → n1' pp, die im Zusammenhang mit der leeren Expansion pp → [] auftritt.

15 Bemerkungen zur Implementierung

Die Idee der vorliegenden Arbeit besteht in der Angabe von Bedingungen, welche die linguistischen Vorkommensbeschränkungen für Koordinationsellipsen in deklarativer Weise spezifizieren. Dies geschieht hier in einem Attribut-Wert-basierten-PATR-ähnlichen Unifikationsformalismus ([Blo91]), man könnte aber auch eine DCG-Grammatik zugrunde legen. Die Kodierung der Vorkommensbeschränkungen mittels in die Grammatik neu eingefügter Merkmale ist vollkommen unabhängig von der späteren Verarbeitung der Grammatik und gestattet die Verwendung derselben Grammatik sowohl für die Analyse als auch für die Generierung von Äußerungen. Das unterscheidet sie von den Ansätzen ([Tru89],[Sed85]). Demgegenüber wird hier die Grammatik über eine Reihe von Zwischenstufen, wobei die leeren Produktionen entfernt werden, kompiliert und durch einen Tomitaparser verarbeitet.[20] Leere Produktionen treten daher nur auf der Ebene

---

[20] Ablaufumgebung ist eine SUN 3/60 Workstation mit IFPROLOG.

der grammatischen Beschreibung auf. Durch die bottom-up gerichtete Verarbeitungsweise kommt es dabei leider zu einem Effizienzverlust, da die Constraints für das Auftreten von Lücken erst beim Zusammenbau der ganzen Konjunktion berücksichtigt werden. Günstiger wäre es, wenn man nur das erste Konjunkt bottom-up parst und beim Vorliegen einer Lücke dann in den weiteren Konjunkten eine top-down Verarbeitungsstrategie wählt, um die syntaktischen Constraints möglichst frühzeitig einzusetzen.

16 Generierung von Linkstilgungslücken aus semantischen Formen

Aus Platzgründen kann auf die hier entstehenden Probleme nicht näher eingegangen werden. Nur soviel sei gesagt: Bei der Sprachanalyse wird eine semantische Form[21] aufgebaut, in der die syntaktischen Lücken rekonstruiert sind z.B.
term-koord(qterm(def,X,and(rot(X),ball(X))),qterm(def,Y,and(gelb(Y),ball(Y))))
für *der rote und der gelbe Ball*. Aus dieser semantischen Struktur erzeugt der Generator[22] eine Wortkette. Dabei entstehen nacheinander sowohl die Verbalisierung ohne Lücke *der rote Ball und der gelbe Ball* als auch die Verbalisierung mit Lücke *der rote und der gelbe Ball*, da beide Verbalisierungen dieselbe Semantik besitzen.

Literatur

[AvE89]   Hiyan Alshawi and Jan van Eijck. Logical forms in the core language engine. In *Proceedings of the 27th Meeting of the ACL*, pages 25–32, 1989.

[Blo91]   Hans Ulrich Block. Compiling trace and unification grammar for parsing and generation. In *Proc. The reversible Grammar Workshop, ACL*, 1991.

[Hoe83]   Tilman Hoehle. Subjektlücken in Koordinationen. Univ. Tübingen, unv. Manuskript, 1983.

[Sed85]   Celestin Sedogbo. A meta grammar for handling coordination in logic grammars. In V.Dahl, editor, *Logic Programming and Natural Language Processing*, pages 153–163. North Holland, 1985.

[Shi84]   Stuart M. Shieber. The design of a computer language for linguistic information. In *10th International Conference on Computational Linguistics (COLING-84)*, pages 362–366, 1984.

[SMSR90] F.C.N. Pereira Stuart M. Shieber, G. van Noord and R.C.Moore. Semantic head driven generation. *Computational Linguistics*, 16:30–43, 1990.

[Tru88]   Hubert Truckenbrodt. Zur Syntax der Koordination. SNS-Bericht 41, Univ. Tübingen, 1988.

[Tru89]   Hubert Truckenbrodt. Koordination und Top-Down-Parsing in Prolog. SNS-Bericht 52, Univ. Tübingen, 1989.

[Wun88]   Dieter Wunderlich. Some problems of coordination in german. In Uwe Reyle und Christian Rohrer, editor, *Natural Language and Linguistic Theories*, pages 289–316. Reidel Publishing Company, 1988.

---

[21]Diese ist an der in ([AvE89]) beschriebenen Form orientiert.

[22]Wir verwenden in unserer Gruppe einen Generator, der auf den Head-Driven Generator ([SMSR90]) zurückgeht.

APPLYING ARTIFICIAL INTELLIGENCE IN DESIGNING FOR QUALITY

B Lees

Department of Computing Science, Paisley College
Paisley PA1 2BE Scotland UK

ABSTRACT

A knowledge-based system is described which is being developed to give advice to engineers in the design of products manufactured in highly automated environments. The aim of the system is to assist a designer to attain the required level of quality of a product at the design stage. A prototype is currently being developed to test this approach in the design of shock absorbers for the automobile industry.

INTRODUCTION

The process of design provides an interesting range of problems to challenge AI techniques. As well as providing more powerful tools for the designer, the application of AI may also help us to understand the complicated reasoning performed by engineers [1]. In this paper, a knowledge-based approach to the optimisation of the quality of products, which are manufactured in highly automated production environments, is described. The emphasis in this approach is to provide *advice* for the human expert designer at various stages in the design process. The resulting system does not assume that there is any fixed sequence of design activities, thus leaving the designer free to adopt his/her preferred style. Advice may be given during, for example, the checking of requirements specifications and the evaluation of product quality.

The system has the ability to intercept transactions between the user and a Computer Aided Design (CAD) system, in order to provide advice when appropriate. But there would be little point in attempting to reason in terms of the geometric data items used by a typical CAD system; these are at too low a level. A more appropriate level to apply knowledge-based support is that of the level of the manufactured *features* of the product: for example, rectangular blocks, cylinders, slots and chamfers.

The long term aim in the project is to provide a generic system, that may be ported to different design environments. However, it is outside the scope of the project to assist in the design of a new *type* of product. Rather, the strength of the system lies in its capability to support the design of a product with a new specification, within an existing product family.

The product design process in initiated by the designer compiling and inputting the customer requirements specification. Once a product design has been specified, the system may evaluate the design in terms of its:

- design consistency and manufacturability
- predicted product quality

From the results of this evaluation advice may be provided to the designer, if requested, to assist him/her to achieve the required quality level.

THE DESIGN ENVIRONMENT

To provide quality support for a new product, it is necessary for the system to maintain several data structures that, collectively, provide a comprehensive product model. The first of these is the *Product Tree*. Modern CAD systems capture and handle design data as primitive geometric data such as lines, arcs, primitive solids and surfaces. However, any machined part can be viewed as the sum of its machined *features*. By using features as design input, the structure of a product being designed may be represented in the form of a Product Tree, which expresses the hierarchical relationships between parts, components and features. The leaves of the Product Tree represent *features* whilst higher nodes represent *parts*. At the highest level, the root of the Product Tree represents the instantiated *product*. From the Product Tree information may be obtained on the overall structure of the product, or, alternatively, on the detailed structure of a sub-assembly or part. It should be noted that, to support this features-based approach, the front end of the system needs to maintain a library of design features so as to be able to translate features into corresponding (lower level) CAD system input. Furthermore, users need to be provided with the facility to create and edit the feature library.

As well as information on the product, there is a need to represent information on the manufacturing environment. For this purpose the *Process Tree* is provided. Each node in the Process Tree references the available manufacturing resources (together with their historic capabilities) which are relevant to the current product.

In addition to these tree structures, information is also held which provides the relationships between the geometry of a product (i.e. its component parts and features as given in the Product Tree) and its functions. Finally, the results of tests on finished products are maintained; such information allows an assessment of the quality of a product to be made.

THE ROLE OF AI

Design is an interesting area of problem solving in which to investigate the application of artificial intelligence methodology [2]. The process of design may be viewed as a search problem, where the goal is to find a composition of parts, processes and features that satisfies the requirements. Typically, only a fraction of the combinations will be able to meet the requirements. As the possible combinations of these are computationally explosive, ways to decrease the search space have to be used. Decomposition of the design into separate smaller design problems decreases this search space significantly. The process of design can then be seen as a process of selecting and instantiating parameters and checking to see if the design still meets the constraints and requirements.

With the aim of creating an integrated quality support environment, the design activities that have been identified as candidates for the application of knowledge-based methods are [3]:

- Search for Matching Requirements Specification
- Feasibility Checking
- Quality Evaluation
- Quality Advice

DESIGN KNOWLEDGE

The knowledge required to support the above-mentioned design activities takes various forms, reflecting the different aspects of the design process, the nature of the product to be designed, the manufacturing environment, and the techniques to be employed to ensure acceptable quality of the product.

Associated with the product are details of the interconnections and interrelationships between components and sub-assemblies. Much of this declarative knowledge is recorded in the product tree. Also, information on the physical characteristics of the manufacturing equipment needs to be accessible - indicating, for example, the function and tolerance capabilities of each machining tool.

Historic knowledge of past performance is also required. To support this, reference may need to be made to data indicating what tolerances have actually been achieved in the past, and also to feedback data from product suppliers and customers. Also needed is knowledge of how previous quality problems were resolved. There is a need to maintain this knowledge to reflect any variation in performance over time

In order to be able to hypothesise as to the cause of any perceived inadequacy in product quality, knowledge of the influences that geometric features have on product functions is also required, this knowledge serving to provide links between the Product Tree and the Function Tree.

DESIGN REASONING

The four system functions for which knowledge-based support is provided each require a different reasoning mechanism. A natural sequence in which these functions might be used would be to start with a search for a matching requirements specification, followed by a feasibility check, and then to proceed to a quality evaluation after which quality advice could be sought. However, the user can use these functions in any order, with the one exception that to obtain quality advice, a quality evaluation must have previously been made. These functions are supported as follows.

Search for Matching Requirements Specification

A search is made for an existing requirements specification (RS) that most closely matches the RS for the new product. If a product range has been specified by the user, then the system will look for an existing product within that range. Otherwise, for each of the newly specified requirements, a search will be made for a corresponding RS having a comparable requirement. Finally the matching RS's are sorted for closeness of fit to the new RS.

Feasibility Check

The feasibility check compares the design data (DD) and the requirements specification to see if they are consistent, with respect to geometrical and functional requirements. The general aim is to detect infeasible designs at an early stage of the design process, before production starts. It is in matching the design data with the functional specification that a knowledge-based approach is used - in the form of constraint propagation. The RS and DD are first converted into the form of rules (a declarative fact may be considered to be a rule without any preconditions). These rules, together with relevant rules from the knowledge base, are then checked for logical consistency, by extended constraint propagation during which each rule in turn is compared with an "environment" consisting of the other rules under consideration. In the event of any conflicts being detected, advice on the handling of such conflicts is offered to the user.

Quality Evaluation

A quality evaluation involves the evaluation of the manufacturing environment and also of product performance. Manufacturing environment evaluation relies on previous manufacturing data in order to detect which specified tolerances can or can not be achieved; the numerical manipulations involved do not require AI methods.

Product performance evaluation is based on the production of a numerical instantiation of the Function Tree that reflects the product's expected behaviour. The first step is to evaluate the leaves, ideally by mapping on to the product's instantiated geometrical features; otherwise, use may be made of historic quality observations, including current tests and/or simulation runs, or equations, if available. Having obtained a numerical evaluation of the leaves, the next step is to transform these into *Quality Values* possessing a quality value scale rating and a verbal meaning. The numerical quality values are then aggregated (using appropriate weights) in order to evaluate the functional behaviour at higher levels of the Product Tree. As a result, an overall evaluation picture is obtained, by mapping the behaviour of the product on to the functional decomposition structure.

Quality Advice

The output from a quality evaluation enables the quality advice mechanism to operate. This essentially involves two activities: (i) *diagnosis*, the interpretation of a quality evaluation, and (ii) *repair*, the formulation and presentation of quality advice. Following a quality evaluation, individual nodes in the Product Tree may be classified as "failed" or otherwise. The quality advice mechanism provides a means of identifying these nodal failures in groups and for advice to be offered on the repair of such failures. This facilitates an interpretation at higher levels of the tree as to the nature of a failure within a complete product assembly.

The quality advice mechanism is user driven and, as is the case with quality evaluation, may be requested for either a fully or partially instantiated design. Although its facilities are only really required when quality inadequacies have been detected, this does not preclude its use to investigate quality aspects when no such failures have been found. During diagnosis, a *Quality Problem Definition* (QPD) is created, which can be described in terms of the function, product and process domains, and which serves to characterise the nature of a quality problem. During the repair phase, the QPD enables case based reasoning techniques to compare or match the current situation to other historic problems, or to identify generic problems.

It should be pointed out that, since quality problems are often very complex and are not always well focussed, the quality advisor will not, in general, be able to determine a solution to a quality failure. However, it *will* perform a search for either a generic or a historic solution path and strategy, and advise the user accordingly.

DISCUSSION

Although the strategic aim is to produce a generic advisory system, the more immediate goal is to develop a prototype system to give advice in the design of a particular type of product. The product chosen for this evaluation exercise is a shock absorber. The manufacturing environment is that of APA Amortiguadores, Spain, who produce a variety of types of shock absorbers for the European, US and Japanese automobile industry. Based on information supplied by the design engineers, a detailed analysis of the product has been carried out, as a result of which its structure may be represented as a product tree in terms of its sub-assemblies, components and features. To facilitate the acquisition of knowledge of the design process, a detailed Petri Net model of the current design procedures employed has been developed.

At the present time, a first prototype has been developed, employing a windows-based user interface, and which partially implements the reasoning mechanisms described above. Current knowledge acquisition activities are directed to the capture of (i) knowledge of the design and manufacturing processes, (ii) knowledge of the product itself, and, in particular, of the influences that the geometrical and functional aspects of the product have on each other, and (iii) general design knowledge, reflecting the considerable experience and expertise of the collaborating design engineers. The system is being developed on Sun workstations, and employs Xview and devGUIDE tools for the user interface. The Common Lisp Object System (CLOS) [4] is being used as a basis for system implementation.

ACKNOWLEDGEMENTS

The research described in this paper is being carried out under ESPRIT Project no. 2178, RA-IQSE, Revision Advisor - An Integrated Quality Support Environment, and is funded by the CEC. The project consortium comprises: CRI A/S, Denmark, AIN, Spain, CTC, Greece, HCS Industrial Automation B.V., Holland, and Paisley College, UK. The author gratefully acknowledges the contribution of all members of the consortium. The cooperation of engineers from APA Amortiguadores Spain in this research is much appreciated.

REFERENCES

1   FORBUS, K.D. Intelligent computer-aided engineering *A.I. Magazine,* Fall 1988, 23-36.
2   BROWN, D.C. and CHANDRASEKARAN B. *Design Problem Solving* Pitman, London, 1989.
3   RA-IQSE CONSORTIUM *Strategy for Reasoning, Knowledge Representation and Knowledge Acquisition in RA-IQSE* November 1990.
4   KEENE S.E. *Object-Oriented Programming in Common Lisp* Addison Wesley, Reading, Mass., 1989.

Automatische Verfeinerung der Wissensbasis durch maschinelles Lernen in einem medizinischen Expertensystem

Bernhard Nagele[†], Gerhard Widmer[†‡], Werner Horn[†‡]

[†]Institut für Medizinische Kybernetik und Artificial Intelligence,
Universität Wien, Freyung 6, A–1010 Wien, und
[‡]Österreichisches Forschungsinstitut für Artificial Intelligence, Wien
E–mail: werner@ai–vie.uucp

MESICAR ist ein Expertensystem der zweiten Generation, welches sehr allgemeine Beschreibungen rheumatologischer Krankheiten beinhaltet. Durch die Anwendung einer detaillierten, hierarchischen Beschreibung der menschlichen Anatomie ist das System in der Lage, Diagnoseentscheidungen zu unterstützen. Der vorliegende Beitrag beschreibt die Erweiterung des Expertensystems um eine Lernkomponente: Das neue System MESICAR–LEARN lernt automatisch verfeinerte Beschreibungen zu häufig auftretenden Krankheiten. Die dafür entwickelte Lernmethode ist eine Kombination von analytischem und empirischem Lernen. Dabei wird MESICARs Wissensbasis als domain theory verwendet. Die erlernten Konzepte werden in eine Krankheitshierarchie integriert und unterstützen so die effiziente und schnelle Diagnose von häufig vorkommenden Fällen.

1. Motivation und Zielsetzung

Expertensysteme der zweiten Generation sind charakterisiert durch ihre Fähigkeit einer prinzipielleren Form des Schlußfolgerns (Steels 1985, 1990). Diese Fähigkeit basiert auf der Verwendung von Basiswissen über die Struktur, die Funktion und das Verhalten der Komponenten der Domäne – oft auch als Tiefenwissen bezeichnet. Die verwendeten Schlußfolgerungsmechanismen sind sehr robust, jedoch ist deren Berechnungsaufwand sehr hoch.

MESICAR (Horn 1989) ist ein Beispiel für solche Expertsysteme der zweiten Generation, da es als Basis zur Erstellung von Diagnosen im rheumatologischen Krankheitsbereich detailliertes Wissen über die menschliche Anatomie verwendet. Durch die Verwendung des Binding (Horn 1991), welches Konsistenzbedingungen festlegt, ist es möglich, Konzepte unabhängig von der anatomischen Lokalisation der Krankheit zu formulieren. Diese Art der Wissensrepräsentation hat den Vorteil, daß allgemein formuliertes Wissen dargestellt werden kann. Es ist somit möglich Wissen, das für viele unterschiedliche Fälle nützlich ist, kompakt und für den Benutzer verständlich darzustellen. Damit jedoch solch allgemein formuliertes Wissen bei einem spezifischen Fall anwendbar wird, muß es für den spezifischen Fall aufbereitet werden. Es wird bei dieser Aufbereitung das spezifische Wissen aus dem allgemeinen Wissen unter Anwendung von Konsistenzbedingungen ermittelt. Der Nachteil dieser Art der Wissensrepräsentation ist somit der hohe Aufwand beim Schlußfolgern. Bei MESICAR sind die Krankheitskonzepte nur in Verbindung mit dem anatomischen Wissen für eine lokalisierte Krankheit verwendbar. Dieses anatomische Wissen ist in einer Heterarchie dargestellt. Die Berechnung des Binding für eine spezifische Krankheit macht den Inferenzprozeß aufwendig.

Um diesen Nachteil für häufig vorkommende Krankheiten zu überwinden, war es wichtig, spezifisches problemorientiertes Wissen in die Wissensbasis von MESICAR aufzunehmen. Für

MESICAR ist dieses spezifische problemorientierte Wissen die Beschreibung von spezifischen Krankheiten deren anatomische Lokalisation fixiert ist. In solchen spezifischen Krankheitskonzepten ist eben die anatomische Lokalisation bekannt und die Berechnung des Binding kann entfallen. Die Akquisition der spezifischen Krankheitskonzepte erfolgt durch Lernen. Der vorliegende Beitrag zeigt, wie dies durch Kombination von analytischen und empirischen Lerntechniken realisiert wurde. Wir bauten MESICAR-LEARN welches ein Learning Apprentice (Mitchell et al. 1985) von MESICAR ist. Inkrementell werden spezifische Krankheitsbeschreibungen[1] durch Generalisierung von Krankheitsinstanzen, welche die Probleme des Patienten darstellen, gebildet. Die generischen Krankheitsbeschreibungen von MESICAR (Kapitel 2) dienen dabei als *domain theory* (Mitchell et al. 1986) für die Lernmethode, welche in Kapitel 3 beschrieben ist. Durch die Aufnahme der spezifischen Krankheitsbeschreibungen in die Wissensbasis von MESICAR mußte natürlich auch der Schlußfolgerungsmechanismus des Expertensystems angepaßt werden. Wie die spezifischen Krankheitsbeschreibungen vom Schlußfolgerungsmechanismus verwendet werden, ist in Kapitel 4 dargestellt. Abschließend (Kapitel 5) werden verschiedene verwandte Lernalgorithmen unserem Ansatz gegenübergestellt.

2. MESICARs Wissensbasis

MESICARs Wissensbasis besteht hauptsächlich aus generischen Krankheitskonzepten und Wissen über die menschliche Anatomie. Ein generisches Krankheitskonzept ist eine komplexe Beschreibung der typischen Form einer Krankheit, bei der von der anatomischen Lokalisation abstrahiert wurde. In Abb. 1 werden Teile des Krankheitskonzeptes *Tendinose*, das heißt eine nicht endzündliche Erkrankung eines Muskel- und Sehnenansatzes, dargestellt.

Abb. 1 gibt einen Eindruck von der Komplexität und Reichhaltigkeit der Wissensbasis von MESICAR. Wir werden im folgenden nur die Faktoren erklären, die für eine grobe Präsentation des Lernalgorithmus im Rahmen dieses Beitrags unmittelbar relevant sind:

- Der "D-Attribute"-Bereich spezifiziert die Attribut-Slots, welche jede Instanz haben kann. Das charakteristische Attribut identifiziert die Instanz, d.h. es ermöglicht die Unterscheidung zwischen verschiedenen Instanzen desselben Krankheitskonzeptes.
- Der "D-Binding" Bereich definiert, woher die Krankheitsinstanz die Werte für die Attribute bekommt.
- Der "Manifestations"-Bereich beinhaltet verschiedene D-M-Ausdrücke. Jeder D-M-Ausdruck verweist auf eine Manifestation (M) welche die Krankheitshypothese D unterstützt oder widerlegt. Jeder D-M-Ausdruck kann für jedes definierte Attribut eine Bewertungsvorschrift (Matching Condition) und eine Vorschrift von Konsistenzbedingungen (D-M-Binding) beinhalten. Das D-M-Binding gibt für ein Attribut einer spezifischen Krankheit an, welche Werte des Attributs bei dieser Krankheit zulässig sind. Für unser Beispiel bedeutet dies unter anderem, daß die anatomische Struktur an welcher eine *Druckschmerzhaftigkeit* festgestellt wurde, in der Region liegen muß, wo der Patient über *Schmerz* klagt.

Diese Beschreibung der Konzepte ist generisch in dem Sinne, daß sie die Erzeugung von Krankheitsinstanzen ermöglicht, die spezielle und detaillierte (anatomische) Informationen enthalten. Diese geben das Krankheitsbild des Patienten wider. Wird das Krankheitsbild "Tennisellbogen am linken Arm" eines Patienten verarbeitet, so erzeugt der Schlußfolgerungsmechanismus von MESICAR die Krankheitsinstanz *Tendinose-1 (Epicondylus radialis humeri)*. In diesem Fall werden in den Slots von *Tendinose-1*, -STRUCTURE und -REGION, die Werte *Epicondylus radialis humeri* bzw. *Ellbogen-vorne-links* eingefüllt.

---

[1] In diesem Artikel wird für den Terminus Krankheitsbeschreibung auch der Terminus Krankheitskonzept gebraucht.

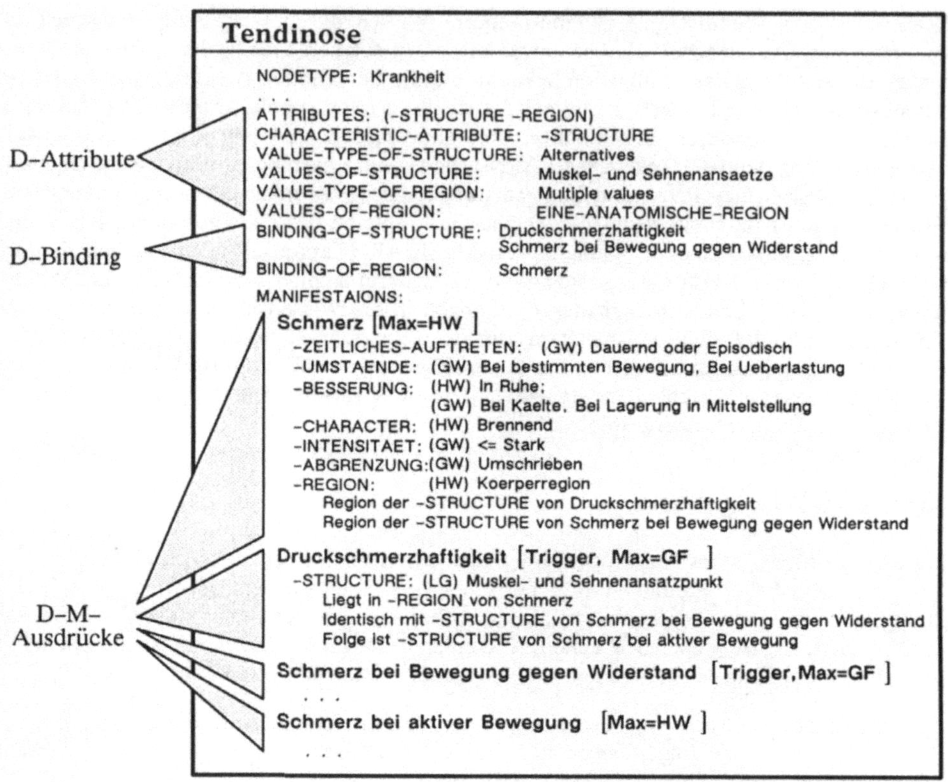

Abb. 1: Beschreibung des generischen Krankheitskonzeptes *Tendinose*.

Die Gesamtheit dieser generischen Krankheitskonzepte, zusammen mit der hierarchischen Beschreibung der Anatomie und den Attributen, definiert das Hintergrundwissen für MESICAR-LEARN. Es wird als domain theory bei der Erzeugung von Erklärungen verwendet.

3. Lernen spezifischer Krankheitsbeschreibungen

MESICARs Inferenzmechanismus erzeugt als Beschreibung des Krankheitsbildes eines Patienten eine oder mehrere Krankheitsinstanzen D_{INST}, die Instanzen eines generischen Krankheitskonzeptes D sind. Ausgehend von diesen Instanzen D_{INST} erzeugt und erweitert MESICAR-LEARN inkrementell spezifische Krankheitsbeschreibungen D_{Spez} unter Führung eines erfahrenen Rheumatologen. In Prinzip wäre das System fähig D_{Spez} aus einer einzigen erfolgreichen Diagnose der Krankheit D (d.h. aus einer Instanz D_{INST}) zu gewinnen. Im allgemeinen aber ist ein solches D_{Spez} erst dann für den Diagnosevorgang nützlich, wenn das System einige leicht unterschiedliche Fälle desselben Problems gesehen hat. Erst dann nämlich kann durch Generalisierung ein allgemeineres D_{Spez} erzeugt werden, welches die meisten Erscheinungsformen dieser spezifischen Krankheit abdeckt.

MESICAR-LEARN unterteilt die Instanzen $D_{INST-1},..., D_{INST-n}$ in positive (richtig diagnostiziert) und negative Trainingsbeispiele (siehe Abb. 2). Die positiven Trainingsbeispiele werden zur Generalisierung, die negativen zur Spezialisierung verwendet. Wenn kein spezifisches Konzept der Krankheit, welche diagnostiziert wurde, existiert, so wird ein solches aus der Erklärung in einer Art *Explanation Based Learning* (Mitchell et al. 1986) gebildet und in die Krankheitshierarchie

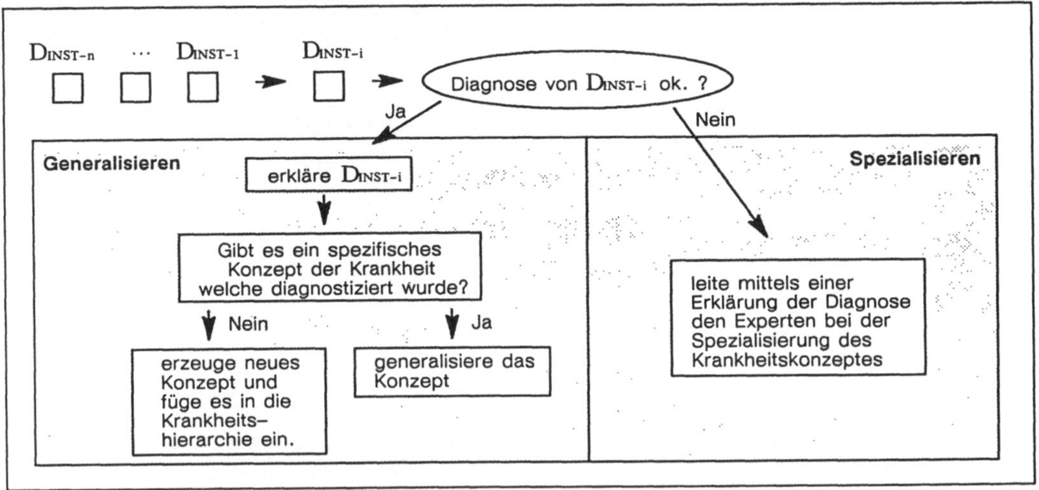

Abb. 2: Grobstruktur des Lernalgorithmus.

eingefügt (Kapitel 3.1). Sollte es ein spezifisches Konzept der Krankheit, welche diagnostiziert wurde, geben, so wird dieses Konzept generalisiert (Kapitel 3.2). Die Erklärung der Diagnose von D_{INST-i} wird in diesem Fall zur Lenkung der induktiven Generalisierung verwendet (Danyluk 1987). Im Fall der Spezialisierung leitet die Erklärung der Diagnose von D_{INST-i} den Rheumatologen (Kapitel 3.3).

3.1 Erzeugen der spezifischen Krankheitsbeschreibung aus einer Erklärung (analytischer Schritt)

Im analytischen Schritt wird mittels einer Art von EBL ein erstes spezifisches Krankheitskonzept D_{Spez} aus der Erklärung von D_{INST} gebildet. Dazu wird zuerst die Erklärung von D_{INST} erzeugt. Diese ist die explizite Darstellung des "Wie und Warum" ein Beispiel zu einem gesuchten Konzept gehört. In unserem System sind die generischen Krankheitskonzepte die *goal concepts* (Mitchell et al. 1986).

Eine Erklärung in MESICAR-LEARN ist ein Baum der Tiefe fünf, der beschreibt, in welcher Form die Krankheit D_{INST} auf der Basis von Manifestationen, die beim Patienten beobachtet wurden, diagnostiziert werden konnte. Der Inhalt der einzelnen Ebenen des Baumes sind:

0: Das Krankheitskonzept D, welches zur Erzeugung der Erklärung verwendet wurde;
1: Zeiger auf jene D-M-Ausdrücke welche zur Diagnose von D_{INST} verwendet wurden;
2: Jene Manifestationen welche Einfluß auf die Diagnose von D_{INST} nahmen;
3: Jene Attribute der Manifestationen für welche Werte vorliegen;
4: Die atomaren Teile der korrespondierenden Matching Conditions zusammen mit den Wert(en) aus der Manifestation.

Als Beispiel für einen solchen Erklärungsbaum ist in Abb. 3 eine Erklärung der Krankheitsinstanz *Tendinose-1 (Epicondylus radialis humeri)*, die das Krankheitsbild "Tennisellbogen" eines Patienten verarbeitet, dargestellt. Es ist dies ein spezieller Fall der generischen Krankheit *Tendinose*, der spezifisch am *Epicondylus radialis humeri*, einem Muskel- und Sehnenansatzpunkt am Ellbogen, auftritt. Wenn wir den Baum der Erklärung mit der entsprechenden Beschreibung des Krankheitskonzeptes in Abb. 1 vergleichen, so sehen wir folgende Charakteristika:

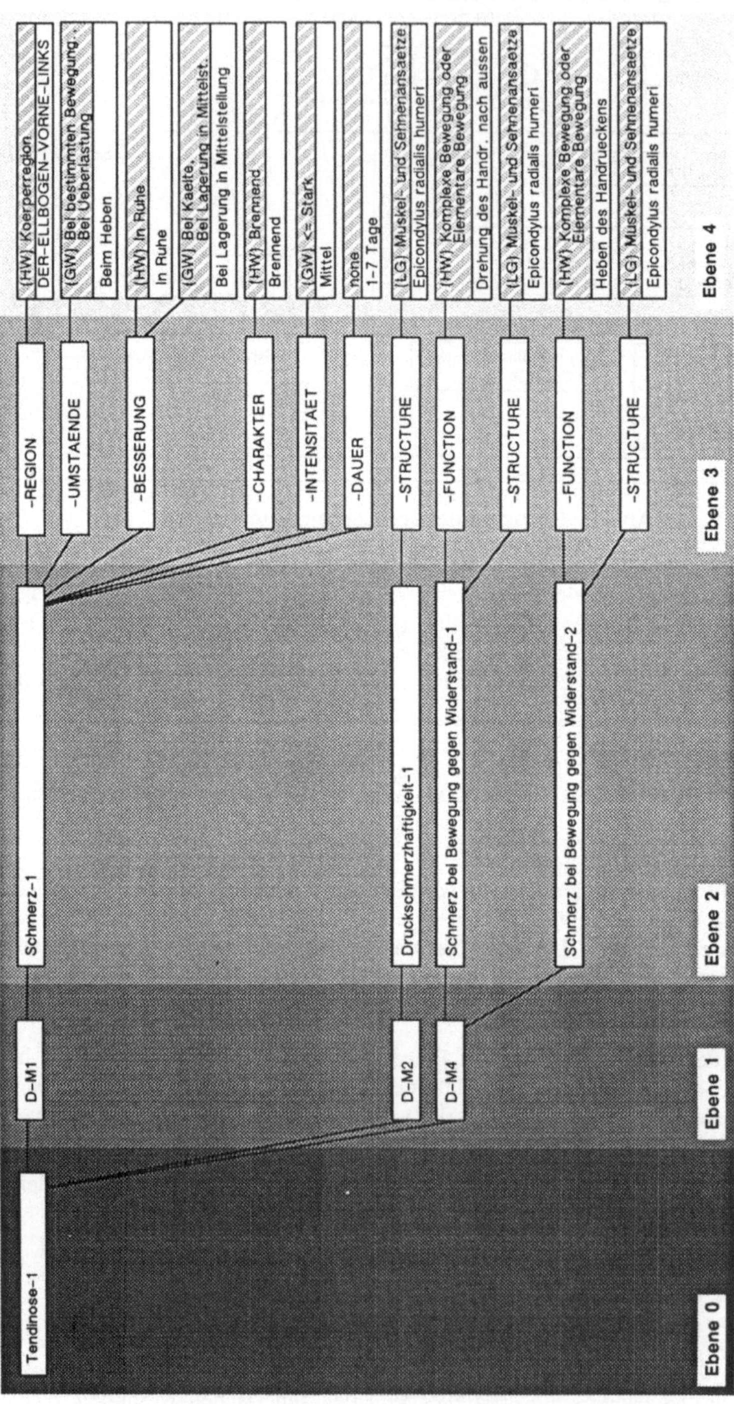

Abb. 3: Erklärung der Krankheitsinstanz *Tendinose-1*.

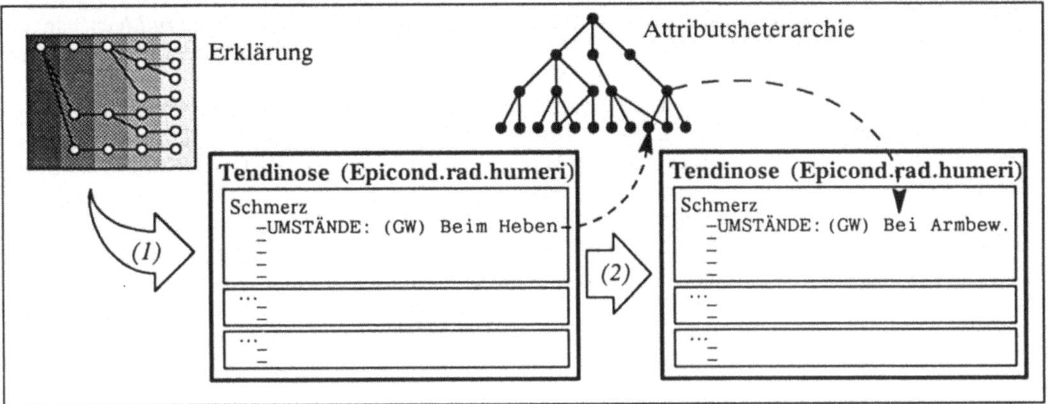

Abb.4: Lernen der spezifischen Krankheitsbeschreibung
Tendinose (Epicondylus radialis humeri).

- Die Struktur des Baumes spiegelt die Struktur der Krankheitsbeschreibung wider;
- nur jene D–M–Ausdrücke wurden verwendet bei welchen die korrespondierenden Manifestationen instanziert und verwendet wurden, d.h. nur die für die tatsächliche Entscheidung relevanten Faktoren kommen in der Erklärung vor. In unserem Beispiel wurde der D–M–Ausdruck *Schmerz bei aktiver Bewegung* nicht dargestellt, weil diese Manifestation nicht gefunden wurde.

Die Struktur des spezifischen Krankheitskonzeptes – in unserem Beispiel *Tendinose (Epicondylus radialis humeri)* – wird analog zur Struktur des generischen Konzeptes direkt aus der Erklärung aufgebaut. Das so gewonnene spezifische Krankheitskonzept wird als Subkonzept D_{spez} in die Krankheitshierarchie eingefügt.[2]

3.2 Inkrementelle Generalisierung (empirischer Schritt)

Das Resultat der analytischen Kompilation aus einem (positiven) Beispiel (Kap. 3.1) ist ein Subkonzept D_{spez}, welches das Erscheinungsbild der Krankheit D an einer bestimmten anatomischen Lokalisation L beschreibt. Dieses D_{spez} ist allerdings sehr speziell – es deckt im wesentlichen nur den Beispielfall ab, aus dem es erzeugt wurde. Werden dem System nun weitere Beispielfälle für die Krankheit D am Ort L bekannt, die sich in einigen Details vom ersten Beispiel unterscheiden, so führen diese zu einer schrittweisen Verallgemeinerung des ursprünglichen D_{spez}, sodaß D_{spez} sich mehr und mehr dem tatsächlichen typischen Krankheitsbild annähert. Abb.4 skizziert die Abfolge der analytischen Erzeugung eines Subkonzepts *Tendinose am Epicondylus radialis humeri* aus der Erklärung eines ersten Beispiels (Schritt 1 – siehe auch Abb.3) und der nachfolgenden empirischen Generalisierung in Reaktion auf ein neues positives Beispiel (Schritt 2). Diese schrittweise Generalisierung (Schritt 2) geht folgendermaßen vor sich:

---

[2] Angemerkt sei hier noch, daß die Attributwerte von D_{spez} Blätter in der Hierarchie der anatomischen Attribute sind. Ebenso sind die Werte in den Matching Conditions der D–M–Ausdrücke (vgl.Kap.2) elementar – das heißt nicht weiter unterteilbar –, wodurch die komplexen Konsistenzbedingungen (D–M–Binding) eliminiert werden können. Durch die nachfolgende Generalisierung kann es allerdings für einzelne Attribute notwendig werden diese Konsistenzbedinungen wiederherzustellen. Dieser (seltene) Fall wird automatisch durch einen aufwendigen Algorithmus behandelt.

Das neue Beispiel unterscheidet sich vom bisherigen Konzept *Tendinose (Epic.rad.hum.)* in der Ausprägung einiger Attribute. Diese Attribute müssen daher im Konzept generalisiert werden. MESICARs Wissensbasis baut auf einem Typsystem auf, d.h. Attribute können einen von mehreren Typen besitzen (z.B. integer, boolean, hierarchisch geordnet, etc.), und abhängig davon werden verschiedene Generalisierungsoperatoren verwendet. Abb.4 skizziert den typischen Fall eines Attributs mit hierarchisch geordneten Werten: dieses Attribut UMSTÄNDE (der Manifestation *Schmerz*) hatte in dem aus dem ersten Beispiel (siehe auch Abb.3) erzeugten Subkonzept den spezifischen Wert *Beim Heben*; im neuen Beispielfall tritt jedoch bei diesem Attribut der Wert *Beim Werfen* auf. MESICAR–LEARN konsultiert in diesem Fall die zu MESICARs Hintergrundwissen gehörende Hierarchie der Werte für UMSTÄNDE und wählt den kleinsten gemeinsamen Oberbegriff (die 'least general generalization') von *Beim Heben* und *Beim Werfen* – nämlich *Bei Armbewegungen* – als Generalisierung, die dann auch in die verallgemeinerte Beschreibung von *Tendinose (Epic.rad.hum.)* eingetragen wird. Hier sind mehrere Dinge anzumerken:

* MESICAR–LEARN verwendet allgemeine Heuristiken, um zu entscheiden, ob zwei verschiedene Werte tatsächlich zu einem gemeinsamen Oberbegriff generalisiert werden sollen. Im Falle der Generalisierung von hierarchisch geordneten Werten hängt diese Entscheidung u.a. davon ab, wie weit die beiden zu verbindenden Begriffe in der Hierarchie voneinander 'entfernt' sind (d.h. ob sie einen gemeinsamen Vater, Onkel, Großvater etc. haben). Im Falle einer nicht gerechtfertigt scheinenden Generalisierung wird nur die Disjunktion des bisherigen Wertes mit dem neuen Wert in das generalisierte Konzept aufgenommen (vorsichtige Generalisierung).

* Bei Attributen, deren Werte nach mehreren Gesichtspunkten hierarchisch geordnet sind (Heterarchie), sind oft mehrere Arten der Generalisierung möglich. Hier kann die Erklärung des Beispiels wichtige Hinweise bezüglich der sinnvollsten Generalisierung liefern (siehe auch Widmer 1991), da das generische Konzept, mit dessen Hilfe die Erklärung aufgebaut wurde, bestimmte Constraints für relevante Attributwerte definiert.

* Das bekannte Problem des *language bias* (Utgoff 1986), daß nämlich die Generalisierungshierarchien inadäquat sein und damit die Formulierung sinnvoller Konzepte unmöglich machen können, zeigt sich in unserem Fall eher als Vorteil: unter der (gerechtfertigten) Annahme, daß MESICARs Wissensbasis für diagnostische Zwecke adäquat strukturiert ist, wirkt sich dieser bias positiv aus, indem medizinisch relevante und sinnvolle Klassen für die Generalisierung zur Verfügung stehen.

Insgesamt gesehen besteht daher die Rolle des analytischen Lernschritts (1) darin, über die Erklärung die für das zu lernende Subkonzept relevanten Manifestationen und Attribute herauszufiltern, während die nachfolgende inkrementelle Generalisierung (2) dann aufgrund weiterer Beispiele den richtigen Grad der Allgemeinheit für die Konzeptbeschreibung findet (vgl. auch Flann & Dietterich 1989).

3.3 Spezialisieren

Bei der inkrementellen Verallgemeinerung (Kap. 3.2) kann es zu Übergeneralisierungen bei einem gelernten Konzept D_{spez} kommen. Diese äußern sich früher oder später darin, daß MESICAR irgendeinen neuen Fall fälschlicherweise als D_{spez} diagnostiziert. In einem solchen Fall muß MESICAR–LEARN das zu ungenaue Konzept D_{spez} *spezialisieren*.

Beim Spezialisieren werden die möglichen Erscheinungsformen eines Krankheitskonzeptes, welche im System dargestellt sind, eingeschränkt. Dieser Vorgang geschieht bei uns händisch durch den Experten, da im System zuwenig Wissen für einen solchen Vorgang vorhanden ist. Das Spezialisieren erfolgt in unserem System im Kontext des momentanen Krankheitsfalles, wobei eine weitreichende Unterstützung des Experten durch die Nutzung der erzeugten Erklärung gegeben werden kann.

Dem Experten wird die Erklärung des Systems wie es zu dieser Diagnose gekommen ist, zur Korrektur vorgelegt. Er kann bei dieser Darstellung des "Wie und Warum" es zu dieser Diagnose gekommen ist, einschränkendem Korrekturen anbringen. Es wird dabei nach jeder vorgenommenen Korrektur die Diagnose neu berechnet und das Ergebnis dem Experten mitgeteilt. Beendet ist der Spezialisierungvorgang wenn die Diagnose des Systems mit jener des Experten übereinstimmt.

3.4 Der Effekt der "domain theory"

In MESICAR–LEARN verwenden wir Erklärungen sowohl zur Erzeugung einer ersten, sehr spezifischen Näherung des zu lernenden Konzeptes – in einer Art analytischen Lernens (EBL) – als auch zur Lenkung der induktiven Generalisierung. Diese Erklärungen stellen einen Fokus auf jene Werte und Attribute dar, welche für das zu erlernende Konzept relevant sind. Die verwendeteten Verallgemeinerungshierarchien sind keine strikten Bäume, so daß mehr als nur eine Generalisierungsmöglichkeit zur Auswahl steht. Hier ist die Information, welche durch die Erklärung zur Verfügung gestellt wird sehr hilfreich. Sie wird verwendet, um den richtigen Vaterknoten auszuwählen. Diese Information sind die Werte aus den atomaren Teilen der Matching Conditions (Ebene 4 in Abb. 3), mit welchen erklärt wurde.

4. Die Verwendung gelernter Konzepte

Die von MESICAR–LEARN gelernten speziellen Krankheitskonzepte sind in Struktur und Repräsentationsform ident mit den generischen Konzepten MESICARs. Deshalb können sie vom Inferenzmechanismus in der gleichen Art und Weise benutzt werden.

Die gelernten Krankheitsbeschreibungen werden als Subkonzepte der generischen Konzepte in die Krankheitshierarchie eingebaut. Die genaue Stelle, an der das Konzept eingeordnet wird, ergibt sich aus dem Wert des charakteristischen Attributs, da das charakteristische Attribut die Lokalisation der Krankheit definiert. Da der Wert des charakteristischen Attributs ein Wert aus der anatomischen Hierarchie ist, ergibt sich eine Korrespondenz zwischen anatomischer und Krankheitshierarchie (siehe Abb. 5).

Der Inferenzmechanismus des Expertensystems MESICAR wurde dahingehend erweitert, daß (gelernte) spezifische Krankheitskonzepte zuerst berücksichtigt werden. Nur wenn die spezifischen Konzepte zur Diagnosefindung nicht ausreichen, greift MESICAR auf sein allgemeines Wissen zurück. Dadurch wird der Diagnoseprozeß in vielen (typischen) Fällen effizienter, und die von MESICAR an den Benutzer gestellten Fragen werden zielgerichteter.

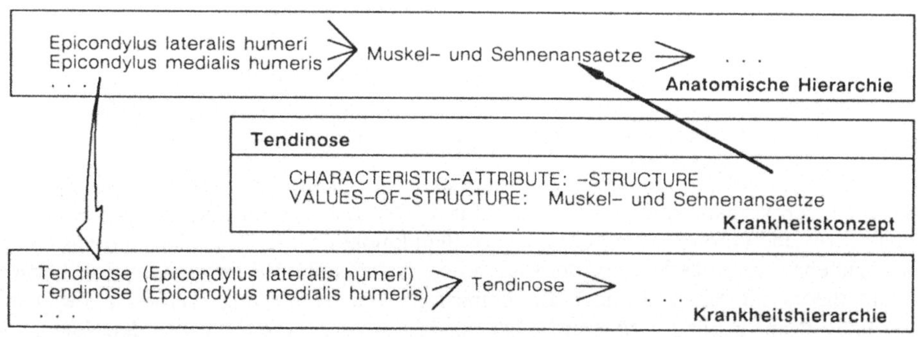

Abb. 5: Anlehnung der Krankheitshierarchie an die Hierarchie der Anatomie.

5. Vergleich mit verwandten Systemen

Wir stellen in diesem Kapitel MESICAR–LEARN dem IOE–Algorithmus (Flann&Dietterich 1989), dem Ansatz von Bergadano&Giordana (1988, kurz B&G–Algorithmus) und dem Ansatz von Widmer (1991, kurz Widmer/91) gegenüber, weil sie im Hinblick auf die Integration analytischen und empirischen Lernens die ähnlichsten bekannten Ansätze sind. Besonderes Augenmerk schenken wir bei diesem Vergleich den Fragen, ob die Systeme inkrementell arbeiten, wie die Systeme sich verhalten wenn das erlernte Konzept zu allgemein ist, und ob das Hintergrundwissen des Systems beim empirischen Generalisieren einen kontextabhängigen *bias* liefert.

Wie Schlimmer und Fisher ausgeführt haben (Schlimmer&Fisher 1986), ist es für Systeme, welche in realen Umgebungen operieren, unerläßlich, inkrementell zu arbeiten. MESICAR–LEARN ebenso wie Widmer/91 erfüllen im Gegensatz zum IOE–Algorithmus und dem B&G–Algorithmus diese Bedingung.

Für inkrementell arbeitende Systeme ist es natürlich schwieriger ein erlerntes Konzept bei Übergeneralisierung einzuschränken (empirisches Spezialisieren) als für nicht inkrementell arbeitende Systeme. Der B&G–Algorithums kann induktiv spezialisieren, da sämtliche Trainingsbeispiele zur Bearbeitung verfügbar sind. Wie komplex inkrementelles Spezialisieren ist, kann man anhand der inkrementellen Version des B&G–Algorithmus (Widmer 1989) erkennen. Das zum Spezialisieren notwendige Wissen ist meist in inkrementell arbeitenden Systemen nicht enthalten. Für ein Lernsystem ist es jedoch wichtig, daß die Möglichkeit der Spezialisierung vorgesehen wurde, da Wissensbasen nie ganz widerspruchsfrei sind. Wir haben daher für diesen Fall bei MESICAR–LEARN die Möglichkeit ”händischer” Spezialisierung vorgesehen, obwohl widerspuchsfreies Hintergrundwissen angenommen werden konnte, da als Wissensbasis jene eines Expertensystemes vorliegt. Weder beim IOE–Algorithmus noch bei Widmer/91 wurde die Möglichkeit des Spezialisierens eines einmal erlernten Konzeptes vorgesehen. Bei Widmer/91 muß jedoch hinzugefügt werden, daß aufgrund der speziellen Eigenschaften der domain theory Übergeneralisierungen im allgemeinen nicht auftreten.

Beim empirischen Generalisieren ist die Frage wichtig, ob der Lernalgorithmus einen kontextabhängigen *bias*, basierend auf dem Hintergrundwissen des Systems, verwendet. Sowohl MESICAR–LEARN als auch Widmer/91 verwenden auch diese Art von bias beim empirischen Generalisieren.

MESICAR–LEARN, Widmer/91 und der IOE–Algorithmus lernen charakteristische Konzeptbeschreibungen (maximal spezifische Beschreibungen). Im Gegensatz dazu lernt der B&G–Algorithmus eine diskriminierende Beschreibung, d.h. eine maximal generelle Beschreibung. Sowohl MESICAR–LEARN als auch Widmer/91 generalisieren möglichst vorsichtig (least general).

6. Conclusio

Der vorliegende Beitrag präsentiert ein auf einem allgemeinen Modell aufbauendes Expertensystem, das seine Wissensbasis aufgrund spezifischer Erfahrungen selbständig verfeinert. Dies führt zu höherer Effizienz und besserer Fokusierung des Problemlösungsvorgangs.

Die Konstruktion und Integration von spezialisiertem Wissen in die Wissensbasis wird durch einen inkrementellen Lernvorgang automatisch ausgeführt. Der Lernalgorithmus ist eine Kombination von analytischem und empirischem Lernen. Vom Standpunkt des maschinellen Lernens ist besonders hervorzuheben, daß das Hintergrundwissen des Systems sowohl im analytischen Lernschritt (als domain theory für EBL) als auch für empirische Generalisierung (Hinweise für plausible Verallgemeinerungen) genutzt wird. Der Effekt für das Expertensystem liegt in der Nutzung einer einheitlichen Wissensbasis, welche sowohl allgemeine Krankheitsbeschreibungen, die ein breites

Spektrum von Krankheitsbildern an beliebigen anatomischen Lokalisationen abdecken, als auch spezifische Krankheitskonzepte für häufig auftretende Fälle integriert. Weiters sollte erwähnt werden, daß das System nur nützliche Krankheitskonzepte erlernt, weil spezifische Beschreibungen nur für jene Krankheitsbilder erzeugt werden, welche bei Patienten aufgetreten sind.

Zusammenfassend sei noch gesagt, daß die präsentierte Methode nicht zur automatischen Erstellung von Wissensbasen gedacht ist. Mittels der vorgestellten Methode sollte ein Expertensystem eher in der Lage sein, seine Wissensbasis automatisch zu verbessern. Dies ist eine wichtige Fähigkeit für Expertensystemen der zweiten Generation, wenn sie erfolgreich in komplexen Domänen eingesetzt werden sollen.

Danksagung

Besonderer Dank sei Dr. Kurt Ammer ausgesprochen, der das umfangreiche rheumatologische Wissen aufbereitet hat. Dank auch an Prof. Robert Trappl, der diese Arbeit unterstützt hat. Die Arbeit an diesem Projekt wurde zum Teil vom *Fonds zur Förderung der wissenschaftlichen Forschung* gefördert. Das Österreichische Forschungsinstitut für Artificial Intelligence wird vom Bundesministerium für Wissenschaft und Forschung unterstützt.

Literatur

Bergadano, F. und Giordana, A. (1988). A Knowledge–Intensive Approach to Concept Induction. In *Proceedings of the Fifth International Conference on Machine Learning*. Los Altos, California: Morgan Kaufmann.

Danyluk, A. (1987). The Use of Explanations for Similarity–Based Learning. In *Proceedings of the Tenth International Joint Conference on Artificial Intelligence (IJCAI–87)*. Los Altos, California: Morgan Kaufmann.

Flann, N. und Dieterich, T. (1989). A Study of Explanation–Based Methods for Inductive Learning. *Machine Learning, 4(2)*187–226.

Horn, W. (1989). MESICAR – A Medical Expert System Integrating Causal and Associative Reasoning. *Applied Artificial Intelligence*, Special Issue on Causal Modelling, 3(2)305–336.

Horn, W. (1991). Utilizing Detailed Anatomical Knowledge for Hypotheses Formation and Hypotheses Testing in Rheumatological Decision Support. *Artificial Intelligence in Medicine*, 3(1)21–39.

Mitchell, T., Mahadevan, S. und Steinberg, L. (1985). LEAP: A Learning Apprentice for VLSI Design, in *Proceedings of the 9th International Joint Conference on Artificial Intelligence (IJCAI–85)*. Los Altos, California: Morgan Kaufmann.

Mitchell, T., Keller, R. und Kedar–Cabelli S. (1986). Explanation–Based Generalisation: A Unifying View. *Machine Learning, 1(1)*47–80.

Schlimmer, J.C. und Fisher, D. (1986). A Case Study of Incremental Concept Induction. In *Proceedings of the Fifth National Conference on Artificial Intelligence (AAAI–86)*. Los Altos, California: Morgan Kaufmann.

Steels, L.(1985). Second Generation Expert Systems, *Future Generations Computer Systems*, 1(4)213–221.

Steels, L. (1990). Components of Expertise, *AI–Magazine*, 11(2)28–49.

Utgoff, P. (1986). Machine Learning of Inductive Bias. Boston, Mass.: Kluwer.

Widmer, G. (1989). An Incremental Version of Bergadano & Giordana's Integrated Learning Strategy. In *Proceedings of the Fourth European Working Session on Learning (EWSL–89)*. London: Pitman.

Widmer, G. (1991). Using Plausible Explanations to Bias Empirical Generalization in Weak Theory Domains. In Y. Kodratoff (Hrsg.), *Proc.Fifth European Working Session on Learning (EWSL–91)*, Berlin: Springer.

Learning Diagnostic Rules for Power Distribution Systems

Andrea Leufke, Angelika Hecht, Regine Meunier, Ruxandra Scheiterer
Siemens AG, ZFE IS INF 3
Otto-Hahn-Ring 6, D-8000 München 83

Abstract

This paper discusses the machine generation of diagnostic rules for fault diagnosis in power distribution systems. The Machine Learning technique that we have implemented processes examples of fault events with the associated diagnoses (from records of previous errors), and derives rules that correctly classify the available examples. In order to formalize relevant domain knowledge and to build adequate diagnostic rules, first order concepts had to be introduced. The paper describes the existing prototype RUDI (Learning **R**ules for **D**iagnosis) and the initial results of the test phase.

1 Introduction

The project we describe contributes to two goals. The first one is to provide a prototypical application of Machine Learning techniques to a real-life problem. The second goal is to study how this approach can be generalized. Therefore the prototype application chosen is not unique, but is representative for a broad range of real-life problems. These problems can be characterized as follows:

There is only a relatively small number of examples available, but each example comprises a huge amount of data. The domain knowledge used for learning comprises relations which are described in first order logic. The concepts to be learned have to be parametrized, i.e. they also describe first order concepts. There is no noise in the classification of the examples, but examples may be incomplete and ambiguous.

2 Domain Description

The problem which is approached in this project has been chosen from the field of message burst analysis in power supply networks.

Power supply networks are monitored and controlled from central control rooms. A power system incorporates protective relays; in the event of a short circuit, circuit-breakers selectively isolate faulty items from the net. Each protective relay monitors a certain part of the network. This part is called a protective zone and may be e.g. a line, a part of

a line or a complete station. For safety reasons some redundancy has to be built into
the protection system of a high energy net. This redundancy is achieved by overlapping
protective zones. That is if an element is faulty, the fault may be detected by more
than one protective devices. The protective devices issue messages to the network control
center, where they are displayed in message lists and mimic diagrams. In the event of
complex faults, several hundred messages may be generated within less than one second;
this is referred to as a message burst.

The control engineer must use the information contained in the message bursts, diagnose the fault location and the fault type rapidly and then take appropriate action. The
control engineer can in principle perform the diagnosis on the basis of his knowledge, but
he is placed under great stress by the large number of messages and the time pressure of
making a diagnosis. A power failure, which takes only a few minutes, already produces
high costs for the power company [Löwe90].

The topology of the network we used consists of about 200 stations and 400 connections
between them. As a station is not a simple node but a complex structure there are about
1500 potential fault locations in a network. The fraction of the topology description which
is currently used for learning comprises about 180kB data.

3 Description of the Learning Task

The learning task comprises the generation of diagnostic rules from examples of message
bursts that have already been correctly diagnosed. A message burst consists of a set of
messages and one or several diagnoses. A message essentially has the form *(location event)*,
where *location* refers to an element in the network and *event* describes what happened
at that location. A diagnosis comprises a fault type and a fault location. The rules
must enable the system to determine the fault types as well as the fault locations for
every new message burst that is recieved. The knowledge that is available consists of
the correctly classified message burst produced by the fault, the underlying topology, the
current breaker status and knowledge about the methods of operation of the protection
equipments.

4 Hypothesis Description Language

For each fault type diagnostic rules of the following form have to be found:

If *Condition part*

Then *diagnosis: fault F_i at location X*

whereby the conditional parts, e.g. the concepts to be learned, are conjunctively
connected terms of disjunctions.

The features used to form the condition part can be partitioned into three classes:
features which refer to events recorded in the message burst, features which describe
properties of elements in the network and finally features which describe the relations of
network elements to the fault location. A condition has the following structure:

Condition = Message part $\wedge$ Relations to fault location $\wedge$ Other relations.

The message part consists of a list of *(location event)* pairs. The possible events are arranged in a class hierarchy, depending on the method of operation of the protection equipment. Therefore an event in the message part of the condition refers to an existing event of the message burst (leaf of the event hierarchy) or it refers to a class of events (interior node).

5 Learning Method

As the data necessary to describe a single example comprises a huge amount of data and there are only a few examples for each class, it is reasonable to learn concepts that describe what discriminates a class from other classes rather than to build concepts which describe all common properties of the elements of a class. Therefore we decided on a discrimination learning techniques. However the approaches which were commercially available had two major disadvantages: first they required a feature vector description of the examples which is not appropriate because of the size of the examples (see above) and second they did not provide the possibility to learn parameterized concepts [Quin86].

The learning method that we have designed generates the diagnostic rules in two steps. First those diagnostic rules are generated that are capable of determining the fault type of an example. The second step involves refining these rules with the object of establishing the fault location. A more detailled description of the algorithm is given in [Meun91].

5.1 Discrimination of the Fault Type

For each fault type $F_i \in$ F diagnostic rules have to be found. Our discrimination strategy compares each positive example (message burst with diagnosis F_i) with all negatives (without diagnosis F_i) and searches for the shortest disjunctions which discriminate the positive example from the negatives.

The most general possible condition is *(event V_1)*, where *event* is the most general event in the event hierarchy (e.g. any event) and V_1 is any location variable. This condition is satisfied by every example of a message burst. Consequently, this condition covers the positive example. However, it also covers all negative examples, and must therefore be specialized. Generally, there are a number of specializations that cover the positive example. These are examined as to whether they exclude all negative examples. If this is not the case, they are specialized further. A distinction can be drawn between two types of specialization: specialization of a feature in a message part by replacement of an event class by a subclass or an element of the class or specialization by the addition of a feature in the message part or in the relation part.

In our learning procedure we give preference to short conditions with more strongly specialized features (former type) over longer conditions with relatively general features (latter type). Only if the event can not be further specialized, a new feature (a message or a relation) is added to the hypothesis. The hypothesis space is therefore divided into subspaces with a growing number of features in the message part, each of which is examined one after the other until hypotheses are found that distinguish the positive examples from the negative examples.

5.2 Determination of the Fault Location

It is true of each of the conditions generated in the first step of the concept development process that they cover at least one positive learning example for the associated fault type, and none of the negative examples. The application of the conditions learned so far, however, does not determine the fault location, because the condition part does not content features that refer to the fault location variable.

To supplement a condition by features with the fault location variable to determine the fault location we use the information given in the positive example: we know the fault location of this.

We map a condition learned so far for a positive example onto the example itself. The topology of the locations to which the variables are bound in the condition part tells us what their relation is to the fault location. Assuming that these realtions are typical, we include them in the relation part of the condition.

Often there are several possibilities to map the condition for a specific fault type onto an example, because the location variables can be bound to different sets of locations in the topology. Various relations to the fault location can then be derived. To determine the final fault location we use as a criterion the number of diagnosed fault locations that are obtained when the extended condition is applied to the positive example. The set of relations used is the one that minimizes the number of diagnoses fault locations.

6 Results

The results presented here are based on 50 examples of classified message bursts. From these, we have derived disjoint learning and test sets. Rules have been learned with respect to 7 different fault types.

Test run: Learning with 11 of the 50 examples, test with the 11 learning examples and test on the 39 test examples

The rules — rewritten here for "line fault" — take the following form:

If   *The message burst includes two locations V_1 and V_2,*
    both locations sent the message "distance protection released",
    V_2 is a line feeder and V_1 is an opposite feeder of V_2
Then   *the fault type is LINE FAULT.*
    The fault location is the line between V_1 and V_2.

For the RUDI diagnoses that we obtained, we assessed 6 features for each example, two for each of the 3 parameters fault type, fault location, and disturbance (= combination of fault type and fault location): the fraction of fault types diagnosed by RUDI that is correct and the fraction of correct fault types that was diagnosed by RUDI — the same for fault locations and incidents. The former is a measure of correctness, and the latter is a measure of completeness.

Test	Learning examples	Test examples
Fault type diagnosed by RUDI correct	100%	95%
Fault location diagnosed by RUDI correct	94%	84%
Disturbance diagnosed by RUDI correct	94%	84%
Correct fault type recognized by RUDI	100%	93%
Correct fault location recognized by RUDI	100%	84%
Correct disturbance recognized by RUDI	100%	84%

7 Conclusions

We have shown that Machine Learning techniques are applicable to message burst analysis. The current results are encouraging. The next step will be to evaluate the performance of our learning procedure by comparison with other learning systems which are able to process first order concepts. A further step will be to improve the strategy for determining the fault location.

8 References

[Lang87] Langley, P.: A General Theory of Discrimination, in Klahr, D., Langley, P., Neches, R. (Eds.), Production System Models of Learning and Development, MIT-Press, 1987, pp. 99-161.

[Löwe90] Löwen, U.: Nedex: Expertensystem zur Störungsanalyse im Hochspannungsnetz, Bulletin SEV\VSE 81 (1990) 3, pp. 37-43.

[Quin86] Quinlan, J.R.: Induction of Decision Trees, in Machine Learning 1 (1) 1986 pp. 81-106.

[Meun91] Meunier, R., Scheiterer, R., Hecht, A.: Lernen von Regeln zur Fehlerdiagnose in Stromversorgungsnetzen in KI 1/1991

Modelling Feature Maps by Attributed Parallel Array Grammars

Rudolf Freund   Martina Kirchmeyer   Friedrich Tafill

Institut für Computersprachen, Technische Universität Wien
A-1040 Vienna, Resselgasse 3, AUSTRIA

Abstract. The notion of n-dimensional attributed parallel array grammars is introduced for describing neural networks. Because of the underlying grid structure,
Kohonen's model of feature maps is especially well suited for being represented
by n-dimensional attributed parallel array grammars. Using our formal description
model we prove that Kohonen's global algorithm can be replaced by a local one.

1. Introduction

Applications of feature mappings have been made in many areas of biology as
well as technics, including sensory mapping, motor control, speech recognition,
vector quantization, and combinatorial optimization. A remarkable survey of
applications in biology as well as for robotics can be found in [RMS].
This paper is dedicated to show how Kohonen's model can be described by means
of n-dimensional attributed array grammars as well as to elaborate some advantages
of this description method for designing networks for application purposes.
In the second section of this paper the definitions needed for the notion of
n-dimensional attributed parallel array grammars are stated and explained by means
of explanatory examples. In the third section n-dimensional attributed parallel array
grammars are used for describing neural networks, especially for Kohonen's model
of (self-organizing) feature maps; moreover we show how Kohonen's algorithm
in a fully connected network can be reduced to a linear algorithm in an equivalent
k-connected network. Simulation results for some well-known problems, which have
been programmed by using a precompiler for MODULA (that has been developed
especially for supporting the implementation of neural networks based on the
description methods proposed in this paper) called the CNS (Cellular Net
Simulator), are presented in the fourth section. Final remarks on the results
achieved in this paper and a preview of future research conclude the paper.

2. Definitions and Preliminary Examples

We adapt the definitions and notations from [Wan] and [Fre] for arrays and
array grammars that are needed for developing the new description method for

neural networks, especially for Kohonen's self-organizing feature maps that we are dealing with in the following sections of this paper.

Definition 2.1. Let $\mathbb{N}$ denote the set of positive integers, i.e. $\mathbb{N} = \{1,2,\dots\}$, and let $n \in \mathbb{N}$. Then an n-dimensional *array* a over an alphabet V is a function $a\colon \mathbb{Z}^n \to V \cup \{\mathcal{B}\}$ with finite support $\mathrm{supp}(a)$, where $\mathrm{supp}(a) = \{v \in \mathbb{Z}^n \mid a(v) \neq \mathcal{B}\}$; $\mathcal{B} \notin V$ is called the background or blank symbol. We also write $a = \prod_{v \in \mathrm{supp}(a)} v\,a(v)$ resp. $a = v_1 a(v_1)\dots v_n a(v_n)$, where $\mathrm{supp}(a) = \{v_i \mid 1 \le i \le n\}$. The set of all n-dimensional arrays over V shall be denoted by V^{*n}.

Usually arrays are regarded as equivalence classes of arrays with respect to linear translations, i.e. only the relative positions of the symbols $\neq \mathcal{B}$ in the plane are taken into account. But for our purposes the formal definition given above turns out to be more convenient.

Example 2.1. Let $V = \{a,b\}$, $a\colon \mathbb{Z}^2 \to \{\mathcal{B},a,b\}$, $a(0,0) = a(0,1) = a$ and $a(1,0) = b$. Then $\mathrm{supp}(a) = \{(0,0),(0,1),(1,0)\}$, and we also write $a = (0,0)a(0,1)a(1,0)b$.

Definition 2.2. Let a_1, a_2 be two n-dimensional arrays over V with $\mathrm{supp}(a_1) \cap \mathrm{supp}(a_2) = \{\}$. Then we define the array $a_1 \vee a_2\colon \mathbb{Z}^n \to V \cup \{\mathcal{B}\}$ by $\mathrm{supp}(a_1 \vee a_2) = \mathrm{supp}(a_1) \cup \mathrm{supp}(a_2)$ and $(a_1 \vee a_2)(v) = a_1(v)$ for $v \in \mathrm{supp}(a_1)$ and $(a_1 \vee a_2)(v) = a_2(v)$ for $v \in \mathrm{supp}(a_2)$.

Example 2.2. $(0,0)a(0,1)a(1,0)b = [(0,0)a] \vee [(0,1)a] \vee [(1,0)b]$.

Definition 2.3. Let $v \in \mathbb{Z}^n$. Then the *translation* $\tau_v\colon \mathbb{Z}^n \to \mathbb{Z}^n$ is defined by $\tau_v(w) = w + v$ for all $w \in \mathbb{Z}^n$, and for any array $a \in V^{*n}$ we get $(\tau_v(a))(w) = a(w - v)$ for all $w \in \mathbb{Z}^n$. For $a \in V^{*n}$ and a non-empty set $Z \subseteq \mathbb{Z}^n$ the *restriction* of a to Z is defined by $a/Z\colon Z \to V \cup \{\mathcal{B}\}$ with $a/Z(v) = a(v)$ for all $v \in Z$. – The vector $(0,\dots,0) \in \mathbb{Z}^n$ shall be denoted by o_n.

An *array production* p *over* V is a triple (a_1,a_2,Z), where $a_1,a_2 \in V^{*n}$ and $Z \subseteq \mathbb{Z}^n$ is a finite set. W. l. o. g. we may assume $\mathrm{supp}(a_1) \cup \mathrm{supp}(a_2) \subseteq Z$ and $o_n \in Z$ in the following. Moreover we say that the array $b_2 \in V^{*n}$ is *directly derivable* from the array $b_1 \in V^{*n}$ by the array production (a_1,a_2,Z), iff there exists an array $b_3 \in V^{*n}$ such that $b_1 = b_3 \vee (\tau_v(a_1)/\tau_v(Z))$ and $b_2 = b_3 \vee (\tau_v(a_2)/\tau_v(Z))$, i. e. the subarray of b_1 corresponding to a_1 is replaced by the array a_2, thus yielding b_2. We also write $b_1 \vdash_p b_2$.

If $p = (a_1,a_2,z)$ is an array production such that $a_1(v) = a_2(v)$ for all $v \in Z - \{o_n\}$, then p is called a *parallel array production*, which can be written in the form $X\prod_{v \in Z - \{o_n\}} v X_v \to Y$, where $X = a_1(o_n)$, $Y = a_2(o_n)$, and $X_v = a_1(v) = a_2(v)$ for all $v \in Z - \{o_n\}$; p is called *propagating*, iff $Y = \mathcal{B}$ implies $X = \mathcal{B}$.

Definition. 2.4 A finite set T of parallel array productions over the alphabet V is called a *table of parallel array productions*. An array $b_2 \in V^{*n}$ is said to be *directly derivable* from the array $b_1 \in V^{*n}$ by T, iff for each $w \in \mathbb{Z}^n$ a parallel array production $X\prod_{v \in Z - \{o_n\}} v X_v \to Y$ exists such that $b_1(w) = X$, $b_2(w) = Y$, and $b_1(v + w) = X_v$ for all $v \in Z - \{o_n\}$, and we write $b_1 \vdash_T b_2$.

Moreover we shall make the convention that the blank symbol $\mathfrak{B}$ can only be replaced in the non-empty context by a symbol of V, i.e. $Y \neq \mathfrak{B}$ is allowed for $X = \mathfrak{B}$ only if $X_v \neq \mathfrak{B}$ for some $v \in Z - \{o_n\}$. As a consequence of this convention changes in an n-dimensional array by using a table of parallel productions are restricted to a finite area of the space $\mathbb{Z}^n$.

Definition 2.5. An ***n-dimensional parallel array grammar*** is a quintuple $G = (n,V,\Sigma,P,A)$ where $n \in \mathbb{N}$ is the dimension of the grammar, V is a set of non-terminal symbols, Σ is a set of terminal symbols such that $V \cap \Sigma = \emptyset$, A with $A \in (V \cup \Sigma)^{*n}$ and $\mathrm{supp}(A) \neq \emptyset$ is the Axiom, and P is a finite set of tables of parallel array productions. G is called *propagating*, iff each production in the tables of P is propagating. An array $b_2 \in V^{*n}$ is said to be ***directly derivable*** from the array $b_1 \in V^{*n}$ in G, iff there is a table T of parallel productions in P such that $b_1 \vdash_T b_2$, and we write $b_1 \vdash_G b_2$; $\vdash_G^*$ denotes the reflexive and transitive closure of the relation $\vdash_G$. The n-dimensional array language generated by G is defined by $L(G) = \{ b \in \Sigma^{*n} \mid A \vdash_G^* b \}$.
Moreover we shall call the quadruple $S = (n,V,\Sigma,P)$ an ***n-dimensional array system***; thus an n-dimensional array grammar is a pair (S,A).

In order to be able to define the important notion of *connectedness* of n-dimensional arrays we need the following definitions:

Definition 2.6. An (undirected) ***graph g*** is an ordered pair (N,E), where N is a finite set of ***nodes*** and E is a set of undirected ***edges*** $\{x,y\}$ with $x,y \in N$. A sequence of different nodes $x_0, x_1, ..., x_l, l \in \mathbb{N}$, is called a *path* of length l in g with the starting-point x_0 and the ending-point x_l, if for all i with $1 \leq i \leq l$ an edge $\{x_{i-1},x_i\}$ in E exists. A graph g is said to be ***connected***, if for any two nodes $x,y \in N$, $x \neq y$, a path in g with starting point x and ending point y exists.

Definition 2.7. Let V be an alphabet and α an n-dimensional array over V. For any $k \in \mathbb{N}$, a graph $g_k(\alpha) = (\mathrm{supp}(\alpha),E_k)$ can be assigned to α such that E_k contains the edge $\{v,w\}$ iff $0 < \|v - w\| \leq k$, where the *norm* $\|v\|$ of a vector $v \in \mathbb{Z}^n$, $v = (v_1,...,v_n)$, is defined by $\|v\| = \max\{ |v_i| \mid 1 \leq i \leq n \}$; α is called ***k-connected*** if $g_k(\alpha)$ is a connected graph. Morerover, if α is k-connected then α is m-connected for all $m > k$, too. The ***norm of an n-dimensional array*** α over the alphabet V is the smallest number $k \in \mathbb{N}$ such that α is k-connected. For a *parallel array production* of the form $X \prod_{v \in U} {}^v X_v \to Y$ the *norm* can be defined as $\max\{ \|v\| \mid v \in U \}$; the ***norm of an n-dimensional parallel array system (grammar)*** $S = (n,V,\Sigma,P)$ ($G = (n,V,\Sigma,P,A)$), $\|S\|$ ($\|G\|$) can be defined as the maximum of the norms of all productions in P (and of the axiom A).

Example 2.3. **Conway's *game of life*** can be described by the two-dimensional array system $S = (2,\emptyset,\{1\},P)$ with $P = P_1 \cup P_2 \cup P_3 \cup P_4$ and

$P_1 = \{ 1 \prod_{v \in U} {}^v X_v \to 1 \mid |\{ v \in U \mid X_v = 1 \}| \in \{2,3\} \},$
$P_2 = \{ 1 \prod_{v \in U} {}^v X_v \to \mathfrak{B} \mid |\{ v \in U \mid X_v = 1 \}| \notin \{2,3\} \},$
$P_3 = \{ \mathfrak{B} \prod_{v \in U} {}^v X_v \to \mathfrak{B} \mid |\{ v \in U \mid X_v = 1 \}| \neq 3 \},$
$P_4 = \{ \mathfrak{B} \prod_{v \in U} {}^v X_v \to 1 \mid |\{ v \in U \mid X_v = 1 \}| = 3 \},$

where U is the environment with $U = \{ v \in \mathbb{Z}^2 \mid \|v\| = 1 \}$; hence $\|S\| = 1$.

In Figure 1 a) to e) four successive derivation steps starting from the axiom α with $\text{supp}(\alpha) = \{(0,0),(1,0),(2,0),(2,1),(1,2)\}$ are depicted showing the periodicity of the evolving structures, because for the array α' in e) we have $\text{supp}(\alpha') = \text{supp}(\alpha) + (1,-1)$.

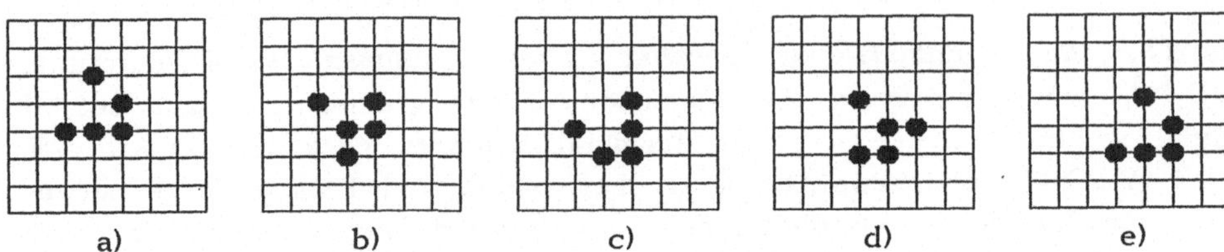

$$a) \qquad b) \qquad c) \qquad d) \qquad e)$$

Figure 1. 'The Glider'

Definition. 2.8. Let V be an alphabet and $\mathcal{A}$ be a set of **attributes** with $\mathfrak{A} \in \mathcal{A}$, $\mathfrak{A}$ being a special attribute called the empty or background attribute. Let $\text{symb}_c: \mathbb{Z}^n \rightarrow (V \cup \{\mathfrak{B}\})$ be an n-dimensional array and $\text{attr}_c: \mathbb{Z}^n \rightarrow \mathcal{A}$ be an attribution function such that $\text{attr}(v) \neq \mathfrak{A}$ only if $v \in \text{supp}(\text{symb}_c)$. Then $c = (\text{symb}_c, \text{attr}_c)$ is called an **n-dimensional attributed array,** symb_c is the *under-lying n-dimensional array* and attr_c is the *associated attribution function.* $V_{\mathcal{A}}^{*n}$ denotes the set of n-dimensional attributed arrays over V with attributes in $\mathcal{A}$.

Definition 2.9. An **attributed parallel array production** is a pair (p,f) where $p = X \prod_{v \in U} vX_v \rightarrow Y$ is a parallel array production and f is an attribute function $f: \mathcal{A}^{|U|+1} \rightarrow \mathcal{A}$ such that we assign a special attribute value *undefined* to $f(a_1,\dots,a_{|U|+1})$ for all attribute vectors $(a_1,\dots,a_{|U|+1})$ lying outside the domain of f. In general we shall not impose any other special restrictions on the set of attributes respectively the attribution functions of attributed arrays or the attribute functions in attributed parallel array productions except that for practical reasons they should be computable within a reasonable amount of time.

Moreover we say that the attributed array $b_2 \in V_{\mathcal{A}}^{*n}$ is *directly derivable* from the attributed array $b_1 \in V_{\mathcal{A}}^{*n}$ by a table T of attributed array productions – abbreviated $b_1 \vdash_T b_2$, – iff for each $w \in \mathbb{Z}^n$ there exists an attributed parallel array production (p,f) with $p = X \prod_{v \in U} vX_v \rightarrow Y$ in T such that $b_1(w) = X$, $b_2(w) = Y$, $b_1(w + v) = X_v$ for all $v \in U, U = \{U_1,\dots,U_{|U|}\}$, and $\text{attr}_{b_2}(w) = f(\text{attr}_{b_1}(w), \text{attr}_{b_1}(w + U_1), \dots, \text{attr}_{b_1}(w + U_{|U|}))$.

Definition 2.10. $S = (n,V,\Sigma,P)$ (respectively $G = (S,A)$) is called an **n-dimensional attributed parallel array system (grammar)** iff P is a set of tables of attributed parallel array productions over $V \cup \Sigma$, n,V,Σ, and A being defined as in Definition 2.5. The notions $\vdash_G$, $L(G)$ etc. are defined in a similar way like for an n-dimensional parallel array system (grammar).

Example 2.3. Assigning attributes to the two-dimensional arrays α we dealt with in Example 2.2 by means of the attribution functions $f_\alpha: \mathbb{Z}^2 \rightarrow \mathbb{Z}^2$ with $f_\alpha(v) = v$ for all $v \in \text{supp}(\alpha)$, this information about the absolute position of a cell in the space $\mathbb{Z}^2$ can be carried on from an axiom by the productions in the attributed parallel array system $S' = (2,\emptyset,\{1\},P')$ with $P' = P_1' \cup P_2' \cup P_3' \cup P_4'$, where P_i' is obtained from P_i by assigning the following attribute functions f_i to the array productions in P_i ($1 \le i \le 4$) – observe that $U = \{U_1,...,U_8\}$, $|U| = 8$:

$f_1(a_1,...,a_9) = a_1$, $f_2(a_1,...,a_9) = \mathfrak{A}$, $f_3 = f_1$, and $f_4(a_1,...,a_9) = a_{i+1} - U_i$ where U_i is the smallest vector in the set $\{v \in U \mid X_v = 1\}$.

The example given above indicates how models of cellular automata extended by suitable sets of attributes respectively attribution functions can be described by means of attributed parallel array systems. In the following chapter we are going to show how the notions explained in this section can be applied to model neural networks.

3. Describing Neural Networks by means of Attributed Parallel Array Systems

Definition 3.1. Let $S = (n,V,\Sigma,P)$ be an n–dimensional attributed parallel array system such that for each attributed parallel array production (p,f) in P with $p = A \prod_{v \in U} vX_v \to B$ either $A \ne \mathfrak{B}$ and $B \ne \mathfrak{B}$ or $U = \emptyset$ and $A = B = \mathfrak{B}$, then S is called an **n–dimensional attributed parallel array system with constant support (n-ASC)**.

Definition 3.2. Let $S = (n,V,\Sigma,P)$ be an n–ASC and Σ be the union of the pairwise disjoint sets Δ, Γ, and Ω such that o is a special symbol in Ω, and let M_x, $x \in \{I,O,N\}$, be pairwise disjoint finite non–empty subsets of $\mathbb{Z}^n$. Then $N = \{n,V,\Delta,\Gamma,\Omega,o,P,M_I,M_O,M_N\}$ is called an **n–dimensional (deterministic) static neural network (n-DSNN)** if the following holds true:

1) $\forall\, a \in \Delta \cup \Gamma$, $(a \to a,id) \in P$, where id is the identity function on $\mathcal{A}$.

2) Each production for a symbol $\alpha \in \Omega$ is of the form $(\alpha\prod_{v \in U_o} vX_v \to \gamma,f)$ for a $\gamma \in \Gamma$, where U_o is a special environment for the output symbols $\alpha \in \Omega$.

3) For each $A \in V \cup \Sigma$ only one environment U exists in the A–productions, i.e. if $(A\prod_{v \in U} vX_v \to B,f)$ is an A–production in P, then each A–production in P is of the form $(A\prod_{v \in U} vY_v \to C,g)$, and moreover $(C,g) \ne (B,f)$ holds true only if $X_v \ne Y_v$ for at least one $v \in U$ or f and g have disjoint domains.

The network N is called **static** because of the assumption that the array system S has constant support , whereas Condition 3) causes the network to be **deterministic**.

With the help of N the functioning of a neural net can be described as follows:

Let $K \in \Delta_{\mathcal{A}}^{*n}$, $L \in \Omega_{\mathcal{A}}^{*n}$, $L' \in \Gamma_{\mathcal{A}}^{*n}$, $M \in V_{\mathcal{A}}^{*n}$ with $supp(K) = M_I$, $supp(M) = M_N$, $supp(L') = supp(L) = M_O$. One learning step of the net M for an input K and an output $L \in (\Omega - \{o\})_{\mathcal{A}}^{*n}$ is defined by $K \vee M \vee L \overset{*}{\models} K \vee M' \vee L' \vdash K \vee M' \vee L'$ for an n–dimensional attributed array $M' \in V_{\mathcal{A}}^{*n}$ with $supp(M') = M_N$, where M' is the new network which is formed out of the previous network M in one learning step. If the output L' of the network M with a given input K is to be calculated, for L a special n–dimensional attributed array L_0 is chosen, where

$L_0 = (symb_0, attr_0)$ with $symb_0(v) = o$ and $attr_0(v) = \mathfrak{A}$ for all $v \in M_O$. In both cases the condition $K \vee M' \vee L' \vdash K \vee M' \vee L'$ assures that M' ends up in a *steady state* with the output L'.

The attributed arrays defined above can be identified with specific layers, i.e. K with the *input-layer*, L (L') with the *output-layer* and M (M') with the *hidden-layer*. The coordinate positions in M_I, M_O, M_N represent the positions of the cells (*neurons*), whereas the elements of V, Δ, Ω, and Γ stand for the possible *states* of the cells. The *connections* of the neurons among each other are determined by the environments used in the productions.
The model described so far could be used for representing different kinds of neural networks, e. g. for feed forward networks with backpropagation as well as for feature mappings. In the sequel we shall specialize on Kohonen's model.

The Model of Kohonen

In the following Kohonen's model of self-organizing feature maps is described using an n-DSNN. For a detailed review of this field in the theory of neural networks the reader is referred to [Ko1], [Ko2], [RMS] and [HKP].
In our representation of Kohonen's model we shall distinguish between three different layers – the input-layer, the hidden-layer and the output-layer, which all shall be assumed to be of the same structure and dimension n. The n + 1-st dimension of the (n + 1)-DSNN is needed to distinguish between the three layers. Thus we shall assume
$M_N = \{ (v,0) \mid v \in M \}$, $M_I = \{ (v,1) \mid v \in M \}$, and $M_O = \{ (v,-1) \mid v \in M \}$ for some finite set $M \subseteq \mathbb{Z}^n$, and in the case n = 1 we take $M = \{ i \mid 0 \leq i \leq m \}$.
The environment U representing the connections of a cell in the hidden-layer is given by $U = U_I \vee U_O \vee U_H$, where $U_I = \{ (o_n,+1) \}$ represents the connection to the corresponding cell in the input-layer, $U_O = \{ (o_n,-1) \}$ represents the connection to the corresponding cell in the output-layer, whereas U_H contains all relative vectors from one cell of the hidden-layer in the neural network to another cell of the hidden-layer in a *fully* connected network, e.g. for $M_N = \{ (i,0) \mid 0 \leq i \leq 1 \}$ we get $U_H = \{ (j,0) \mid -1 \leq j \leq 1 \}$.
Except for $\mathfrak{A}$ all the other attributes are assumed to be of the form (val,t,x) where val $\in \mho$ is the weight of a cell in the neural network, $\mho$ being the set of possible weights, t serves for counting the learning steps, and the vector x may represent additional attributes serving for special purposes described together with the corresponding algorithms. Hence we define
$\underline{val}: \mathcal{A} \to \mho$, $\underline{val}(val,t,x) = val$; $\underline{t}: \mathcal{A} \to \mathbb{N} \cup \{0\}$, $\underline{t}(val,t,x) = t$;
$\underline{x(i)}: \mathcal{A} \to range(\underline{x(i)})$, $\underline{x(i)}(val,t,x) = $ i-th component of the vector x.

The following productions of an n-dimensional attributed parallel array system describe Kohonen's algorithm for feature maps, i.e. the excitation centre w_0 for the input v_I is determined by the competitive condition $\|v_I - \underline{val}(attr(w_0))\| \leq \|v_I - \underline{val}(attr(w))\|$ for all $w \in M_N$.

For the following let $U_H = \{U_1,\dots,U_u\}$, $U_0 = o_{n+1}$, and moreover $a \in \Delta$, $b \in \Omega$:

1) $(S(o_n,-1)b(o_n,1)a \to F_{a,b},h_1)$, $h_1: \mathcal{A}^3 \to \mathcal{A}$,

$h_1(x,y,z) = (\underline{val}(attr(x)),\underline{t}(attr(x)),\underline{val}(attr(x)) - \underline{val}(attr(z)))$

i.e. $h_1(attr(w),attr(w + (o_n,-1)),attr(w + (o_n,1)) = (\underline{val}(attr(w)),\underline{t}(attr(w)),$
$$\underline{val}(attr(w)) - \underline{val}(attr(w + (o_n,1)))).$$

2) $(F_{a,b}\Pi_{v \in U_H}{}^v X_v \to W_{a,b},h_2)$, $h_2: \mathcal{A}^{u+1} \to \mathcal{A}$,

$h_2(y_1,\dots,y_{u+1}) = \underline{if}\ [(\|\underline{x(1)}(y_1)\| \le \|\underline{x(1)}(y_i)\|)$ for all i with $1 < i \le u + 1)$ $\underline{and}$
$(\ f(U_{i-1})$ for all i such that $(1 < i \le u + 1\ \underline{and}\ \|\underline{x(1)}(y_1)\| = \|\underline{x(1)}(_i)\|)\ ]\ \underline{then}\ y_1$
e.g. $[\ f(U_i) = $ true iff $U_i < o_{n+1}]$ assures only one winner to be computed.

3) $(F_{a,b}\Pi_{v \in U_H}{}^v X_v \to L_{a,b},h_3)$, $h_3: \mathcal{A}^{u+1} \to \mathcal{A}$,

$h_3(y_1,\dots,y_{u+1}) = \underline{if}\ [\|\underline{x(1)}(y_1)\| > \|\underline{x(1)}(y_i)\|$ for some i with $1 < i \le u + 1]\ \underline{or}$
$[(\|\underline{x(1)}(y_1)\| \le \|\underline{x(1)}(y_i)\|$ for all $i > 1$ with $1 < i \le u + 1)\ \underline{and}\ ($not $f(U_{i-1})$
for some i with $(1 < i \le u + 1\ \underline{and}\ \|\underline{x(1)}(y_1)\| = \|\underline{x(1)}(y_i)\|))\ ]\ \underline{then}\ y_1.$

4) $(b(o_n,1)L_{a,b} \to l_{a,b},h_4)$, $(b(o_n,1)W_{a,b} \to w_{a,b},h_4)$, with $h_4: \mathcal{A}^2 \to \mathcal{A}$,

$h_4(x,y) = (\|\underline{x(1)}(y)\|,\underline{t}(y)).$

5) $(W_{a,b}\Pi_{v \in U_H}{}^v X_v \to S,h_{5,b})$, $(L_{a,b}\Pi_{v \in U_H}{}^v X_v \to S,h_{5,b})$ with $h_{5,b}: \mathcal{A}^{u+1} \to \mathcal{A}$,

$h_{5,o}(y_1,\dots,y_{u+1}) = (\underline{val}(y_1),\underline{t}(y_1))$ and for $b \ne o$
$h_{5,b}(y_1,\dots,y_{u+1}) = (g(\underline{val}(y_1),\underline{x(1)}(y_1),\underline{t}(y_1),U_k),\underline{t}(y_1) + 1)$ where $X_{U_k} = W_{d,e}$ for
some $d \in \Delta$, $e \in \Omega$; $g(x,y,t,v) = x + \varepsilon(t) * h(v,t) * y$, e.g. $h(v,t) = \exp(-v^2/2\sigma(t)^2)$,
g representing Kohonen's learning rule for the adaptation of the weights.

6) $(S(o_n,-1)c(o_n,1)a \to S,h_6)$ with $c \in \Gamma$ and $h_6: \mathcal{A}^3 \to \mathcal{A}$, $h_6(x,y,z) = x$,

i.e. $h_6(attr(w),attr(w + (o_n,-1)),attr(w + (o_n,1))) = attr(w).$

7) $(b(o_n,1)Y \to b,h_7)$ with $Y \in \{S\} \cup \{F_{d,e} \mid d \in \Delta, e \in \Omega\}$, $h_7: \mathcal{A}^2 \to \mathcal{A}$, $h_7(x,y) = x.$

The productions 6) and 7) are needed to guarantee the steady state of the network after the successful computation of the winner (the excitation centre), which is labelled by $W_{a,b}$, whereas the loosers are labelled by $L_{a,b}$. The productions 5) show the main difference between a learning step and a mere computation step: After a computation step the attributes of the neurons in the hidden layer are just the same as at the beginning of the computation (see function $h_{5,o}$), whereas in a learning step – by the functions $h_{5,b}$, $b \ne o$ – the weights are adapted according to Kohonen's learning rule, and moreover the time component is incremented.

We are now going to show how this *global* adaption rule can be simulated by bounded local actions in an n-DSNN N' with $\|N'\| = k$ (in most cases we even may assume $k = 1$); observe that $\|v\| \le k$ for all $v \in U_H$:

1) $(S(o_n,-1)b(o_n,1)a \to F_{a,b},h_1)$, $h_1: \mathcal{A}^3 \to \mathcal{A}$,

$h_1(x,y,z) = (\underline{val}(x),\underline{t}(x),\underline{val}(x) - \underline{val}(z),\|\underline{val}(x) - \underline{val}(z)\|,o_{n+1},o_{n+1});$
$\underline{x(3)}$, $\underline{x(4)}$: relative position with respect to the global resp. local winner.

2) $(F_{a,b}\Pi_v \in U_H{}^v X_v \to W_{a,b'},h_2)$, $(W_{a,b'}\Pi_v \in U_H{}^v X_v \to W_{a,b'},h_2)$, $h_2: \mathcal{A}^{u+1} \to \mathcal{A}$,

$h_2(y_1,\dots,y_{u+1}) = \underline{if}\ [\underline{x(2)}(x_1) < \underline{x(2)}(y_i)$ for all i with $1 < i \le u + 1]$
$\underline{or}\ [(\underline{x(2)}(y_1) \le \underline{x(2)}(y_i)$ for all i with $1 < i \le u + 1)$
$\underline{and}\ (\underline{x(3)}(y_i) + U_{i-1} < \underline{x(3)}(y_1)$ for all $i > 1$ with $\underline{x(2)}(y_1) = \underline{x(2)}(y_i))\ ]\ \underline{then}\ y_1.$

3) $(Y \prod_{v \in U_H} {}^v X_v \to L_{a,b}', h_3)$ with $Y \in \{F_{a,b}, W_{a,b}', L_{a,b}', L_{a,b}''\}$, $h_3: \mathcal{A}^{u+1} \to \mathcal{A}$,
$h_3(y_1, \ldots, y_{u+1}) = \underline{if}$ $[\underline{x(2)}(y_1) > \underline{x(2)}(y_i)$ for some i with $1 < i \leq u + 1]$
$\underline{or}$ $[(\underline{x(2)}(y_1) \leq \underline{x(2)}(y_i)$ for all i with $1 < i \leq u + 1)$
$\underline{and}$ $(\underline{x(3)}(y_i) + U_{i-1} \geq \underline{x(3)}(y_1)$ for some $i > 1$ with $\underline{x(2)}(y_1) = \underline{x(2)}(y_i))]$
$\underline{then}$ $(\underline{val}(y_1), \underline{t}(y_1), \underline{x(1)}(y_1), \underline{x(2)}(y_k), \underline{x(3)}(v) + v, v)$, where
v is that vector $U_k \in U_H$ with $((\underline{x2}(y_k) \leq \underline{x2}(y_j)$ for $k \neq j)$ and
$(\underline{x3}(y_k) + U_{k-1} < \underline{x3}(y_j) + U_{j-1}$ for all $j \neq k$ with $\underline{x2}(y_k) = \underline{x2}(y_j)))$.

4) $(W_{a,b}' \prod_{v \in U_H} {}^v X_v \to W_{a,b}, h_4)$, where for all $v \in U_H$,
$X_v \in \mathcal{L}''$, $\mathcal{L}'' = \{L_{d,e}'' \mid d \in \Delta, e \in \Omega\}$, $h_4: \mathcal{A}^{u+1} \to \mathcal{A}$, $h_4(y_1, \ldots, y_{u+1}) = y_1$.

5) $(L_{a,b}' \prod_{v \in U_H} {}^v X_v \to L_{a,b}'', h_5)$ with $h_5: \mathcal{A}^{u+1} \to \mathcal{A}$,
$h_5(y_1, \ldots, y_{u+1}) = \underline{if}$ $[(\underline{x2}(y_1) = \underline{x2}(y_i))$ $\underline{and}$ $(\underline{x3}(y_1) = \underline{x3}(y_i) + U_{i-1})$ for all i
with $1 < i \leq u + 1]$ $\underline{and}$ $[X_{U_i} \in \mathcal{L}''$ for all i with $\underline{x4}(U_i) = -U_{i-1}]$ $\underline{then}$ x_1.

6) $(L_{a,b}'' \prod_{v \in U_H} {}^v X_v \to L_{a,b}, h_6)$, where for some $v \in U_H$
$X_v \in \{W_{d,e}, L_{d,e} \mid d \in \Delta, e \in \Omega\}$, and $h_6: \mathcal{A}^{u+1} \to \mathcal{A}$, $h_6(y_1, \ldots, y_{u+1}) = y_1$.

7) $(W_{a,b} \prod_{v \in U_H} {}^v X_v \to S, h_{7,b})$, $(L_{a,b} \prod_{v \in U_H} {}^v X_v \to S, h_{7,b})$, $h_7: \mathcal{A}^{u+1} \to \mathcal{A}$,
$h_{7,o}(y_1, \ldots, y_{u+1}) = (\underline{val}(y_1), \underline{t}(y_1))$ and for $b \neq o$
$h_{7,b}(y_1, \ldots, y_{u+1}) = (g(\underline{val}(y_1), \underline{x(1)}(y_1), \underline{t}(y_1), \underline{x(3)}(y_1)), \underline{t}(y_1) + 1)$.

8) $(S(o_n, -1)c(o_n, 1)a \to S, h_8)$ with $c \in \Gamma$ and $h_8: \mathcal{A}^3 \to \mathcal{A}$, $h_8(x, y, z) = x$.

9) $(b(o_n, +1)Y \to b, h_9)$ with $Y \in \{S\} \cup \{F_{d,e}, W_{d,e}', L_{d,e}', L_{d,e}'' \mid d \in \Delta, e \in \Omega\}$,
$h_9: \mathcal{A}^2 \to \mathcal{A}$, $h_9(x, y) = x$.

10) $(b(o_n, 1)L_{a,b} \to l_{a,b}, h_{10})$, $(b(o_n, 1)W_{a,b} \to w_{a,b}, h_{10})$, with $h_{10}: \mathcal{A}^2 \to \mathcal{A}$,
$h_{10}(x, y) = (\| \underline{x(1)}(y) \|, \underline{t}(y))$.

During the first of the three phases of the simulation algorithm described above informations about the relative positions with respect to the local respectively the global winner cell are passed from one cell to another such that finally the informations from the global winner cell reach all the other cells of the hidden layer. When affirmative 'answers' from its entire environment allow the excitation centre to enter the winning state $W_{a,b}$, in the third phase the looser cells successively are forced to enter a loosing state $L_{a,b}$. Hence the number of derivation steps equals $3*d$, where d is the maximal distance between the winner cell and another cell in the hidden-layer with respect to the underlying graph $g_k(M)$ of the network M with $supp(M) = M_N$ (see Definitions 2.1 and 3.2). Thus the time complexity of the local algorithm described above is $3*d_{max}$, where d_{max} is the maximal distance of nodes in $g_k(M)$. Summarizing these considerations we can state the following theorem:

Theorem 3.1. For any n–DSNN $N = \{n, V, \Delta, \Gamma, \Omega, o, P, M_I, M_O, M_N\}$ modelling a fully connected neural network based on Kohonen's global adaption rule, an equivalent n–DSNN N' with $\| N' \| = k$ exists which only uses a linear local adaption algorithm provided that $k \geq \| a \|$ where a is any n-dimensional array with $supp(a) = (M_I \cup M_O \cup M_N)$.

4. Examples of Kohonen Feature Mappings

In order to be able to simulate some examples of Kohonen feature mappings we have developed the CNS (Cellular Net Simulator) supporting the design and implementation of neural networks described by means of our new concept of n-dimensional attributed parallel array grammars using the programming language MODULA II. For a detailed discussion of the following examples the reader is referred to [RMS] and [HKP].

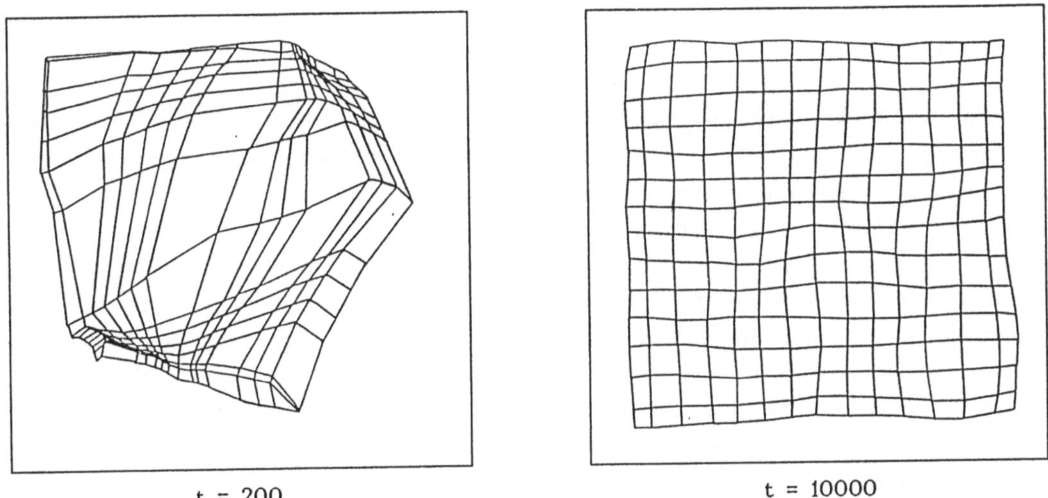

t = 200   t = 10000

Figure 2. Square grid.

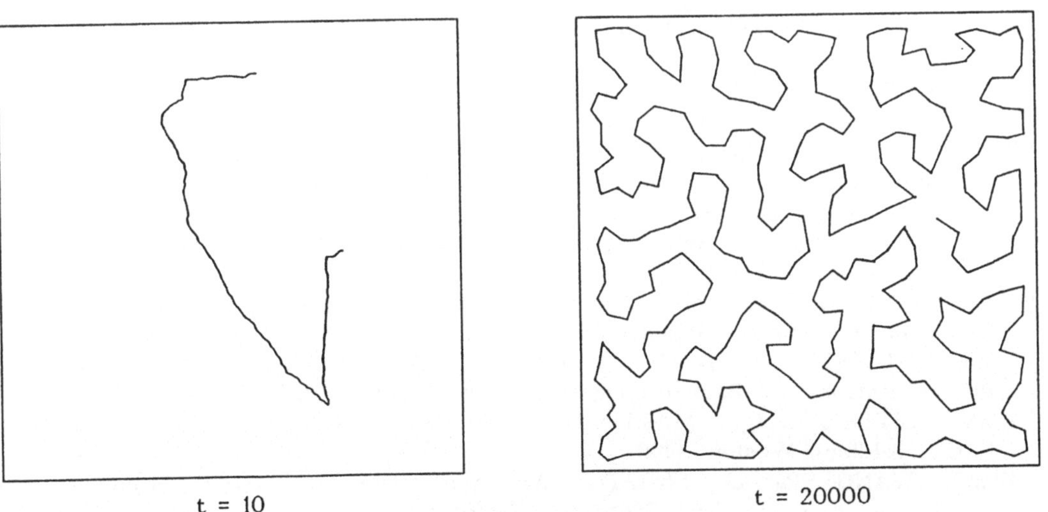

t = 10   t = 20000

Figure 3. 'Peano' curve.

In Figure 2 the results of a Kohonen feature mapping from a square region $\mathcal{N} = \{(x,y) \mid 1 \leq x,y \leq 1000\}$ of the plane onto a 15×15 array is depicted. Using a uniform probability distribution for the random input patterns the weights of the cells organize themselves into a square grid ($\varepsilon(t) = 0.9 * (0.05/0.9)^{(t/t_{max})}$, $\sigma(t) = 5 * 0.2^{(t/t_{max})}, t_{max} = 10000$). Figure 3 shows the development of a map from the two-dimensional square $\mathcal{N}$ to a one-dimensional chain of 300 neurons using the adaption rule parameters $\varepsilon(t) = 10 * 0.1^{(t/t_{max})}$, $t_{max} = 20000$, $\sigma(t) = 50 * 0.02^{(t/t_{max})}$ and yielding a space-filling (Peano) curve.

5. Conclusion

As the examples in the previous section show, the CNS is a good tool for supporting the simulation of various applications of Kohonen's feature maps. Our notion of attributed parallel array grammars has turned out to be well suited for describing neural networks, especially in the case of feature mappings with underlying structures that can be represented as n-dimensional arrays. The reduction of Kohonen's algorithm in a fully connected network to a linear algorithm in an equivalent k-connected network makes it possible to design these networks within parallel computer architectures with bounded neighbourhood connections. Hence, besides exploring models with multiple hidden-layers future research will also be concerned with simulating various extended versions of Kohonen's model on a transputer workstation.

6. References

[Fre]: FREUND, Rudolf: N-Dimensionale Sprachen. Thesis, Technical University of Vienna, 1982.

[HKP]: HERTZ, John A., KROGH, Anders S., PALMER, Richard G.: Introduction to the Theory of Neural Computation. Santa Fe Institute. Addison Wesley, 1991.

[Kem]: KEMKE, Christel: Modelling Neural Networks by Means of Networks of Finite Automata. Proceedings of the IEEE - First Interntional Conference on Neural Networks, San Diego,CA, 21-24, June (1987).

[Ko1]: KOHONEN, T.: Self-Organized Formation of Topologically Corrected Feature Maps. Biological Cybernetics 43: 59-69 (1982).

[Ko2]: KOHONEN, T.: Self-Organization and Associative Memory. Springer Series in Information Sciences 8, Heidelberg, 1984.

[RHW]: RUMELHART, D. E., HINTON, G. E., WILLIAMS, R. J.: Learning Representations by Back-Propagating Errors. Nature 323: 533-536 (1986).

[RMS]: RITTER, Helge, MARTINETZ, Thomas, SCHULTEN, Klaus: Neuronale Netze. Addison-Wesley, 1990.

[Wan]: WANG, Patrick Shen-Pei, An Application of Array Grammars to Clustering Analysis for Syntactic Patterns, *Pattern Recognition*, Vol. 17, No. 4, 441 - 451 (1984).

Design of the SNNS Neural Network Simulator

Andreas Zell, Niels Mache, Tilman Sommer, Thomas Korb

Universität Stuttgart,
Institut für Parallele und Verteilte Höchstleistungsrechner (IPVR),
Breitwiesenstr. 20-22, D-7000 Stuttgart 80,
E-mail: zell@informatik.uni-stuttgart.de

ABSTRACT

SNNS is a neural network simulator for Unix workstations developed at the Universität Stuttgart. It is a tool to generate, train, test and visualize artificial neural networks. The simulator consists of a simulator kernel, a graphical user interface based on X-Windows to interactively construct and visualize neural networks, and a compiler to generate large neural networks from a high level network description language. Applications of SNNS currently include printed character recognition, handwritten character recognition, recognition of machine parts, stock prize prediction, noise reduction in a telecom environment and texture analysis, among others. We also give preliminary design decisions for a planned parallel version of SNNS on a massively parallel SIMD-computer with more than 16,000 processors (MasPar MP-1216) which has been installed at our research institute recently.

Keywords: connectionism, neural networks, network simulators, network description language

1. THE SNNS NEURAL NETWORK SIMULATOR

SNNS (Stuttgart Neural Network Simulator) is an efficient and portable neural network simulation environment for Unix workstations. It is a software tool to generate, train, test and visualize artificial neural networks. The simulator consists of three major components: a simulator kernel that operates on the internal representation of the neural networks, a graphical user interface to interactively construct and change small neural nets, and a compiler to generate the internal representation of large neural networks from a high level network description language. The whole network simulator has been developed in C on various Unix workstations. The graphical user interface was implemented under X-Windows X11 Release 4.0 with the MIT Athena widget set, for maximal portability.

The SNNS simulator kernel operates on the internal representation of the neural networks and performs all operations of the learning and recall phase. It is loosely coupled with the network compiler by a network description file containing an intermediate form of the network and more closely with the graphical user interface via an interface of function calls. The definition of learning and propagation rules is part of the network definition program, learning can be supervised or not. The simulator kernel is written in C for efficiency and portability and has already been ported to a number of architectures (Sun 3 and Sun 4 under SunOS 4.0, DECStation 2100 / 3100 under Ultrix-32, HP 9000/345 under Unix Sys V.3, IBM PC 386 under AT&T Unix Sys. V and SCO Xenix V, IBM RISCSystem/6000 under AIX). We achieved 1.1 M CPS (connections per second) on a DECStation 3100 and more than 2.2 M CPS on an IBM R/6000 Model 520[1]. This indicates that SNNS it is a rather fast software neural network simulator.

The graphical user interface, based on X-Windows, is a tool to construct the topology and visualize and modify small to medium sized nets interactively with an integrated graphical editor. It can also be used to generate and save test patterns for small networks. To economize on screen space the display elements are kept in separate windows and thus can be arbitrarily arranged or hidden if desired. There are various ways

---

[1]These performance numbers were obtained with multi-layer perceptron network topologies with full connectivity between adjacent layers during forward activation (recall) mode. We used continuous (float) units and weights, the standard logistic activation function and no speedup techniques like table lookup etc. The numbers for online backpropagation in learning mode are slower by a factor of between two and three.

to display or modify nodes and links or selected sets of them. An integrated help facility aids the novice with the interface. Networks can be modified through the user interface during simulation. Units can be introduced, removed, or have their activation values changed, connections among the units can be inserted, deleted, redirected, or have their strengths modified. In contrast to most other simulators the modifications can be done in a simple manner directly in the visual representation of the network topology.

Our network description language Nessus is a high level procedural language. Its main task is to describe the topology of the network being simulated. We are able to specify parameters like network topology, activation functions and graphical display information of regular topologies, in a convenient way. However, the ASCII network description file may also be generated by any other program which can generate a file in the proper intermediate form.

The Nessus compiler can generate the internal representation of large neural networks from this network description language. The compiler was implemented in C with the aids of lex and yacc and can generate large networks very rapidly. In fact, most of the time spent in generating large networks with this compiler is attributable to writing the often several megabytes of data in a network description file of a large network. We have successfully generated networks with more than 10.000 nodes and more than one million weights with the compiler but have not attempted to train these networks.

The structure of the whole SNNS simulator can be visualized as in figure 1.

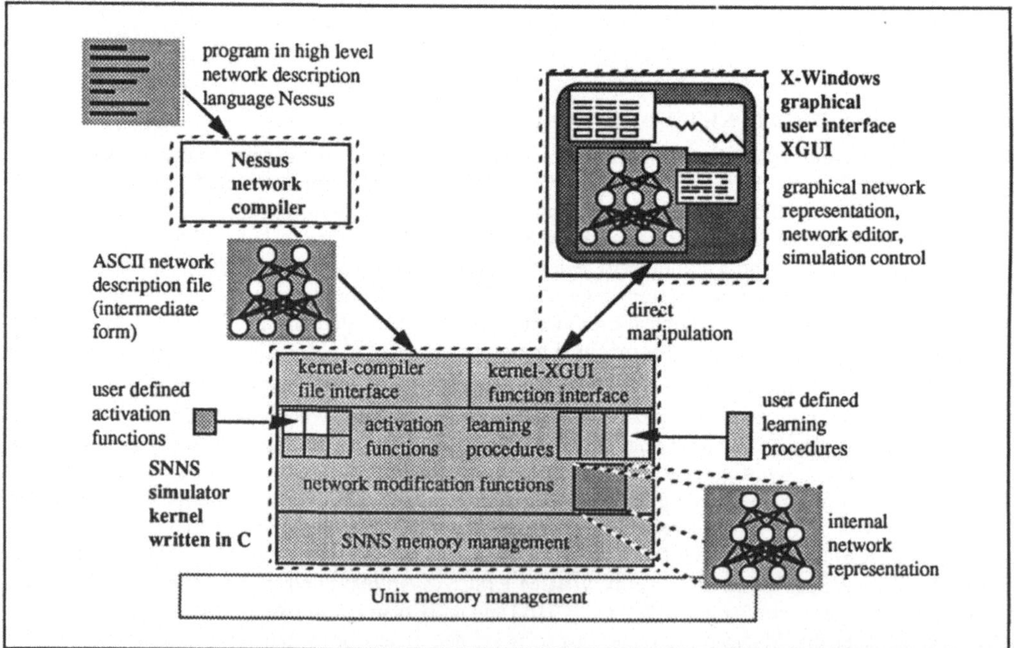

Fig. 1: Structure of the SNNS network simulator consisting of 3 parts: simulator kernel, graphical user interface and network compiler. The dashed line indicates that the kernel and the graphical user interface are linked together, whereas the network compiler is a different application.

2. SIMULATOR KERNEL

The kernel performs activation propagation and learning. Learning can be supervised or not. Networks can be modified through the user interface during simulation. Units may be introduced, removed, or have their activation values changed. Connections among the units may be inserted, deleted, redirected, or have their strengths modified, if needed.

2.1. Simulator kernel layers

The simulator kernel is structured into three layers of increasing abstraction. The innermost layer are the memory management functions. They provide functions for the allocation and disallocation of network data structures in large blocks of contiguous memory, thus enhancing the standard Unix memory management. The next layer comprises all functions that modify the network, including propagation and learning functions. The kernel may easily be extended with user defined activation functions or additional learning procedures written in C. The next layer consists of two different interfaces: the function interface consists of all functions that the kernel provides to the X graphical user interface. Also, any other application program, who wants to call the network simulator kernel as a subroutine may do so via this function interface. The second interface consists of the file I/O interface to the network compiler.

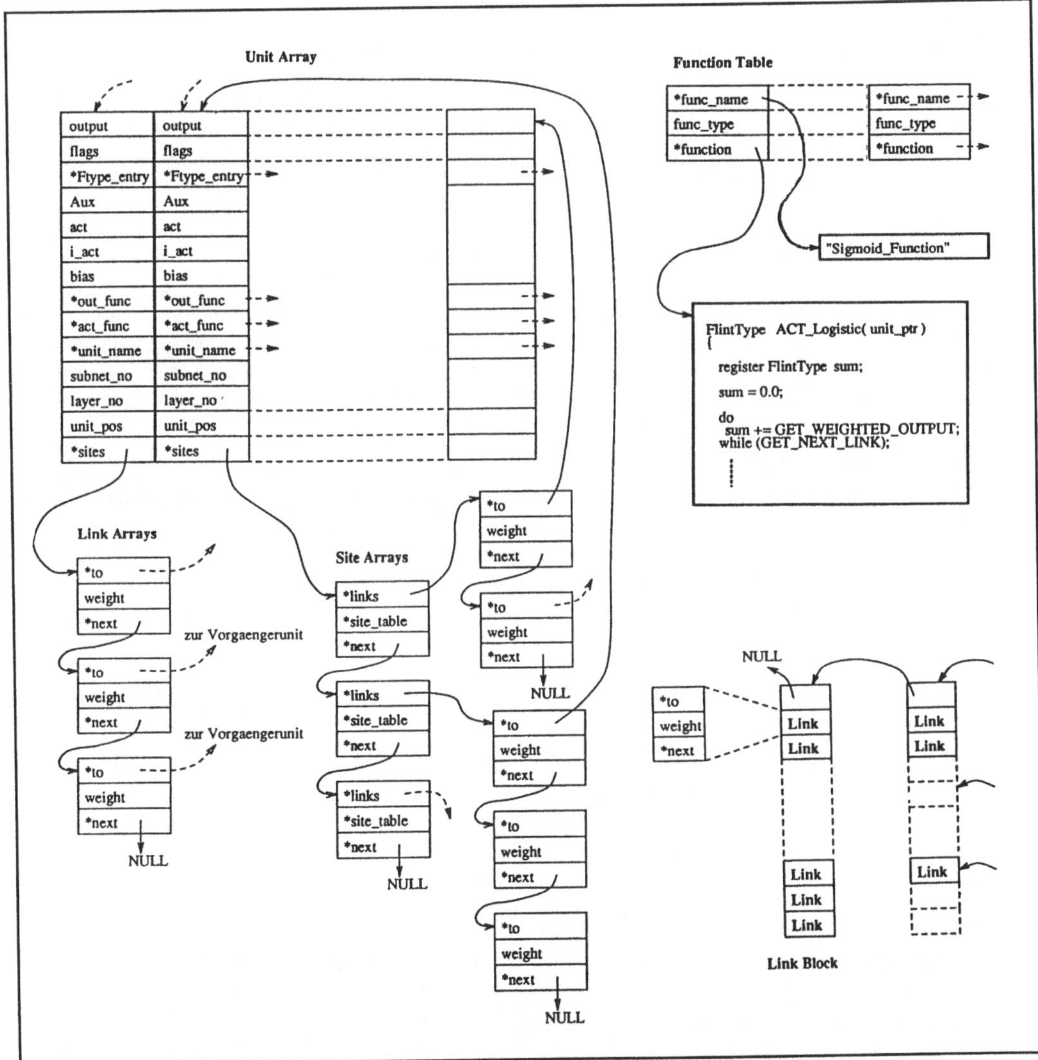

Fig. 2: SNNS simulator kernel internal data structures (simplified)

2.2. Internal data structures

A dynamic unit array was chosen for efficiency reasons to hold the contents of the units. If more units are requested than are available in the unit array, the SNNS memory management demands a new larger array from the operating system and efficiently copies all data and pointers to substructures to the new array, disallocating the old unit array. The main internal data structures are represented graphically in fig. 2. The internal data structures are similar to those in the Rochester Connectionist Simulator [Goddard et al. 89].

Currently about a dozen activation and output functions are already supplied with the simulator, but it is very easy to write other transfer functions in C, then compile and link them to the simulator kernel. They then show up in the user interface and can be chosen from a menu.

Five different modes of forward dynamic activation spreading can be selected: synchronous firing, random order, random permutation, topologic order, and fixed order. In synchronous mode, all cells (quasi) simultaneously compute their new activation, then they all change their output. In random order one cell is chosen at random, its new activation and output values are computed and propagated before any other cell is updated. In random permutation a permutation of the cell numbers guarantees that every cell is updated after one full sweep through the network). In fixed order, the cells are updated according to their internal cell number, while topologic order first performs a topologic sort of the network (provided it is acyclic). This guarantees that a change of activation in the input layer is reflected all way up to the output layer in one sweep through the network.

The simulator allows the generation of new links or units at run time. For testing purposes any property of a cell or connection may be inspected or changed between cycles at run time.

The kernel does not differentiate between feedforward and feedback networks since we wanted to allow experimentation with feedback networks as well. In order to test the feedforward property of networks the kernel offers a topological sort of the network to help the user to detect cycles when working with learning rules like standard back-propagation. Similarly, the simulator kernel does not possess a layer concept, but regards the network as flat. The layer concept may be imprinted on the network by the network compiler.

3. SNNS GRAPHICAL USER INTERFACE

Even for small neural networks a text-based or a numerical representation of the network and its activities is usually inadequate. A graphical representation of the network is necessary to display the dynamics of the simulation. But for larger networks with many units and connections even a graphical display can be rather confusing. Therefore, a graphical user interface must contain appropriate tools to efficiently constrain the number of objects and the amount of information displayed.

3.1. Network visualization

The graphical user interface consists of the following windows which can be positioned and controlled independently:

- a *manager panel* with info panel (above), below the menu button GUI, with which other windows may be opened, a message line and a status information line
- several *graphical displays* of the network
- a *remote panel* to control the activity of the simulator (like with a TV remote control)
- a *control panel* which is used to control learning and to test the network
- several *help windows* for context sensitive help

A number of popup windows (transient shells) are only visible on request and block all other windows of SNNS. These are

- a *file panel* to load and store networks and patterns
- a *setup panel* to control the graphical appearance of the networks
- a *confirmer* to demand user confirmations and to display important messages
- a *list panel* to choose several alternatives from a list

- a *layer panel* to individually select the layer of units (note our layers are unlike the usual hierarchical layers of neural networks: they have nothing to do with network topology but only with the visual display. They are similar to overhead transparencies such that units may belong to several layers. One or many layers of units may be displayed in a window.

Figure 3 shows a version of the current graphical user interface. Not visible here are a help panel with context sensitive help, a text panel to record a session with the simulator which can be loaded and replayed and a setup panel to control the display of units and links.

Units are usually displayed as growing boxes or growing bars in a raster of positions. The user can control the raster size of the graphic window, the visual representation of units (activation values, output values, number, name) and the display of links (directed, undirected, weight). Connections and units can be displayed selectively, i.e. the user may choose to display only those units whose activations or outputs exceed a given display threshold or only those links whose weights are in a certain range. This allows watching the growth of units and the establishing or deterioration of strong links during learning.

With the proliferation of color workstations in our department our simulator now can utilize color displays. It then gives a color coded display of the units activations or outputs and uses color to indicate weight sign and strength. This is not only an improvement of looks but can convey more information in the same area.

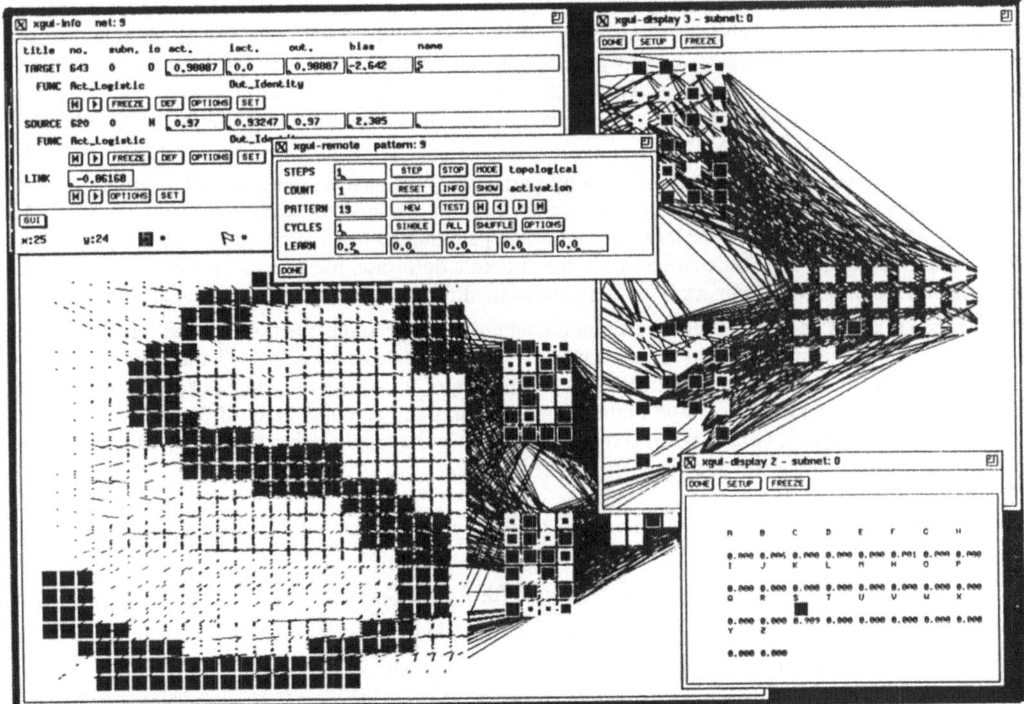

Fig. 3: Graphical user interface of SNNS: manager panel (top left), remote panel (center) and three graphical network displays showing various aspects of a letter recognition network: overall network topology and unit activations (bottom left), links whose weights are in a selected range (top right), names and activation of output units (bottom right).

This graphical user interface is a much improved successor to our earlier NetSim interface [Zell et al. 89] which was influenced by the original (SunView) RCS interface [Goddard et al. 89].

3.2. Network editing

The graphical interface is not only used to display a neural network but to generate and manipulate it as well. Therefore, the user has a powerful set of operations (insertion, deletion, copying, moving) at his use. These operations may be applied to individual units or to selections of units and may affect links as well, like 'copy all selected units with their input links' or 'delete all links into the selected units'. These operations allow a quick and convenient generation of networks. For networks which fit on a display screen and have a regular topology it is is usually more convenient to use the graphical interface of the simulator to generate the networks than to use the network compiler. The interactive graphical network editing facilities are especially useful for networks with simple or repetitive but not completely regular topology. We consider these capabilities one of the distinguishing aspects of SNNS.

4. NEURAL NETWORK DESCRIPTION LANGUAGE NESSUS

4.1. The Nessus Language

Nessus is a procedural language especially suited to describe the topology of neural networks. It was developed after experiences we gained with the implementation of a declarative language, Nesila. This earlier language had some nice features like topology descriptions in a set theoretic notation with so called *where clauses* specifying arbitrary and even nested conditions for groups of nodes to be connected. It also eliminated the necessity to declare variables before their use and even allowed the use of variables before their declaration. This was made possible by the single assignment rule of the language and a two phase compiler. However, this language was hard to implement and took too long to generate large networks, for which it was originally designed. Therefore we fell back to a standard procedural language which is now implemented very efficiently.

A Nessus program is divided into the following parts: program header, constant definition part, type definition part, structure definition part, variable declaration part and topology modification part. The interesting and unusual parts are the structure definition part and the topology modification part. The idea here is to define regular topologic structures in the structure definition part which can be later combined, extended and modified in various ways in the topology modification part.

The program in fig. 4 describes a letter recognition network similar to the one displayed in fig. 3, with the difference that the hidden layer units are displayed as one 4x12 matrix instead of two 4x6 matrices. In this network all units are of a single type stdUnit. They are arranged in three layers: an input layer of 576 units in a 24*24 matrix, a hidden layer of 48 units in a 4*12 matrix and an ouput layer of 26 units with names "A", .. "Z" in a 8*4 matrix (which is not completely filled). In the topology modification part these layers are connected with random weights.

4.2. The Network Compiler

Our compiler performs the following tasks:

- translation of a network definition into an input file for the simulator kernel

- combining of source files and intermediate representation files to networks, and

- computing the layout of the generated networks for the graphical interface.

We used Lex and Yacc to construct the scanner and the LALR-parser, mainly because the language was undergoing several changes during implementation. The programmer can define output and activation functions or learning rules as C functions which are included in a library. These functions may automatically be linked to the simulator kernel by the compiler.

The compiler supports debugging of Nessus programs indicating the positions of detected errors in the source file. The format of error messages is compatible with the EMACS editor, thus providing a comfortable programming environment. If compilation is initiated from within EMACS, the editor automatically positions on the line in which the first error occurred, even for files that are linked in.

```
network recogLetter();        {network recognizes letters displayed by a 24*24 input matrix}
const  Letters = ["A".."Z"];  {output units are named "A", "B", .. "Z"}
typedef                       {unit type without sites - same for all units}
    unit with actfunct Act_Logistic, act 0: stdUnit;
structure
    cluster[576] of stdUnit with iotype input matrix (24,24) at (12,12): inLayer;
                              {input layzer: 24x24 matrix to display letters}
    cluster[48] of stdUnit matrix (4,12) at (16,12): hidLayer;
                              {hidden layer: 48 units in a 4x12 matrix, center (16,12), default type}
    cluster[26] of stdUnit with iotype output get name from Letters
                    matrix (8,4) at (22,12): outLayer
                              {output layer: 26 char units, 8x4 matrix, center (22,12)}
var unit: x, y;
begin                         {define connectins between layers}
    foreach x in inLayer do
        foreach y in hidLayer do
            x-> y : random  {fully connect input to hidden layer with random weights}
        end
    end;
    foreach x in hidLayer do
        foreach y in outLayer do
            x-> y : random  {fully connect hidden to output layer with random weights}
        end
    end
end.
```

Fig. 4: Nessus program to generate letter recognition network

5. RECENT MODIFICATIONS TO SNNS

Since the simulator kernel and graphical user interface are now efficient enough in our view, the inclusion of other popular network paradigms other than the numerous variations of back propagation is given priority now. We already have implemented Hopfield networks, ART 1 [Carpenter, Grossberg 88], Quickprop and Counterpropagation [Hecht-Nielsen 88]. We continue to implement further network paradigms.

At the same time we are trying to facilitate installation and porting SNNS to other Unix workstation platforms that we can access in our department and that support X11R4. We are considering a port to OSF/Motif.

It is planned to distribute SNNS via anonymous ftp free of charge under a GNU-style copyright and license agreement, including source code. We only need to charge a nominal fee for the printed user manuals and postage. Currently all written documentation is in German, but we hope to have an English version of the documentation by the time this article appears.

6. APPLICATIONS OF SNNS

SNNS is used by a number of co-workers and students in our department as well as some cooperating research institutions. Some applications so far include

* *printed character recognition*: the goal is here to recognize printed individual characters of a variety of fonts in different sizes scanned by an OCR scanner. The characters are already segmented and are rotated only slightly. The neural net models examined here are various variants of backpropagation, counterpropagation and quickprop.

- *handwritten character recognition*: scale and position invariant recognition of single handwritten characters. The same models are examined plus more specialized models like the neocognitron.

- *recognition of machine parts*: two dimensional binary and gray scale images of relatively flat machine parts are to be recognized with a neural net classifier system. The machine parts may be rotated to any degree. Part of the image preprocessing will be done with conventional technology.

- *stock prize prediction*: based on the previous time behaviour of selected stock and economic indices, a short term prediction of selected stock values and direction of movement is being investigated. Here, the adaline, madaline and backpropagation models will be compared for this task.

- *recognition and classification of exogenic and endogenic components of event correlated brain potentials*: this research is done in collaboration with a medical psychology research group in Tübingen who is in charge of the experimental setup and the choice of network model.

- *noise reduction in natural language communication in a telecom environment*: together with an industry partner specializing in telefone and mobile phone equipment, the application of neural networks for noise reduction and later on for recognition of a limited subset of spoken language in a noisy telecom environment is being investigated.

- *texture and object recognition*. This larger joint project with another federal research institution and an industry partner will use SNNS for research on texture and object recognition for real world vision problems, like materials inspection and image segmentation of objects differentiated by textures. Here SNNS will be used to evaluate various neural network models which will later be trained on a massively parallel neural network simulation system on a SIMD computer (see below).

The first of these applications are performed as student projects, the last three are cooperation projects. Results of these projects have not been published yet. It is expected that the range of applications of SNNS will increase significantly in the near future.

7. RELATED WORK

Some ideas in the SNNS simulator were inspired by the Rochester Connectionist Simulator RCS, [Goddard et al. 89], some also by the Esprit II Research Project 2059 Pygmalion Neurocomputing Simulator [Pygmalion 90 a-c], both Unix workstation simulators implemented in C with a graphical user interface under X-Windows. Other popular simulators, like P3 [Zipser, Rabin 86], the PDP-Simulators [McClelland 86] and NeuralWorks Professional II [NeuralWare 90] and the Axon language [Hecht-Nielsen 88] were analyzed but did not have a great impact on our own system. Recently have we been able to obtain the UCLA SFINX neural network simulator [Mesrobian et al 89].

8. A PARALLEL NEURAL NETWORK SIMULATION ENVIRONMENT

In a successor project a massively parallel simulation system for neural networks on a SIMD-computer with more than 16.000 processors (MasPar MP-1216) is being developed. The goal of this project is to enable the simulation of large neural networks, mainly for the tasks of image processing, feature extraction and pattern and object recognition.

The MasPar MP-1216 delivers a peak performance of 30,000 MIPS (32 bit addition) and 1,500 resp. 600 MFLOPS (32 bit resp. 64 bit). Communication bandwidth is up to 1500 MB/s peak global router and up to 24 GB/s peak X-net communication. It can be programmed with parallel versions of C (MPL) and Fortran. MPPE (MasPar parallel programming environment), an integrated graphical tool set based on X-Windows, facilitates program development and debugging. An overview of the MasPar MP-1216 architecture is given in fig. 5.

The sequential simulator SNNS will be the starting point for the parallel simulator to be implemented. The parallel simulator will consist of a massively parallel simulator kernel running on the MasPar, an X-Windows based graphical user interface to visualize the networks on graphic workstations, and a modified description language. Tools for the analysis of network performance, for measurements of learning behaviour and for tests about scalability of the models will be developed and integrated into the system.

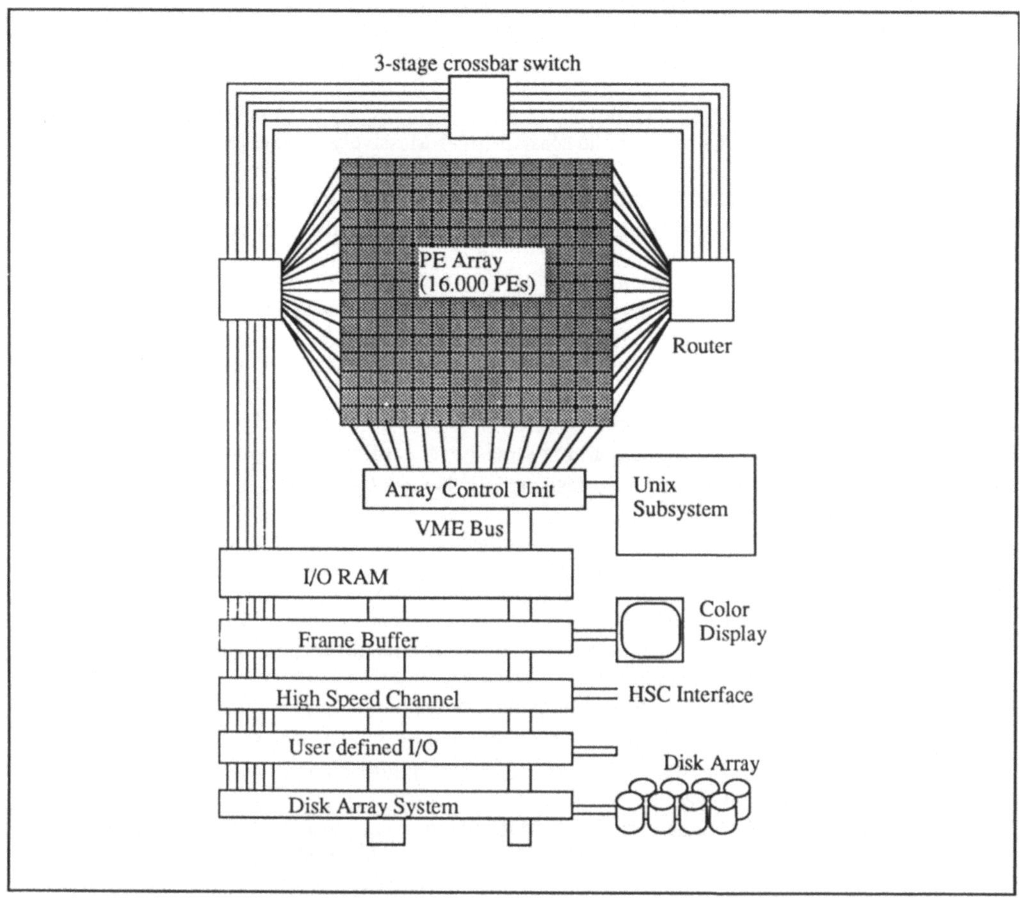

Fig. 5: MasPar MP-1 architecture

We are currently investigating the benefits of different approaches to parallelization of the kernel, as given in [Singer 90], [Grajski et al. 90], [Chinn et al. 90] and [Zhang et al. 89]. The studies of [Grajski et al. 90] showed that 9.8 M CUPS (connection updates per second) for learning and 18.4 M CUPS during recall can be obtained with "vanilla" backpropagation benchmarks on a 16K PE MasPar MP-1216. These studies suggest that for networks with regular topology, between a tenfold and a hundredfold increase in performance of a massively parallel SIMD system against a workstation simulator can be obtained.

The implementation of the parallel simulator will be done in MPL, a parallel extension of C.

9. SUMMARY

We have given an overview of SNNS, a neural network simulator for Unix workstations. SNNS is a tool to generate, train, test and visualize artificial neural networks. Its graphical user interface enables the interactive construction, manipulation and visualization of the neural networks under simulation. A number of applications of SNNS are currently in development, among them character and object recognition problems, adaptive control problems and prediction problems. Future work will include the incorporation of additional connectionist models and learning procedures in SNNS, the development of other applicatons and the development of a massively parallel version of SNNS, a parallel neural network simulation environment on our MasPar MP-1216 SIMD-computer.

REFERENCES

[Carpenter, Grossberg 88] Carpenter, G.A., Grossberg, S.: The ART of Adaptive Pattern Recognition by a Self-Organizing Neural Network, IEEE Computer, March 1988, pp. 77-88

[Chinn et al. 90] G. Chinn, K.A. Grajski, C. Chen, C. Kuszmaul, S. Tomboulian: Systolic Array Implementations of Neural Nets on the MasPar MP-1 Massively Parallel Processor, MasPar Corp. Int. Report

[Eckmiller 90] R. Eckmiller (Ed.): Advanced Neural Computers, North Holland, 1990

[Eckmiller et al. 90] R. Eckmiller, G. Hartmann, G. Hauske (Ed.): Parallel Processing in Neural Systems and Computers, North Holland, 1990

[Goddard et al. 89] Goddard, N.H., Lynne, K.J., Mintz, T., Bukys, L.: The Rochester Connectionist Simulator: User Manual, Tech Report 233 (revised), Univ. of Rochester, NY, 1989

[Grajski et al. 90] K.A. Grajski, G. Chinn, C. Chen, C. Kuszmaul, S. Tomboulian: Neural Network Simulation on the MasPar MP-1 Massively Parallel Processor, Internat. Neural Network Conference, Paris, France, 1990

[Hecht-Nielsen 88] Hecht-Nielsen, R.: Neurocomputing, Addison-Wesley, 1990

[Hinton 89] Hinton, G.E.: Connectionist Learning Procedures, Artificial Intelligence 40(1989), p.185-234

[NeuralWorks 90a, b, c] NeuralWorks Professional II: Neural Computing, Users Guide, Reference Guide, NeuralWare Inc., 1990

[McClelland, Rumelhart 87] McClelland, J.A., Rumelhart, D.E., the PDP Research Group: Explorations in Parallel Distributed Processing, MIT Press, Cambridge MA, 1987

[Mesrobian 89] E. Mesrobian, M. Stilber, J. Skrzypek: UCLA SFINX: Structure and Function in Neural Networks, Report No. UCLA-MPL-TR 89-8, Comp. Science Dept., UCLA, 1989

[Pygmalion 90a] M. Hewetson: Pygmalion Neurocomputing, Graphic Monitor Tutorial v 1.1 & Graphic Monitor Manual, Dept. Comp. Science, University College, London

[Pygmalion 90b] J. Taylor: Pygmalion Neurocomputing, Algorithm Library v 1.0, ditto

[Pygmalion 90c] M. B. R. Vellasco: Pygmalion Neurocomputing, nC Tutorial & nC Manual v 1.02, ditto

[Recce, Treleaven 89] Recce, M., Treleaven, P.C.: Parallel Architectures for Neural Computers, Neural Computers, Springer, 1989, pp. 487-495

[Rumelhart, McClelland 86] Rumelhart, D.E., McClelland, J.A., the PDP Research Group: Parallel Distributed Processing, Vol. 1, 2, MIT Press, Cambridge MA, 1986

[Singer 90] A. Singer: Implementations of Artificial Neural Networks on the Connection Machine, Thinking Machines Corp. Tech. Rep. RL 90-2, Jan. 1990 (also to appear in Parallel Computing, summer 1990)

[SNNS 91a] A. Zell, Th. Korb, N. Mache, T. Sommer: SNNS, Stuttgarter Neuronale Netze Simulator, Benutzerhandbuch, Universität Stuttgart, Fakultät Informatik, Bericht Nr. 1/91, (in German)

[SNNS 91b] A. Zell, Th. Korb, N. Mache, T. Sommer: SNNS, Stuttgarter Neuronale Netze Simulator, Nessus-Handbuch, Universität Stuttgart, Fakultät Informatik, Bericht Nr. 3/91, (in German)

[Touretzky 89] Touretzky, D.: Advances in Neural Information Processing Systems 1, Morgan Kaufmann, 1989

[Touretzky et al. 88] Touretzky, D., Hinton, G., Sejnowski, T.: Proc. of the 1988 Connectonist Models Summer School, June 17-26, Carnegie Mellon University, Morgan Kaufmann, 1988

[Zhang et al. 89] X. Zhang, M. Mckenna, J.P. Mesirov, D. L. Waltz: An efficient implementation of the Back-propagation algorithm on the Connection Machine CM-2, Thinking Machines Corp. TR

[Zell et al. 89] A. Zell, Th. Korb, T. Sommer, R. Bayer: NetSim, ein Simulator für Neuronale Netze, Informatik Fachberichte 216, D. Metzing (Hrsgb.) GWAI-89, 13th German Workshop on Artificial Intelligence, Eringerfeld, Sept. 89, Springer, pp. 134-143 (in German)

[Zell et al. 90] A. Zell, Th. Korb, T. Sommer, R. Bayer: A Neural Network Simulation Environment, Proc. Applications of Neural Networks Conf., SPIE Vol. 1294, pp. 535-544

[Zell et al. 91] A. Zell, Th. Korb, N. Mache, T. Sommer: Recent Developments of the SNNS Neural Network Simulator, Proc. Applications of Neural Networks Conf., SPIE Vol. 1294, 1991

[Zipser, Rabin 86] D. Zipser, D.E. Rabin: P3: A Parallel Network Simulation System, in [Rumelhart, McClelland 86]

Deductive Generalization and Meta-Reasoning
or
How to Formalize Genesis

Gernot Salzer
Technische Universität Wien
Karlsplatz 13/E185-2, A-1040 Wien/Austria
salzer@csdec1.tuwien.ac.at

Abstract

When using resolution for showing the unsatisfiability of logic formulas one often encounters infinite sequences of structurally similar clauses. We suggest to use deductive generalization to derive a small number of meta-clauses subsuming these infinite sequences. Resolution is extended by meta-unification in order to resolve meta-clauses instead of ordinary ones.

As a step towards a unification procedure for general meta-terms we investigate the unification of monadic ones. We describe an algorithm yielding a finite, complete and orthonormal set of unifiers. First experiments show the usefulness of our approach: theorem provers save space as well as time, proofs become considerably shorter.

> *And the Lord God formed man from the dust*
> *of the ground and breathed into his nostrils the*
> *breath of life; and man became a living soul.*
>
> *(Genesis 2:7)*

1   Introduction

Inspecting the clause dumps generated by automated theorem provers one finds a lot of clauses that are neither tautologies nor subsumed by other clauses—and therefore cannot be eliminated—but nevertheless are similar to each other with regard to their structure. Whereas a mechanical theorem prover has to keep all these clauses, since none is redundant, a human theorem prover would use some adequate abbreviation instead.

Suppose our task were to formalize genesis as it is described in [Gid 75]. According to this best-seller Adam was the founder of the human race (we disregard the minor fact that there was also involved a rib named Eve). Using clause logic we could formalize this fact as

$$Human(adam) \quad\quad \leftarrow$$
$$Human(offspring(x)) \quad \leftarrow \quad Human(x)$$

stating that Adam as well as the offspring of a human is human. By resolution ([Ro 65a])
we are able to infer the new facts

$$Human(\mathit{offspring}(adam)) \leftarrow, \ Human(\mathit{offspring}(\mathit{offspring}(adam))) \leftarrow, \ \ldots$$

Clearly, $Human(\underbrace{\mathit{offspring}(\cdots \mathit{offspring}(adam)\cdots))}_{m \text{ times}} \leftarrow$ holds for arbitrary m. Though all
these new clauses are of the same shape, an automatic theorem prover would generate
them one by one. The goal of this paper is to develop a method that enables a theorem
prover to deal with sequences of structurally similar clauses in a more intelligent and
more efficient way.

One approach is to use some generalization mechanism like *mathematical induction*
([Da 68]) or *least common generalization* ([Pl 70], [Pl 71], [Re 70]). The latter method
yields $Human(x) \leftarrow$, stating that all individuals are human. This assertion seems a little
bit too strong, since now also $Human(serpent) \leftarrow$ holds; thus inductive generalization
changes the set of possible models.

Another method for reducing the number of retained clauses is the simplification
of terms by rewrite rules, f.i. *demodulation* ([Wo 67]) and *narrowing* ([Sl 74]). If the
equation $\mathit{offspring}(x) = x$ would hold, the rewrite rule $\mathit{offspring}(x) \to x$ would collapse
mankind to a species consisting of a single human named *adam* since all clauses are
reduced to the normalform $Human(adam) \leftarrow$. Logical completeness is preserved only if
the set of reduction rules is complete ([KB 70]), i.e., if it has certain termination and
uniqueness properties.

In [Sa 90a] we proposed a different approach called *deductive generalization*: instead
of affecting the set of models or requiring equational theories with canonical systems
of rewrite rules, we extend the language of first-order logic by meta-literals to capture
infinite sequences of clauses. Accordingly, meta-unification is used to unify these meta-
literals. In this way a theorem prover saves space as well as time since replacing an
infinite set of first-order clauses by a single meta-clause reduces the search space. Furthermore, instead of resolving the original clauses one by one, a macro-inference rule
(*meta-resolution*) uses the meta-clauses to derive new ones, which again represent infinite sets of ordinary resolvents. Example 3 shows that meta-resolution is able to refute
clause sets in constant time where conventional resolution takes time at least proportional
to the logarithm of the length of input clauses.

In the next section we review deductive generalization and meta-terms as presented
in [Sa 90a]. The reader not familiar with the basic terminology of automated theorem
proving is referred to [CL 73] or [Lo 78]. For the other sections, however, this terminology
is not necessary since those are self-contained.

As a step towards a general unification procedure for meta-terms this paper investigates the unification of monadic meta-terms. These can be most conveniently written
as strings with repetitions (R-strings). Section 3 introduces the terminology concerning
R-strings and defines their normalform; in section 4 we describe a unification algorithm
for R-strings. Finally, section 5 discusses related work as well as experimental results.

2   Deductive Generalization and Meta-terms

Our first step is to describe and characterize the situations giving rise to sequences of
similar clauses. To handle positive and negative literals in a uniform way we prefer to

view clauses as disjunctions instead of writing them in logic programming style (as done in the introduction).

In [Sa 90a] we identified clauses of the form $P \vee Q$ as a source of structurally similar resolvents. Let $T = P \vee Q$ be a clause such that Q is an instance of the dual of P, i.e., $Q = \overline{P}\lambda$ for some substitution λ, and such that the variables of Q are a subset of those of P. Furthermore, let $C = L_1 \vee \cdots \vee L_i \vee \cdots \vee L_k$ be any clause that can be resolved with T, where L_i and P are the literals resolved upon and μ is the most general unifier of L_i and $\overline{P}$. By $C^{(n)}$ we denote the clauses generated by T from C, defined as:

- $C^{(0)} = C$

- For $n \geq 1$ $C^{(n)}$ is the binary resolvent of $C^{(n-1)}$ and (a renamed copy of) T, where $C^{(n-1)}$ is resolved upon its i-th literal and T upon P.

Then the following proposition holds:

Proposition 1 *$C^{(n)}$ is defined for all $n \geq 1$ and is given by*

$$C^{(n)} = L_1\mu \vee \cdots \vee \overline{P}\lambda^n\mu \vee \cdots \vee L_k\mu.$$

Proof By induction on n. The details can be found in [Sa 90b].

Corollary 2 *If μ, the most general unifier of L_i and $\overline{P}$, is a match of $\overline{P}$ onto L_i, i.e. $\overline{P}\mu = L_i$, then $C^{(n)}$ is given by $C^{(n)} = L_1 \vee \cdots \vee \overline{P}\lambda^n\mu \vee \cdots \vee L_k$ for all $n \geq 0$.*

Thus the sequence of resolvents generated by T from C is infinite; moreover, the clauses differ from each other in one literal only.

Example 1 *Abbreviating the names in the introductory example we obtain the clauses $C = H(a)$ and $T = \neg H(x) \vee H(o(x))$. Since $H(o(x))$ is an instance of $H(x)$ via the substitution $\lambda = \{x \leftarrow o(x)\}$ and $\mu_1 = \{x \leftarrow a\}$ is a match of $H(x)$ onto $H(a)$, we may apply corollary 2 and obtain $C^{(n)} = H(x)\lambda^n\mu_1$, i.e. the clauses $H(a)$, $H(o(a))$, $H(o(o(a)))$ etc.*

A second possibility is to resolve T with $T' = \neg H(y) \vee H(o(y))$, that is, with a renamed copy of itself. $\mu_2 = \{x \leftarrow o(y)\}$ is a match of $H(x)$ onto $H(o(y))$, therefore corollary 2 yields the sequence $T'^{(n)} = \neg H(y) \vee H(x)\lambda^n\mu_2$.

One way to represent the clauses $C^{(n)}$ in a compact form is to replace n by a formal meta-variable α and to identify the resulting meta-clause C^α with $\{C^{(n)} \mid n \geq 0\}$. With respect to meta-unification we permit arbitrary linear combinations of meta-variables as exponents of substitutions. Thus we extend the syntax of first-order logic obtaining a weak second-order language. The step from C and T to C^α is referred to as *deductive generalization*.

Example 2 *Continuing example 1 we get the meta-clauses*

$$\begin{aligned} M_1 &= H(x)\{x \leftarrow o(x)\}^\alpha \{x \leftarrow a\} \text{ and} \\ M_2 &= \neg H(y) \vee H(x)\{x \leftarrow o(x)\}^\alpha \{x \leftarrow o(y)\} \end{aligned}$$

describing all resolvents of C and T.

The introduction of meta-clauses into a theorem prover saves space that would otherwise be needed to store the represented clauses seperately. To make the new concept really useful we would like to resolve meta-clauses instead of working with the (usually infinitely) many ordinary clauses. Resolving two meta-clauses M_1 and M_2 means to check each clause represented by M_1 and each clause represented by M_2 for resolvents. The set of resolvents—in most cases of infinite cardinality—should again be representable by a finite number of meta-clauses. In this way proofs may become considerably shorter.

Example 3 *Let C be the set $\{C, T, D\}$ of clauses, where C and T are the same as in example 1, and $D = \neg H(\underbrace{o(\cdots o(a)\cdots))}_{m \text{ times}}$ with $m \geq 0$. C is unsatisfiable for arbitrary m; the length of the shortest refutation using resolution is proportional to $\log m$. Using meta-resolution we first derive the meta-clause M_1 of example 2; then we resolve it with D, where the meta-unifier involved is $\{\alpha \leftarrow m\}$, and obtain the empty clause in one step independent of the size of m.*

At the heart of every resolution procedure is a unification algorithm for terms. Thus in our case we have to investigate the unification of meta-terms. The next example illustrates what we expect from meta-unification.

Example 4 *The meta-term $t_1 = x\{x \leftarrow f(g(x))\}^\alpha\{x \leftarrow u\}$ represents the set*

$$\{u, f(g(u)), f(g(f(g(u)))), \ldots\},$$

whereas $t_2 = f(y)\{y \leftarrow g(f(y))\}^\beta\{y \leftarrow v\}$ stands for

$$\{f(v), f(g(f(v))), f(g(f(g(f(v))))), \ldots\}.$$

Though each term of t_1 is unifiable with each term of t_2 there are only two basic kinds of most general unifiers: the unifiers look either like $\{u \leftarrow f(v)\}$, $\{u \leftarrow f(g(f(v)))\}$ etc. or like $\{v \leftarrow g(u)\}$, $\{v \leftarrow g(f(g(u)))\}$ etc. Thus meta-unification should yield the following two meta-unifiers:

$$\lambda_1 = \{u \leftarrow f(y)\{y \leftarrow g(f(y))\}^\gamma\{y \leftarrow v\}, \beta \leftarrow \alpha + \gamma\}$$
$$\lambda_2 = \{v \leftarrow g(x)\{x \leftarrow f(g(x))\}^\gamma\{x \leftarrow u\}, \alpha \leftarrow 1 + \beta + \gamma\}$$

We start the investigation of meta-unification by restricting function symbols to monadic ones. In this case we choose the simpler representation of meta-terms as *strings with repetitions* (R-strings). Monadic function symbols and constant symbols are interpreted as the elements of an alphabet serving as basis for the corresponding R-strings.

Example 5 *Writing the meta-terms of example 4 as R-strings we get*

$$t_1 = (fg)^\alpha u, \qquad \lambda_1 = \{u \leftarrow f(gf)^\gamma v, \beta \leftarrow \alpha + \gamma\},$$
$$t_2 = f(gf)^\beta v \text{ and } \lambda_2 = \{v \leftarrow g(fg)^\gamma u, \alpha \leftarrow 1 + \beta + \gamma\}.$$

3 R-strings and their normal forms

In the following, Σ denotes an alphabet (i.e., a finite set of atomic symbols) and V_R and V_T enumerable sets of $\mathcal{R}$- resp. $\mathcal{T}$-variables with $\Sigma \cap V_R = \emptyset$, $\Sigma \cap V_T = \emptyset$ and $V_R \cap V_T = \emptyset$. The elements of V_T are ordered by some arbitrary but fixed total ordering denoted by $\prec$. V is used as abbreviation for the set $V_R \cup V_T$ of variables. The set $\{0, 1, 2, \ldots\}$ of numerals is denoted by $\mathcal{N}$. In the examples below we assume that $\{a, b, \ldots, h\} \subseteq \Sigma$, $\{u, v, w, x, y\} \subseteq V_R$ and $\{\alpha, \beta, \gamma, \delta, \alpha_1, \beta_1, \ldots\} \subseteq V_T$ with $\alpha \prec \beta \prec \gamma \prec \delta \prec \alpha_1 \prec \beta_1 \prec \ldots$

A string (word) over Σ is a finite sequence of symbols from Σ; the empty string is denoted by ϵ. The set of all strings over Σ with, respectively without, ϵ is denoted by Σ^* resp. Σ^+. The length of a string w, denoted by $|w|$, is the number of symbols in w; $|\epsilon|$ is defined as 0. w repeated n times is abbreviated by w^n; w^0 equals ϵ.

Definition 1 *The set $\mathcal{T}$ of numerical terms is the smallest set satisfying:*

- $\mathcal{N} \subseteq \mathcal{T}$
- $V_T \subseteq \mathcal{T}$
- $n(t) \in \mathcal{T}$ *iff* $n \in \mathcal{N}$ *and* $t \in \mathcal{T}$
- $t_1 + t_2 \in \mathcal{T}$ *iff* $t_1, t_2 \in \mathcal{T}$

In case that $t \in V_T$ we simply write nt instead of $n(t)$.

Definition 2 *The set $\mathcal{E}$ of E-words is given by $\{(w)^t \mid w \in \Sigma^+, t \in \mathcal{T}\}$.*

Definition 3 *The set $\mathcal{R}$ of R-strings is given by $(\Sigma \cup \mathcal{E})^* \cdot (\{\epsilon\} \cup V_R)$.*

R-strings and numerical terms are called expressions. Let e be an expression or a set of expressions. The set of variables occurring in e is denoted by $\mathrm{var}(e)$; $\mathrm{var}_R(e) = \mathrm{var}(e) \cap V_R$ and $\mathrm{var}_T(e) = \mathrm{var}(e) \cap V_T$. An expression e is called *ground* iff $\mathrm{var}(e) = \emptyset$.

By R-strings we just get a convenient tool to handle monadic meta-terms. Since in the language of first order logic there are no variables for function symbols, the elements of V_R may appear at the end of an R-string only. If $\mathcal{R}$-variables were also to appear within an R-string we would face the much harder problem of general string unification ([Ma 77]). However, an E-word $(w)^t$ can be regarded as typed variable, where w and t restrict the possible ways of substituting strings for that variable.

An R-string can be thought of as an abbreviation for a set of strings without variables. We formalize this idea by defining a function $\mathcal{M}$ that assigns a set of words to each R-string as its meaning.

Definition 4 *A substitution σ is a mapping $\sigma : V \to (\mathcal{T} \cup \mathcal{R})$ such that*

- *the set $\mathrm{dom}(s) = \{v \in V \mid \sigma(v) \neq v\}$ is finite and*
- *$\sigma(v) \in \mathcal{T}$ resp. $\sigma(v) \in \mathcal{R}$ iff $v \in V_T$ resp. $v \in V_R$.*

$\mathrm{dom}(s)$ *is called the* domain *of s, $\mathrm{rg}(s) = \{\sigma(v) \mid v \in \mathrm{dom}(s)\}$ the* range *of s.*

Let $\mathrm{dom}(s) = \{v_1, \ldots, v_n\}$ and $t_i = \sigma(v_i)$ for $1 \leq i \leq n$. Then σ can be written as the set $\{v_1 \leftarrow t_1, \ldots, v_n \leftarrow t_n\}$, where the $v_i \leftarrow t_i$ are called the components *of σ; the empty set determines the identity substitution. Usually substitutions are written in postfix notation, i.e., $t\sigma$ instead of $\sigma(t)$.*

σ is called ground *iff all expressions in $\mathrm{rg}(\sigma)$ are ground.*

The domain of substitutions is extended to arbitrary expressions in the usual way: only the variables in an expression are affected by substitutions, all other symbols remain unchanged. Thus substitutions are functions of type $(\mathcal{T} \cup \mathcal{R}) \to (\mathcal{T} \cup \mathcal{R})$. The composition $\tau \circ \sigma$ of substitutions τ and σ is usually written in postfix notation as $\sigma\tau$.

Definition 5 *Let r be an R-string. The* meaning $\mathcal{M}(r)$ *of r is the set of all pairs $(\sigma, \bar{r})$, where σ is a ground substitution with $\mathrm{dom}(\sigma) = \mathrm{var}(r)$ and $\bar{r}$ is the string obtained from $r\sigma$ by replacing each E-word $(w)^c$ by w^i with i being the natural number corresponding to the numeral c.*

Note that for all $(\sigma_1, \bar{r}_1), (\sigma_2, \bar{r}_2) \in \mathcal{M}(r)$ we have $\bar{r}_1 = \bar{r}_2$ if $\sigma_1 = \sigma_2$; the converse is not true in general as can be seen in the next example.

Example 6 *Let r be the R-string $(ab)^{1+\alpha}(a)^\beta(b)^\beta$. As meaning of r we get:*

$$\mathcal{M}(r) = \{ \ (\{\alpha \leftarrow 0, \beta \leftarrow 0\}, ab), \quad (\{\alpha \leftarrow 0, \beta \leftarrow 1\}, abab), \quad \ldots,$$
$$(\{\alpha \leftarrow 1, \beta \leftarrow 0\}, abab), (\{\alpha \leftarrow 1, \beta \leftarrow 1\}, ababab), \ldots,$$
$$\vdots \qquad\qquad\qquad \vdots \qquad\qquad \ddots \}$$

$\mathcal{M}$ *is not injective: the R-string $a(ba)^\alpha b(a)^\beta(b)^\beta$ has the same meaning as r.*

The function $\mathcal{M}$ defines an equivalence relation between R-strings: two R-strings are equivalent iff $\mathcal{M}(r) = \mathcal{M}(s)$. This equivalence can be decided by the means of normal forms: each equivalence class contains a unique R-string to which all equivalent R-strings can be reduced by a simple algorithm.

Definition 6 *A numerical term t is in* normal form *iff $t = c_0 + c_1 v_1 + \cdots + c_n v_n$ with $c_0 \in \mathcal{N}$, $c_i \in \mathcal{N} \backslash \{0\}$, $v_i \in V_T$ for $1 \leq i \leq n$ and $v_1 \prec \ldots \prec v_n$.*

Definition 7 *A word $w \in \Sigma^+$ is* prime *iff there is no word $\overline{w} \in \Sigma^+$ with $|\overline{w}| < |w|$ such that $w = \overline{w}^n$ for some $n \geq 2$.*

Definition 8 *An R-string r is in* normal form *iff*

- *for each E-word $(w)^t$ in r the word w is prime and t is in normal form containing no constant part, i.e., $t = c_1 v_1 + \cdots + c_n v_n$*
- *r contains no subword of the form $(w_1 w_2)^t w_1$ with $w_1 \in \Sigma^+$*
- *r contains no subword $(w)^{t_1}(w)^{t_2}$*

The algorithm for obtaining the normal form of an R-string is listed in table 1 and is illustrated by the next example.

Example 7 *Let r be the R-string $(ba)^\alpha b(abab)^{\beta+1} a$. By the intermediate steps*

$$r_1 = (ba)^\alpha b(ab)^{2(\beta+1)} a, \qquad r_2 = (ba)^\alpha b(ab)^{2+2\beta} a,$$
$$r_3 = (ba)^\alpha babab(ab)^{2\beta} a \ and \ r_4 = bababa(ba)^\alpha(ba)^{2\beta}$$

we obtain $NF(r) = bababa(ba)^{\alpha+2\beta}$.

Theorem 3 *Let r and s be R-strings. Then $\mathcal{M}(r) = \mathcal{M}(s)$ iff $NF(r) = NF(s)$.*

The proof of this theorem is given in full detail in [Sa 90b].

$$\overline{r} \leftarrow \mathbf{NF}(r)$$

[r is an arbitrary R-string; $\overline{r}$ is in normal form, where $\mathcal{M}(\overline{r}) = \mathcal{M}(r)$.]

(1) **[Making E-words prime]** Let r_1 be the R-string obtained from r by replacing each E-word $(w)^t$ in r by $(\overline{w})^{c(t)}$, where $\overline{w}$ is the word of smallest length satisfying $w = \overline{w}^i$ and c is the numeral evaluating to i.

(2) **[Normalization of numerical terms]** r_2 is obtained from r_1 by replacing all numerical terms in r_1 by their normal forms.

(3) **[Removing constant numerical terms]** r_3 is obtained from r_2 by replacing all E-words of the form $(w)^{c_0}$ by w^i and all E-words of the form $(w)^{c_0 + c_1 v_1 + \cdots + c_n v_n}$ by $w^i (w)^{c_1 v_1 + \cdots + c_n v_n}$, where c_0 is the numeral corresponding to i.

(4) **[Shifting E-words to the right]** r_4 is obtained from r_3 by replacing substrings of the form $(w_1 w_2)^t w_1$ with $w_1 \in \Sigma^+$ by $w_1 (w_2 w_1)^t$ until r_4 contains no more substrings of that kind.

(5) **[Joining E-words with the same base]** r_5 is obtained from r_4 by replacing substrings of the form $(w)^{t_1}(w)^{t_2}$ by $(w)^t$, where t is the normal form of $t_1 + t_2$, until r_5 contains no more substrings of that kind.

r_5 is the result of the algorithm.

Table 1: Algorithm computing the normal form of an R-string

4 Unification of R-strings

Definition 9 *A substitution λ is a* unifier *of two R-strings r and s iff* $\mathcal{M}(r\lambda) = \mathcal{M}(s\lambda)$.

A unification algorithm for R-strings faces two tasks: on the one hand the symbols of the R-strings have to correspond to each other, on the other hand the exponents allow for certain multiples of the E-words only. $\mathcal{R}$-variables cause no troubles since each R-string contains at most one of this kind. $\mathcal{T}$-variables however may appear at different places within an R-string; replacing such a variable in one place may change the exponents in others.

For the sake of a simpler treatment we separate these tasks; moreover, we deal with normal forms only. In this case the general unification procedure for arbitrary R-strings can be divided into five steps:

1. Compute the normal forms, denoted by r and s, of the R-strings to be unified.

2. Replace all E-words $(w_i)^{t_i}$ in r and s by $(w_i)^{v_i}$, where the v_i are new $\mathcal{T}$-variables appearing nowhere else; the strings obtained in this way are denoted by r' and s'. Thus the number of different $\mathcal{T}$-variables in r' and s' is the same as the number of E-words.

3. Obtain the unifiers of r' and s'. These unifiers describe how the exponents have to relate to each other for the strings to be equal.

4. Solve the linear Diophantine equations obtained from the exponents of r resp. s and the unifiers of step 3.

5. Putting together the solutions of step 4 and the unifiers of step 3 we obtain the unifiers of r and s.

Example 8 *Consider the unification of $(aaa)^\beta(a)^\alpha$ and $(aa)^\gamma(a)^{\gamma+\beta+1}$. Our first step is to normalize the R-strings; we obtain $r = (a)^{\alpha+3\beta}$ and $s = a(a)^{\beta+3\gamma}$. Next we replace the exponents by new T-variables: $r' = (a)^{\alpha_1}$ and $s' = a(a)^{\beta_1}$. The unification algorithm of table 2 applied to r' and s' yields the set $\{\{\alpha_1 \leftarrow 1 + \beta_1\}\}$ containing only one unifier. This unifier is a constraint for the exponents of r and s: the exponent in r, corresponding to α_1, has to exceed the one in s, corresponding to β_1, by one, i.e., $\alpha + 3\beta = 1 + \beta + 3\gamma$ respectively*

$$\alpha + 2\beta - 3\gamma = 1. \tag{1}$$

We are interested in all nonnegative integer values of α, β and γ satisfying (1); that means we have to solve a Diophantine equation over the set of natural numbers. Algorithms for this task can be found in [CF 89], [La 89] and [Sa 91a]; using the latter one we finally obtain a complete and orthonormal set of unifiers for the original R-strings:

$$\begin{aligned}
\{ \ &\{\alpha \leftarrow 1 + 3\gamma, \beta \leftarrow 0\}, \\
&\{\alpha \leftarrow 3\delta_1, \beta \leftarrow 2 + 3\delta_2, \gamma \leftarrow 1 + \delta_1 + 2\delta_2\}, \\
&\{\alpha \leftarrow 1 + 3\delta_1, \beta \leftarrow 3 + 3\delta_2, \gamma \leftarrow 2 + \delta_1 + 2\delta_2\}, \\
&\{\alpha \leftarrow 2 + 3\delta_1, \beta \leftarrow 1 + 3\delta_2, \gamma \leftarrow 1 + \delta_1 + 2\delta_2\} \ \}
\end{aligned}$$

This section is devoted to the unification of restricted R-strings according to step 3. We start with a formal definition of 'restricted'.

Definition 10 *The set $\overline{\mathcal{R}}$ of restricted R-strings is the set of all $r \in \mathcal{R}$ satisfying:*

- *r is in normal form*
- *Each E-word in r is of the form $(w)^v$ with $v \in V_T$.*
- *Each $v \in V_T$ occurs at most once in r.*

The unification algorithm for restricted R-strings is listed in table 2. Note the difference between $\{\emptyset\}$ and $\emptyset$. The former is a set containing one unifier, viz. the identity substitution, whereas the latter is the empty set of unifiers signalling non-unifiability.

Recursive calls to *UNIFY* are used to unify substrings of r and s. An auxiliary function $\diamond$ augments the partial unifiers obtained in this way by further components; it is defined as

$$\lambda \diamond \sigma = \lambda \circ \sigma - \{v \leftarrow t \in \lambda \mid v \in \mathrm{var}(\mathrm{rg}(\sigma))\}$$

The domain of $\diamond$ is extended to allow for sets of substitutions as first argument:

$$\{\lambda_1, \ldots, \lambda_n\} \diamond \sigma = \{\lambda_1 \diamond \sigma, \ldots, \lambda_n \diamond \sigma\}$$

$$\Lambda \leftarrow \textbf{UNIFY}(r, s)$$

$[r$ and s are elements of $\overline{\mathcal{R}}$ with $\mathrm{var}_T(r) \cap \mathrm{var}_T(s) = \emptyset$. Λ is a finite, complete and orthonormal set of unifiers for r and s. If $\Lambda = \emptyset$ then no unifiers exist.]

(1) $[\mathcal{R}$-variables] If $r \in V_R$ or $s \in V_R$ (w.l.o.g. $r \in V_R$) then

    (1.1) If $r = s$ then return $\{\emptyset\}$
    (1.2) else if r does not occur in s then return $\{\{r \leftarrow s\}\}$
    (1.3) else if $s = (w)^\alpha s'$ then return $UNIFY(r, s') \diamond \{\alpha \leftarrow 0\}$
    (1.4) else return $\emptyset$

(2) [**Empty words**] else if $r = \epsilon$ or $s = \epsilon$ (w.l.o.g. $r = \epsilon$) then

    (2.1) If $r = s$ then return $\{\emptyset\}$
    (2.2) else if $s = (w)^\alpha s'$ then return $UNIFY(r, s') \diamond \{\alpha \leftarrow 0\}$
    (2.3) else return $\emptyset$

(3) [**Symbols from** Σ] else if $r = ar'$ and $s = bs'$ with $a, b \in \Sigma$ then

    (3.1) If $a = b$ then return $UNIFY(r', s')$
    (3.2) else return $\emptyset$

(4) [**E-words**] else (w.l.o.g. $r = (u)^\alpha r'$)

    (4.1) If $u = v_1 v_2$ and $s = v_1 (v_2 v_1)^\beta s'$ then
        return $[UNIFY(r', v_1(v_2 v_1)^\gamma s') \diamond \{\beta \leftarrow \alpha + \gamma\}] \cup$
                $[UNIFY(v_2(u)^\gamma r', s') \diamond \{\alpha \leftarrow 1 + \beta + \gamma\}]$
    (4.2) else return $[UNIFY(r', s) \diamond \{\alpha \leftarrow 0\}] \cup$
                $[UNIFY(u(u)^\gamma r', s) \diamond \{\alpha \leftarrow 1 + \gamma\}]$
    where γ is a new $\mathcal{T}$-variable appearing nowhere else.

Table 2: Unification algorithm for restricted R-strings

Example 9

$UNIFY((a)^\alpha, (a)^\beta x) =$

$\begin{aligned}
&= \; [UNIFY(a(a)^\gamma, x) \diamond \{\alpha \leftarrow 1 + \beta + \gamma\}] \cup [UNIFY(\epsilon, (a)^\gamma x) \diamond \{\beta \leftarrow \alpha + \gamma\}] \\
&= \; [\{\{x \leftarrow a(a)^\gamma\}\} \diamond \{\alpha \leftarrow 1 + \beta + \gamma\}] \cup [(UNIFY(\epsilon, x) \diamond \{\gamma \leftarrow 0\}) \diamond \{\beta \leftarrow \alpha + \gamma\}] \\
&= \; \{\{\alpha \leftarrow 1 + \beta + \gamma, x \leftarrow a(a)^\gamma\}\} \cup [(\{\{x \leftarrow \epsilon\}\} \diamond \{\gamma \leftarrow 0\}) \diamond \{\beta \leftarrow \alpha + \gamma\}] \\
&= \; \{\{\alpha \leftarrow 1 + \beta + \gamma, x \leftarrow a(a)^\gamma\}\} \cup [\{\{\gamma \leftarrow 0, x \leftarrow \epsilon\}\} \diamond \{\beta \leftarrow \alpha + \gamma\}] \\
&= \; \{\{\alpha \leftarrow 1 + \beta + \gamma, x \leftarrow a(a)^\gamma\}\} \cup \{\{\beta \leftarrow \alpha, x \leftarrow \epsilon\}\} \\
&= \; \{\{\alpha \leftarrow 1 + \beta + \gamma, x \leftarrow a(a)^\gamma\}, \{\beta \leftarrow \alpha, x \leftarrow \epsilon\}\}
\end{aligned}$

Theorem 4 $UNIFY(r, s)$ *terminates for all* $r, s \in \overline{\mathcal{R}}$ *with* $\mathrm{var}_T(r) \cap \mathrm{var}_T(s) = \emptyset$ *and yields a finite, complete and orthonormal set of unifiers for r and s.*

The proof as well as the formal definitions for *complete* and *orthonormal* can be found in

$$Level\ 1$$

1:	$P(i(e), x, x)$	from clash [ass2,linv,lid,lid]
2:	$P(i(i(x)), e, x)$	from clash [ass2,linv,linv,lid]

$$Level\ 2$$

3:	$P(x, i(x), e)$	from clash [ass1,2,lid,linv]
4:	$P(x, e, x)$	from clash [ass1,2,lid,2]
⋮	⋮	⋮
9:	$P(i(i(i(i(x)))), e, x)$	from clash [ass2,2,lid,2]

$$Level\ 3$$

10:	$P(e, i(i(x)), x)$	from clash [ass1,3,linv,2]
⋮	⋮	⋮
73:	$P(i(e), x, i(i(i(i(x)))))$	from clash [ass2,1,9,4]

$$Level\ 4$$

$$\vdots$$

Table 3: Hyper-resolvents from group axioms

[Sa 90b]. Intuitively, completeness and orthonormality of the set of unifiers means that each ground unifier of r and s is uniquely represented by exactly one unifier in the set.

The worst-case complexity of $UNIFY$ can be shown to be exponential, since:

$$|UNIFY(\ (a)^{\alpha_n}(b)^{\beta_n}\cdots(a)^{\alpha_1}(b)^{\beta_1}x,\ (a)^{\gamma_n}(c)^{\delta_n}\cdots(a)^{\gamma_1}(c)^{\delta_1}y\ )| \geq \binom{2n}{n} \geq 2^n,$$

i.e., the cardinality of the set of unifiers grows exponentially for the above type of unification problem. The complexity of the unifcation algorithm for arbitrary R-strings depends on the complexity of solving Diophantine equations, which is still an open problem according to [La 89].

5   Discussion

The idea of investigating clauses of the type $\neg P \vee Q$, where P and Q are unifiable after proper renaming, is not new at all. Reynolds ([Re 70]) calls them transformations and applies least common generalization. Bibel ([Bi 88]) uses the term 'cycles' and describes the precompilation of such clauses when containing arithmetic functions.

In the context of logic programming much attention is devoted to the question whether a query to a logic program gives rise to infinite computations or an infinite set of answers. The simplest programs of interest are such consisting of clauses of the above kind. Work along this line can be found in [SBV 89] and [De 90], for instance. The latter author also introduces meta-structures (weighted graphs) as a means to describe the repeated resolution of clauses with two literals; additionally, he gives a unification algorithm for weighted graphs yielding an approximate unifier. The application of these results to automated theorem proving is limited, however, since many of them only hold for unification without occur-check.

Level 1

1:	$P((i)^\alpha e, x, x)$	from [ass2,linv,-,lid] and lid via cor. 2
2:	$P((i)^{2\alpha+1}x, x, e)$	from [ass2,linv,-,lid] and linv via cor. 2
3:	$P((i)^{2\alpha+2}x, e, x)$	from [ass2,linv,-,lid] and linv via cor. 2

Level 2

4:	$P(x, (i)^{2\alpha+1}x, e)$	from clash [ass1,3,1,2]
5:	$P(x, e, (i)^{2\alpha}x)$	from clash [ass1,3,1,3]
6:	$P(e, x, i^{2\alpha}x)$	from clash [ass1,2,2,3]
7:	$P((i)^\alpha e, e, (i)^\beta e)$	from clash [ass2,1,2,1]
8:	$P((i)^\alpha e, (i)^\beta e, e)$	from clash [ass2,1,3,1]
9:	$P((i)^\alpha e, (i)^{2\beta}x, x)$	from clash [ass2,1,3,3]

Level 3

10:	$P((i)^\alpha e, (i)^\beta e, (i)^\gamma e)$	from clash [ass2,9,7,7]
11:	$P((i)^{2\alpha}x, (i)^\beta e, (i)^{2\gamma}x)$	from clash [ass1,5,8,5]
12:	$P((i)^\beta e, (i)^{2\alpha}x, (i)^{2\gamma}x)$	from clash [ass1,7,9,6]
13:	$P((i)^{2\alpha}x, (i)^{2\gamma+1}x, (i)^\beta e)$	from clash [ass1,6,4,7]
14:	$P((i)^{2\gamma+1}x, (i)^{2\alpha}x, (i)^\beta e)$	from clash [ass2,2,5,7]

Table 4: Meta-hyper-resolvents from group axioms

A clause $P \rightarrow Q$ can be viewed also as a (global) rewrite rule ([De 90]). In [Pu 87] Purdom proves a result analogous to proposition 1: a rewrite rule causes endless rewritings, if (a part of) the right-hand side is an instance of the left-hand side.

To demonstrate the usefulness of our method we choose the group axioms represented without equality predicate (see [Lo 78]):

associativity 1:	$\neg P(x, y, u) \vee \neg P(y, z, v) \vee \neg P(x, v, w) \vee P(u, z, w)$
associativity 2:	$\neg P(x, y, u) \vee \neg P(y, z, v) \vee \neg P(u, z, w) \vee P(x, v, w)$
left identity:	$P(e, x, x)$
left inverse:	$P(i(x), x, e)$

This clause set is quite a good test for proof strategies since the law of associativity written in this form is responsible for a fast growing number of resolvents that have to be dealt with.

Positive hyper-resolution ([Ro 65b]) with level-saturation and subsumption is rather restrictive since it generates only unit clauses (facts) when applied to a set of Horn clauses. Nevertheless, this strategy applied to the above clauses yields an infinite number of non-redundant resolvents (see table 3).

Looking closer at the intermediate results of the first level, we find the partial clash $\neg P(x, y, z) \vee P(i(x), z, y)$ obtained from [ass2,linv,-,lid]. Since this clause fulfills all necessary requirements stated in section 2 and both unit clauses—left identity as well as left inverse—are instances of $P(x, y, z)$, corollary 2 yields the meta-clauses 1, 2 and 3 of table 4 (with arguments written as R-strings). Observe that these meta-clauses subsume all of the ordinary hyper-resolvents of level 1 as well as the two input unit clauses.

On the next level six new meta-resolvents are derived, and level 3 contains only five of them. But since the latter ones subsume all preceding as well as all succeeding clauses, the resolution process stops with the five clauses 10–14 describing all of the infinitely many ordinary hyper-resolvents sketched in table 3. Moreover, since hyper-resolution is complete for sets of Horn clauses, the termination without contradiction proves the satisfiability of the group axioms.

These first experiments show that deductive generalization and meta-reasoning indeed enhance the capabilities of theorem provers. At the moment, however, our method is subject to two essential limitations:

1. So far we have focused our attention to monadic meta-terms only. Though the results can be generalized to some extent in order to cope with function symbols of arities higher than one, it is still an open problem how to unify general meta-terms.

2. In section 2 we require that the clause T may not introduce any new variables. Due to this restriction deductive generalization cannot be applied to such standard examples in logic programming like the *append*-clause. To get rid of this limitation we most probably would have to extend our notion of meta-terms by periodical variables in the style of [De 90].

References

[Bi 88] W. Bibel. Advanced Topics in Automated Deduction. *Advanced Topics in Artificial Intelligence*, LNCS 345, 41–59. Springer Verlag, New York, 1988.

[CF 89] M. Clausen and A. Fortenbacher. Efficient Solution of Linear Diophantine Equations. *J. Symbolic Computation* 8 (1989), 201–216.

[CL 73] C. L. Chang and R. C. T. Lee. *Symbolic Logic and Mechanical Theorem Proving*. Academic Press, New York, 1973.

[Da 68] J. L. Darlington. Automatic Theorem Proving with Equality Substitutions and Mathematical Induction. *Machine Intelligence* Vol. 3 (B. Meltzer and D. Mitchie eds.), 113–127. Edinburgh University Press, 1968.

[De 90] P. Devienne. Weighted graphs: a tool for studying the halting problem and time complexity in term rewriting systems and logic programming. *Theoretical Computer Science* 75 (1990), 157–215.

[Gid 75] The Gideons, eds. *The Holy Bible*. National Publishing Company, 1975.

[KB 70] D. E. Knuth and P. B. Bendix. Simple Word Problems in Universal Algebra. *Computational Problems in Abstract Algebra* (J. Leech ed.), 263–297. Pergamon Press, 1970.

[La 89] D. Lankford. Non-negative Integer Basis Algorithms for Linear Equations with Integer Coefficients. *J. Automated Reasoning* 5 (1989), 25–35.

[Lo 78] D. W. Loveland. *Automated Theorem Proving: A Logical Basis*. North Holland, Amsterdam, 1978.

[Ma 77] G. S. Makanin. The Problem of Solvability of Equations in a Free Semigroup. *Mat. Sb.* 103(145) (1977), 147–236. English translation in *Math. USSR Sb.* 32.

[Pl 70]   G. D. Plotkin. A Note on Inductive Generalization. *Machine Intelligence* Vol. 5 (B. Meltzer and D. Mitchie eds.), 153–163. Edinburgh University Press, 1970.

[Pl 71]   G. D. Plotkin. A Further Note on Inductive Generalization. *Machine Intelligence* Vol. 6 (B. Meltzer and D. Mitchie eds.), 101–124. Edinburgh University Press, 1971.

[Pu 87]   P. Purdom. Detecting Looping Simplifications. 2nd *Int. Conf. on Rewriting Techniques and Applications '87*, LNCS 256, 54–61. Springer Verlag, New York, 1987.

[Re 70]   J. C. Reynolds. Transformational Systems and the Algebraic Structure of Atomic Formulas. *Machine Intelligence* Vol. 5 (B. Meltzer and D. Mitchie eds.), 135–151. Edinburgh University Press, 1970.

[Ro 65a] J. A. Robinson. A Machine Oriented Logic based on the Resolution Principle. *J. ACM* Vol. 12 No. 1 (1965), 23–41.

[Ro 65b] J. A. Robinson. Automatic Deduction with Hyper-Resolution. *Int. J. Comput. Math.* 1 (1965), 227–234.

[Sa 90a] G. Salzer. Deductive Generalization for Clause Logic. *Year-book of the Kurt-Gödel-Society 1989*, 47–59, Wien, 1990.

[Sa 90b] G. Salzer. *Unification of Strings with Repetitions.* TR E1803/S03, Technische Universität Wien, 1990.

[Sa 91a] G. Salzer. *Unique Representation of the Nonnegative Solutions of Linear Diophantine Equations.* TR E1803/S04, Technische Universität Wien, 1991.

[SBV 89] D. Schreye, M. Bruynooghe, K. Verschaetse. On the Existence of Nonterminating Queries for a Restricted Class of Prolog-Clauses. *Artificial Intelligence* 41 (1989/90), 237–248.

[Sl 74]   J. R. Slagle. Automated Theorem-Proving for Theories with Simplifiers, Commutativity, and Associativity. *J. ACM* Vol. 21 No. 4 (1974), 622–642.

[Wo 67]   L. Wos, G. A. Robinson, D. F. Carson and L. Shalla. The Concept of Demodulation in Theorem Proving. *J. ACM* Vol. 14 No. 4 (1967), 698–709.

A Generalized Factorization Rule Based on the Introduction of Skolem Terms*

Uwe Egly
FG Intellektik / FB Informatik
TH Darmstadt
Alexanderstraße 10
D–6100 Darmstadt
e-mail: xiisuegl@ddathd21.bitnet

Abstract

In this paper, we describe a factorization rule which is based on the introduction of Skolem terms. This rule generalizes non-unifiable terms to a new term not occurring elsewhere in the clause set. Clauses of the form $p(x, t_1) \vee p(y, t_2)$ are factorized to $p(x, m)$ where t_1, t_2 are ground terms and m is a new constant not occurring in the Herbrand universe of the original clause set. A refutation of $p(x, m)$ implies a refutation of $p(x, t_1) \vee p(y, t_2)$ but not vice versa. We extend this factorization rule in several ways and show that the application of such rules may increase the performance of automated theorem provers. A linear resolution proof of exponential length may collapse into a linear resolution proof of linear length.

1   Introduction

While problem reduction methods play a very important role in human problem solving, their potential is not widely explored in the field of automated theorem proving. Bledsoe [1971] described several reduction rules which reduce a given problem to one or two easier problems depending on the chosen rule. Although the rules are equivalences, they are directed and only one implication is used performing the reduction. As a consequence, the reduced problem is provable (refutable) iff the given problem is provable (refutable). Besides these rules, there is another rule providing a simple clause splitting mechanism. The subclauses of a clause which is decomposable into two or more subclauses sharing no variables may be treated independently. As an effect of such a clause split, the original clause set is split into two or more new clause sets containing all but the decomposed clause and exactly one subclause. The split's effect on the (linear) resolution proof tree is its decomposition into subtrees. The length of the proof for the original problem is less[1] or equal the sum of the lengths of all proofs for the subproblems.

In order to get stronger results, Baaz and Leitsch [1985] introduced a correct but incomplete reduction rule which decomposes a clause into independent subclauses whereas the subclauses share exactly one variable before the application of the rule. Performing the split may effect the search space inspected by an automated theorem prover [Baaz and Leitsch, 1985; Egly, 1990]. This splitting rule has been generalized in order to handle an arbitrary number of variables in common. This enhanced splitting rule is based on function introduction and re-skolemization.

---

*This research was supported by the Federal Ministry for Research and Technology within the project TASSO under grant no. ITW 8900 A7.

[1]due to factorization

Since the subclauses resulting from the decomposition replace the original clause, completeness is not preserved[2]. The introduction of functional terms may yield an exponential reduction of the proof's length measured in clause instances required for the proof [Baaz and Leitsch, 1990]. More recently, Baaz and Leitsch [1991] proved that even non-elementary cut-offs are possible.

As opposed to the application of a splitting rule to a clause which belongs to the original clause set, splitting a deduced clause has to be performed during run time without the intervention of a human being (at least if we assume an automated theorem prover). Implementing such advanced splitting rules in an automated theorem prover causes several difficulties due to the duplication of the clause set generated so far. The duplication of the clause set and the separation of the proof search have to be performed in order to preserve correctness. If we would use deduced clauses of one subproblem in order to solve the other then this would yield unsound effects. As an example, let C be a clause set and let $L_1 \vee C_1$ be the clause which is decomposed into subclauses L_1 and C_1. If $\neg L_1$ is deduced from $C \cup \{C_1\}$ and if we would use this clause in order to solve L_1 then $\Box$ would be obtained. But if we try to refute the original clause in a similar way, a tautology $L_1 \vee \neg L_1$ occurs. Another difficulty is the non-availability of heuristic knowledge (except in simple cases [Baaz and Leitsch, 1985]) controlling the application of the splitting rules. Therefore, in this paper we investigate another mechanism called generalized factorization which has similar effects on the search space like a splitting rule. Some of the different factorization rules behave like a an extended splitting rule, whereas others do not correspond to a splitting rule.

The main idea is to factorize clauses of the form $p(x, t_1) \vee p(y, t_2)$ to $p(x, m)$ whereas t_1, t_2 are ground terms and m is a new Skolem constant. Therefore, this generalized factorization extends the Herbrand universe of the original clause set. As a consequence, such a generalized factor can neither be generated by the usual resolution rule nor by the usual factorization rule. The introduction of the rule is based on the observation that two or more literals in a resolvent with the same predicate symbol and with the same sign are not unifiable due to different ground terms on the same position.

This kind of factorization is correct but not complete since the factor replaces the original clause. A refutation of $p(x, m)$ implies a refutation of $p(x, t_1) \vee p(y, t_2)$ but not vice versa. Extensions of this factorization can handle more complicated cases but then, new (functional) Skolem terms rather than Skolem constants possibly have to be introduced depending on the variable distribution in the clause. Applying this generalized factorization rule may yield a linear proof length[3] in contrast to an exponential length for the original problem.

In the following, some definitions are given in section 2. In section 3, we re-examine an example presented in [Baaz and Leitsch, 1990] in order to show what subproblems are generated and how they are determining the length of the proof. In section 4, generalized factorization rules are introduced producing correct but generalized factors of the original clause which cannot be produced with the usual factorization rule. Applying these factorization rules yields a linear proof length in the example presented in section 3. An extension of this example can be refuted applying generalized factorization while the splitting rule (without a 'look-ahead' for possible substitutions) fails. In section 5, we conclude.

---

[2]If the subclauses are simply added, sat–equivalence is preserved.

[3]The length of a proof is the number of clauses occurring in the proof.

2 Definitions and Notation

A *literal* is either an atom formula or a negated atom formula in first order logic. Let $|L|$ denote the atom of a literal L. We define the duality of quantifiers by

$$\sim q = \begin{cases} \forall, & \text{if } q = \exists \, ; \\ \exists, & \text{if } q = \forall \, . \end{cases}$$

A *clause* is a disjunction of literals. The empty clause is denoted by $\square$. The *literal set* of a clause $C = L_1 \vee \ldots \vee L_n$ is defined as the set of all literals occurring in the clause C. Here, $LS(C) = \{L_1, \ldots, L_n\}$. Furthermore, LS^{-1} is the inverse function which yields a clause for a given literal set (e. g. if $S = \{L_1, \ldots, L_m\}$ then $LS^{-1}(S) = L_1 \vee \ldots \vee L_m$).

If two or more literals (with the same sign) of a clause C have a most general unifier (mgu) σ, then $LS^{-1}(LS(C)\sigma)$ is called a *factor* of C.

Let C_1 and C_2 be two clauses (called parent clauses) with no variables in common. Let L_1 and L_2 be two literals with complementary signs in C_1 and C_2, respectively. If $|L_1|$ and $|L_2|$ have a most general unifier (mgu) σ, then the clause

$$LS^{-1}\left((LS(C_1\sigma) - L_1\sigma) \cup (LS(C_2\sigma) - L_2\sigma)\right)$$

is called a *binary resolvent* of C_1 and C_2. The literals L_1 and L_2 are called the literals resolved upon.

A *resolvent* of two (parent) clauses C_1 and C_2 is one of the following binary resolvents: a binary resolvent of C_1 and C_2, a binary resolvent of C_1 and a factor of C_2, a binary resolvent of a factor of C_1 and C_2, or a binary resolvent of a factor of C_1 and a factor of C_2.

Given a set $\mathcal{C}$ of clauses and a clause $C_0 \in \mathcal{C}$, a *linear deduction* of C_n from $\mathcal{C}$ with top clause C_0 is a deduction of the form shown below where

1. for $i = 0, 1, \ldots, n-1$, C_{i+1} is a resolvent of C_i (called a center clause) and B_i (called a side clause), and

2. each B_i is either in $\mathcal{C}$, or is a C_j for some $j, j < i$.

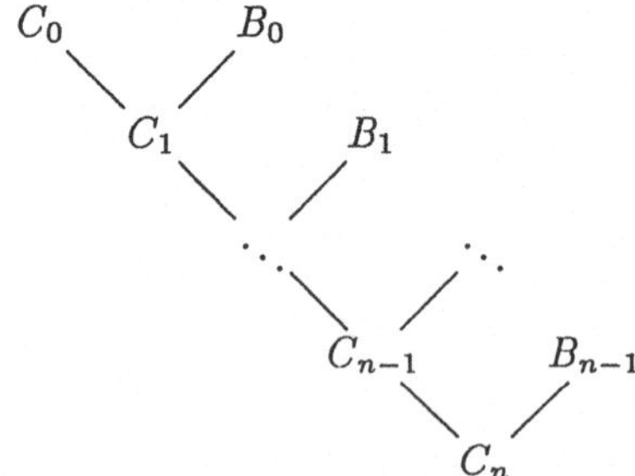

A *simple split*[4] decomposes a clause into independent subclauses which share no variables.

$$\frac{\mathcal{C} \cup \{C_1 \vee C_2\}}{\mathcal{C} \cup \{C_1\} \qquad \mathcal{C} \cup \{C_2\}} \; SP_1$$

---

[4] The rules should be read from top to bottom as follows. Instead of trying a refutation of $C_1 \vee C_2$ from $\mathcal{C}$, try two refutations of C_1 from $\mathcal{C}$, C_2 from $\mathcal{C}$. Refutations of both subproblems imply a refutation of the original problem.

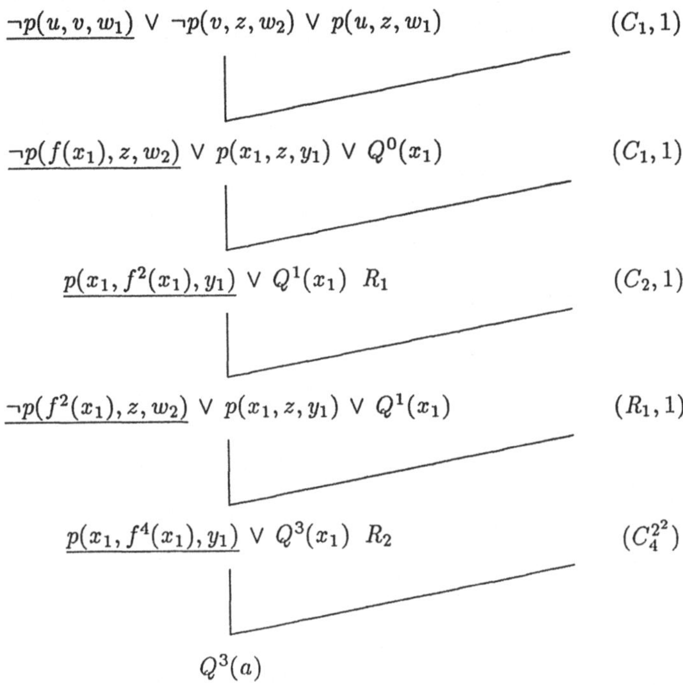

Figure 1: A linear deduction of $Q^3(a)$.

A simple split is only applicable if the clause is decomposable into variable independent subclauses. A more general splitting rule is based on the introduction of Skolem terms into the different subclauses. We consider the universal closure $UC(C)$ of a clause C. Let

$$(\forall x_1)\ldots(\forall x_n)[(\forall y_1)\ldots(\forall y_k)\, C_1 \vee (\forall z_1)\ldots(\forall z_l)\, C_2]$$

be the universal closure of a clause $C = C_1 \vee C_2$ and $x_1,\ldots,x_n$ are the variables occurring in both subclauses, $y_1,\ldots,y_k$ occur in C_1, and $z_1,\ldots,z_l$ occur in C_2. Let $q_i \in \{\exists,\forall\}$. The following rule SP_2 describes the split.

$$\frac{C \cup \{(\forall x_1)\ldots(\forall x_n)\,[(\forall y_1)\ldots(\forall y_k)\, C_1 \vee (\forall z_1)\ldots(\forall z_l)\, C_2]\}}{C \cup \{(q_1 x_1)\ldots(q_n x_n)\,(\forall y_1)\ldots(\forall y_k)\, C_1\} \qquad C \cup \{(\sim q_1 x_1)\ldots(\sim q_n x_n)\,(\forall z_1)\ldots(\forall z_l)\, C_2\}}\ SP_2$$

The application of this rule is shown in the next section.

3　An Example

Consider the following clause set $C_n = \{C_1, C_2, C_3, C_4^n, C_5^n\}$ taken from [Baaz and Leitsch, 1990]:

$$
\begin{aligned}
C_1 &= p(x, f(x), y) \vee q(y, f(y), x) \\
C_2 &= \neg p(u, v, w_1) \vee \neg p(v, z, w_2) \vee p(u, z, w_1)
\end{aligned}
$$

$$C_3 = \neg q(u, v, w_1) \lor \neg q(v, z, w_2) \lor q(u, z, w_1)$$
$$C_4^n = \neg p(a, f^{2^n}(a), z)$$
$$C_5^n = \neg q(a, f^{2^n}(a), z)$$

C_1 is split into two independent subclauses using rule SP_2 from the previous section in the following way. First, we consider $UC(C_1) = (\forall y)(\forall x)[p(x, f(x), y) \lor q(y, f(y), x)]$. In principal, there are four different possibilities for the quantifiers. Here, we choose the form

$$(\exists y)(\forall x)p(x, f(x), y) \lor (\forall y)(\exists x)q(y, f(y), x).$$

Skolemization yields the clause $p(x, f(x), m) \lor q(y, f(y), g(y))$ with the new Skolem terms m and $g(y)$. Decomposing the clause yields a decomposition of the clause set. C_n is unsatisfiable if both clause sets $(C_n - C_1) \cup \{p(x, f(x), m)\}$ and $(C_n - C_1) \cup \{q(y, f(y), g(y))\}$ are unsatisfiable. There is a (linear) resolution refutation which has length linear in n.

Let n be 2 and let

$$Q^k(x) = \bigvee_{i=0}^{k} q(y_{i+1}, f(y_{i+1}), f^i(x))$$

in this example. Let $f^0(t) = t$ for any term t. Figure 1 shows a linear deduction of $Q^3(a)$ with top clause C_2. For the $2n + 1$ linear resolution steps, we need $4n + 3$ different clause instances. The result is the clause $Q^3(a)$ which is an abbreviation for the clause

$$q(y_1, f(y_1), a) \lor q(y_2, f(y_2), f(a)) \lor q(y_3, f(y_3), f^2(a)) \lor q(y_4, f(y_4), f^3(a)).$$

Obviously, the q–literals are not unifiable because of their last argument. Although this clause is decomposable into 2^n independent subclauses by a simple split SP_1, the length of the whole refutation is exponential [Baaz and Leitsch, 1990]. Assuming the existence of a refutation of $Q^3(a)$, an application of a simple split separates the linear deduction Δ into deductions Δ_i, $(i = 1, \ldots, 2^n)$ corresponding to exactly one literal of $Q^3(a)$.

What we would need is a generalized factorization rule which reduces $Q^3(a)$ to $q(y_1, f(y_1), m)$ whereas m is a new constant symbol not occurring in the Herbrand universe of C. But this factorization step would be exponential w.r.t. the number of literals occurring in the clause because there are 2^n literals in $Q^{2^n-1}(a)$. In the following, we explain, how the number of occurrences of q–literals in the center clauses can be bound to a constant by subsequent applications of generalized factorization rules.

Consider the resolvent named R_2 in figure 1. Obviously, it is of the form

$$p(x, f^4(x), y_1) \lor q(y_1, f(y_1), x) \lor \underbrace{q(y_2, f(y_2), f(x)) \lor q(y_3, f(y_3), f^2(x)) \lor q(y_4, f(y_4), f^3(x))}_{\displaystyle \underbrace{q(y_2, f(y_2), f(r)) \lor q(y_3, f(y_3), f^2(r)) \lor q(y_4, f(y_4), f^3(r))}_{\displaystyle q(y_2, f(y_2), f(m))}}$$

The first two literals are 'connected' by the variables x and y_1, the others have only the variable x in common. As indicated in the picture, the latter q–literals may be made independent by the introduction of a new Skolem constant r (the mechanism is the same as performing a split). The different terms $r, f(r)$ and $f^2(r)$ are generalized to a new constant m. Since a refutation of $q(y_2, f(y_2), f(m))$ implies refutations for $q(y_{l+1}, f(y_{l+1}), f^l(r))$ $(l \geq 2)$, all literals of this form may be deleted. The result is a generalized factor of the form

$$p(x, f^4(x), y_1) \lor q(y_1, f(y_1), x) \lor q(y_2, f(y_2), f(m)).$$

This factor may be used as a side clause in subsequent deduction steps replacing the use of R_2[5]. If $n \geq 3$ then the last resolution step in figure 1 is replaced by a resolution against the first literal of C_2. The resulting resolvent is resolved with the current factor as a side clause yielding

$$p(x, f^8(x), y_1) \vee q(y_1, f(y_1), x) \vee q(y_2, f(y_2), f(m)) \vee q(y_3, f(y_3), f^4(x)) \vee q(y_4, f(y_4), f(m)).$$

Applying usual factorization and generalized factorization yields the clause

$$p(x, f^8(x), y_1) \vee q(y_1, f(y_1), x) \vee q(y_2, f(y_2), f(m_2)).$$

Further resolution steps are performed similarly. The maximal number of occurrences of q–literals is bound to four.

If all p–literals are resolved to $\Box$ then there are two remaining literals to solve, namely $q(y_1, f(y_1), a) \vee q(y_2, f(y_2), f(s))$. These literals are either factorized using $FACT_1$ (described in section 4) or the splitting rule SP_1 may be applied. Factorization yields the subproblem $q(y_1, f(y_1), o)$, whereas o is a new constant. Since the number of linear resolution steps required for resolving the p–literals to $\Box$ is linear in n, the number of applications of the generalized factorization rule is also linear in n. Taking into account the result that a refutation of $q(y_1, f(y_1), o)$ requires a number of resolution steps which is also linear in n, the whole problem can be solved with a number of resolution steps linear in n. Therefore, the number of clauses used in the proof is also linear in n.

As opposed to an application of SP_2, generalized factorization would neither introduce functional (Skolem) terms in this example nor would the clause set be split into several parts. However, several applications of the generalized factorization rule are requiered to get the reduction of the proof complexity. One application of SP_2 yields the decomposition of the original clause set. Generalized factorization rules are described in the next section.

4 Generalized Factorization

In this section, we introduce four factorization rules based on the introduction of Skolem terms. A short correctness proof for each rule is given for two reasons; the restrictions on variables become clear and it is shown that all rules are based on quantificational theorems introducing existential quantifiers. For all rules, c_1 denotes the rest of the clause and it may represent more than one literal. The symbol r is a variable for literals. For instance, $r(y_1, t_1)$ means that there are terms y_1 and t_1 occurring in r. Then, $r(y_1, t_1)$ may be of the form $p(g(y_1), y_1, t_1)$. The first generalized factorization rule $FACT_1$ is applicable to clauses of the form $c = r(y_1, t_1) \vee r(y_2, t_2) \vee c_1$ with t_1 as well as t_2 are ground terms. Neither y_1 nor y_2 occur in c_1.

$$\frac{C \cup \{r(y_1, t_1) \vee r(y_2, t_2) \vee c_1\}}{C \cup \{r(y_1, m) \vee c_1\}} \; FACT_1$$

The correctness of $FACT_1$ is proven by the following deduction: $r(y_1, t_1) \vee r(y_2, t_2) \vee c_1 \vdash_{PL}$ $(\exists z)((\forall y_1)r(y_1, z) \vee (\forall y_2)r(y_2, z)) \vee c_1 \vdash_{PL} (\exists z)(\forall y_1)r(y_1, z) \vee c_1$. The satisfiability of $C_1 = C \cup \{r(y_1, t_1) \vee r(y_2, t_2) \vee c_1\}$ implies the satisfiability of $C_2 = C \cup \{(\exists z)(\forall y_1)r(y_1, z) \vee c_1\}$. C_2 is sat–equivalent to $C \cup \{r(y_1, m) \vee c_1\}$.

Clause $r(y_1, t_1) \vee r(y_2, t_2) \vee c_1$ may be decomposed by a simple split SP_1 yielding three subproblems $(C - c) \cup \{r(y_1, t_1)\}$, $(C - c) \cup \{r(y_2, t_2)\}$, and $(C - c) \cup \{c_1\}$. As an alternative to the decomposition, $FACT_1$ may be tried (i. e. if a refutation cannot be found within a given

---

[5]A split would also be possible. If $q(y_2, f(y_2), f(m))$ is refutable, we may use the unit clause $\neg q(m_1, f(m_1), f(z))$ as a lemma (m_1 is a new constant).

time limit or if the problem decomposes to a large number of subproblems like in the example above). A simple split can be easily incorporated into $FACT_1$.

$$\frac{C \cup \{r(y_1, t_1) \vee r(y_2, t_2) \vee c_1\}}{C \cup \{r(y_1, m)\} \qquad C \cup \{c_1\}}$$

Applying $FACT_1$, the clause which has to be factorized has to be decomposable into independent subclauses. In the next rule, a clause is considered which is not decomposable into independent subclauses because of n variables (denoted by a variable vector $\vec{x}$). Here, a Skolem term is introduced. It is not sufficient to generalize t_1 and t_2 to a common constant not occurring elsewhere in the clause set. There is a short counter example. Consider the clause $s(x, t_1) \vee s(x, t_2)$. Assume, there is a single unit clause $\neg s(g(y), y)$ and t_1, t_2 are different ground terms. There is no deduction of $\square$ from these two clauses because t_1 and t_2 are not unifiable. But if t_1 and t_2 are replaced by the same constant m then the unit clause $s(x, m)$ occurs. A single resolution step between $s(x, m)$ and $\neg s(g(y), y)$ yields $\square$. The introduction of a Skolem term $h(x)$ prevents the unification and therefore, no resolution step is possible. This factorization rule is as follows.

$$\frac{C \cup \{r(\vec{x}, t_1) \vee r(\vec{x}, t_2) \vee c_1(\vec{x})\}}{C \cup \{r(\vec{x}, h(\vec{x})) \vee c_1(\vec{x})\}} \; FACT_2$$

$FACT_2$ is correct because the formula $(\forall \vec{x})(r(\vec{x}, t_1) \vee r(\vec{x}, t_2) \vee c_1(\vec{x})) \rightarrow (\forall \vec{x})((\exists z) r(\vec{x}, z) \vee c_1(\vec{x}))$ is valid. $FACT_1$ and $FACT_2$ factorize only literals where the usual factorization rule is not applicable due to a clash of two ground terms.

Factorization may be extended to the case where the occur check prevents a successful unification. Let $\vec{t}$ be a term vector and the terms do neither contain variables from the variable vectors $\vec{x}, \vec{y}$ nor the variable z. Then the rule is as follows.

$$\frac{C \cup \{r(\vec{x}, z) \vee r(\vec{y}, f(\vec{t}, z))\}}{C \cup \{r(\vec{y}, f(\vec{t}, m))\}} \; FACT_3$$

The correctness of $FACT_3$ is shown by an application of the constant introduction rule of [Baaz and Leitsch, 1985]. Thus, we get $r(\vec{x}, z) \vee r(\vec{y}, f(\vec{t}, m))$ from $r(\vec{x}, z) \vee r(\vec{y}, f(\vec{t}, z))$. Ordinary factorization yields $r(\vec{y}, f(\vec{t}, m))$.

As opposed to $FACT_3$, $FACT_4$ handles additional literals in the clause. All parts of the clause depend on each other due to a common variable. The factorization rule is as follows.

$$\frac{C \cup \{r(\vec{x}, z) \vee r(\vec{y}, f(\vec{t}, z)) \vee c_1(z)\}}{C \cup \{r(\vec{x}, m) \vee c_1(z)\}} \; FACT_4$$

The application of the constant introduction rule to $r(\vec{x}, z) \vee r(\vec{y}, f(\vec{t}, z)) \vee c_1(z)$ yields $r(\vec{x}, m) \vee r(\vec{y}, f(\vec{t}, m)) \vee c_1(z)$. Grounding all variables in t and applying $FACT_1$, we get $r(\vec{x}, m) \vee c_1(z)$.

In both r–literals, the variable z may occur in a term if both variables have a common prefix (e. g. in $r(\vec{x}, g(g(z)))$ and in $r(\vec{y}, g(g(g(f(\vec{t}, z)))))$) '$g(g($' is that prefix).

As mentioned above, the rules $FACT_1$ and $FACT_4$ are sufficient to refute the clause set of the example in section 3 with length linear in n. Only a Skolem constant is introduced in this case.

Example 4.1 Test problem 59 in [Pelletier, 1986]
Consider the following clause set $C = \{C_1, C_2, C_3\}$.

$$
\begin{aligned}
C_1 &= \neg p(x) \lor \neg p(f(x)) \\
C_2 &= p(f(x)) \lor p(x) \\
C_3 &= \neg p(x) \lor p(f(x))
\end{aligned}
$$

C_2 is factorized yielding $p(f(m))$. Resolving the second literal of C_3 against the second literal of C_1 with an additional ordinary factorization step yield $\neg p(x)$. $\square$ is deduced immediately by a further resolution step between $\neg p(x)$ and $p(f(m))$. If no factorization rule is applied, the refutation of the original clause set is one step longer.

An application of SP_2 to clause C_2 is also possible. The subclauses are either $p(f(m))$ and $p(x)$ or $p(f(x))$ and $p(m)$. In the former case, $p(f(m))$ is refuted in the same way like before and the refutation of $p(x)$ takes two resolution steps. In the latter case, $p(m)$ is refuted in a similar way like $p(f(m))$ and $p(f(x))$ is refuted in two steps.

Example 4.2
Let the clause set be $C = \{C_1, C_2, C_3, C_4, C_5, C_6\}$ with

$$
\begin{aligned}
C_1 &= p(x) \lor p(f(x)) \\
C_2 &= \neg p(x) \lor \neg p(f^n(x)) \\
C_3 &= p(f(x)) \lor \neg p(f^n(x)) \\
C_4 &= \neg p(x) \lor p(f^{n-1}(x)) \\
C_5 &= \neg p(x) \lor p(f^{n+1}(x)) \\
C_6 &= p(x) \lor \neg p(f^{n+1}(x))
\end{aligned}
$$

The clauses C_3 to C_6 are dependent from C_1 and C_2. Generating all possible resolvents of C_1 and C_2 yields the dependent clauses. C_1 is factorized to $C_1' = p(f(m))$ as well as C_2 is factorized to $C_2' = \neg p(f^n(m))$. C' denotes the clause set $\{C_1', C_2, C_3, C_4, C_5, C_6\}$ and C'' denotes the clause set $\{C_1, C_2', C_3, C_4, C_5, C_6\}$. Table 1 summarizes run time measurements for refutations of C, C', and C'' for different n obtained with SETHEO [Letz *et al.*, 1991; Schumann *et al.*, 1989]. The different columns have the following meaning. Depth is the depth of the search tree plus one. The number of inferences forming the proof is denoted by '# of inf'. The number of failed unifications tried during the search for the proof is denoted by '# of failed'. The field 'instructions' refers to the total number of abstract machine instructions executed during the search for the proof. Time denotes the run time on a SUN SPARC station 1+[6] as presented by SETHEO.

Note that the introduction of a new constant and the deletion of a literal decreases the number of possible inferences. All possible resolutions with the first literal of clause C_2 are no longer possible as well as resolutions between C_2' and the second literal of clause C_5. If we factorize C_1 to $C_1' = p(f(m))$ then no inferences are possible between C_1' and the second literals of C_2, C_3, and C_6. Furthermore, all resolutions with the first literal of C_1 are no longer possible.

Example 4.3
Reconsider the example in section 3 and replace the clauses C_4^n by C_{41}^n and C_5^n by C_{51}^n with

$$
\begin{aligned}
C_{41}^n &= \neg p(f(a), f^{2^n+1}(a), f(z)) \\
C_{51}^n &= \neg q(f(a), f^{2^n+1}(a), f(z)).
\end{aligned}
$$

---

[6]The run time in the first row is 0 due to the inaccuracy in time measurement precision.

clause set	n	depth	# of inf	# of failed	instructions	time
C	4	7	11	6864	12631	283 ms
C'	4	5	7	287	662	0 ms
C''	4	7	6	773	1570	33 ms
C	6	9	15	246538	452045	18.8 s
C'	6	6	9	3045	6627	200 ms
C''	6	9	8	12184	24579	850 ms
C	8	11	19	8869604	16261011	1154 s
C'	8	7	11	16597	35834	1.7 s
C''	8	11	10	191365	387658	22.1 s
C	10	–	–	–	–	–
C'	10	8	13	216167	462182	31.4 s
C''	10	13	12	3000358	6099089	521 s

Table 1: Measurements for refutations of C, C', and C''

The Herbrand universe is not changed due to these replacements. Without an additional 'look-ahead' for possible substitutions, the top–level split is no longer possible[7]. The reason is the inability to unify a newly introduced Skolem term with the term $f(z)$. Using generalized factorization, a similar deduction occurs in this example (compared with the deduction in figure 1). The only difference is the last clause containing two q–literals. The clause $q(y_1, f(y_1), a) \vee q(y_1, f(y_1), f(m))$ rewrites to $q(y_1, f(y_1), f(a)) \vee q(y_2, f(y_2), f(m))$ which is replaced by $q(y_1, f(y_1), f(m))$. The last clause is refutable.

5 Conclusion

We have introduced several new factorization rules based on the introduction of Skolem terms which may exponentially reduce the length of a proof. Some examples have been considered which show the increase of a prover's performance if these factorization rules are used. The application of a generalized factorization rule introduces new Skolem terms restricting the search space of an automated theorem prover similarly to the application of a splitting rule (refer to [Egly, 1990] for results). Due to this introduction, the resolution process terminates frequently in the case of a satisfiable clause set. Another advantage of the factorization rule in comparison to a splitting rule is that it is unnecessary to decompose the clause set. Furthermore, the number of literals occurring in the factorized clause decreases. This generalized factorization rule will be implemented in a prover which is based on a connection calculus [Neugebauer and Schaub, 1991] i. e. a calculus based on the connection method [Bibel, 1987].

6 Acknowledgments

The author would like to thank Wolfgang Bibel, Torsten Schaub, Josef Schneeberger, and the two referees for their constructive criticism and for their useful comments on an earlier draft of this paper.

---

[7]To be fair, there is such a possibility to combine a split with a 'look-ahead search' for possible substitutions [Baaz and Leitsch, 1989].

References

[Baaz and Leitsch, 1985] M. Baaz and A. Leitsch. Die Anwendung starker Reduktionsregeln in automatischen Beweisen. *Proc. of the Austrian Acad. of Science II*, 194:287–307, 1985. In German.

[Baaz and Leitsch, 1989] M. Baaz and A. Leitsch. A Strong Reduction Method for Clause Logic. Technical Report 8901, Technische Universität Wien, Institut für Computersprachen, Abteilung für Anwendungen der Formalen Logik, Getreidemarkt 9, A-1060 WIEN, Austria, 1989.

[Baaz and Leitsch, 1990] M. Baaz and A. Leitsch. A Strong Problem Reduction Method Based on Function Introduction. In *ISSAC 90*, pages 30–37. ACM–Press, 1990.

[Baaz and Leitsch, 1991] M. Baaz and A. Leitsch. Complexity of Resolution Proofs and Function Introduction. Technical Report TR–9101, Technische Universität Wien, Institut für Computersprachen, Abteilung für Anwendungen der Formalen Logik, Getreidemarkt 9, A-1060 WIEN, Austria, 1991.

[Bibel, 1987] W. Bibel. *Automated Theorem Proving*. Vieweg Verlag, Braunschweig, second edition, 1987.

[Bledsoe, 1971] W. W. Bledsoe. Splitting and Reduction Heuristics in Automatic Theorem Proving. *Artificial Intelligence*, 2:57–78, 1971.

[Chang and Lee, 1973] C. L. Chang and R. C. Lee. *Symbolic Logic and Mechanical Theorem Proving*. Academic Press, New York, 1973.

[Egly, 1990] U. Egly. Problem-Reduction Methods and Clause Splitting in Automated Theorem Proving. Master's thesis, Technische Universität Wien, Institut für Computersprachen, Abteilung für Anwendungen der Formalen Logik, Getreidemarkt 9, A–1060 WIEN, 1990.

[Letz *et al.*, 1991] R. Letz, J. Schumann, S. Bayerl, and W. Bibel. SETHEO — A high-performance theorem prover for first-order logic. *Journal of Automated Reasoning*, 1991.

[Neugebauer and Schaub, 1991] G. Neugebauer and T. Schaub. A pool-based connection calculus. Technical Report AIDA-91-2, FG Intellektik, FB Informatik, TH Darmstadt, Alexanderstraße 10, D–6100 Darmstadt, January 1991.

[Pelletier, 1986] F. J. Pelletier. Seventy-Five Problems for Testing Automatic Theorem Provers. *Journal of Automated Reasoning*, 2:191–216, 1986.

[Schumann *et al.*, 1989] J. Schumann, N. Trapp, and M. van der Koelen. SETHEO/PARTHEO Users Manual. Report FKI-121-89, Institut für Informatik, Technische Universität München, Arcisstr. 21, D–8000 München 2, Germany, December 1989.

On Exploiting the Structure of Martin-Löf's Theory of Types*

Andrew Ireland

Department of Artificial Intelligence
University of Edinburgh
Edinburgh, EH1 1HN, Scotland.

Abstract

Program synthesis in Martin-Löf's Theory of Types is a theorem proving activity. We demonstrate how the rich structure of the theory may be exploited in the automation of this activity. Basic properties of data type constructors are shown to exhibit a general structure in the way in which they are expressed and derived. A proof procedure for negation is developed based upon these properties. As a consequence our proof procedure may be extended uniformly to incorporate new data types.

1 Introduction

Martin-Löf's Theory of Types [Mar82, NPS90] is a rich logic in which provably correct programs can be synthesized. Specifications and programs are expressed within the theory as types and objects respectively. Proof corresponds to demonstrating that a type is non-empty. Because of the constructive nature of the logic this involves constructing an object that inhabits the type. Program synthesis within the theory is therefore a theorem proving activity. This paper investigates how the rich structure of the theory can be exploited in the automation of this activity. In particular we develop a proof procedure for negation based upon general properties of data type constructors.

We have been greatly influenced by the work of Backhouse in particular his explanation of the rules of Type Theory[Bac86]. We make use of his terminology and draw upon many of his notational conventions[BCM89].

2 Deriving properties of data types

Given an arbitrary data type constructor we show how uniqueness, closure and cancellation properties may be expressed within the theory. These properties are exploited

---

*The work described here was funded by the *Carnegie Trust for the Universities of Scotland* and was carried out at Stirling University in partial fulfilment of the requirements for the Ph.D. degree.

in the development of our proof procedure for negation presented in §3. For each property, inspection of the corresponding derivation reveals a general structure. This general structure provides the basis for automating the derivation of these properties. A detailed account of this work appears in [Ire89].

Uniqueness properties

An uniqueness property states that distinct object constructors build distinct object expressions. Consider, for instance, the uniqueness property for the *List* type[1]

$$(\forall h : T)(\forall t : List(T))\neg(h :: t =_{List(T)} nil)$$

Let Θ denote an arbitrary data type constructor with k introduction rules, defining canonical object constructors $\theta_1, \ldots, \theta_k$, then for each pair of distinct constructors θ_i and θ_j there exists an uniqueness property expressed by the type[2]

$$(\forall p_{i1} : B_{i1}) \ldots (\forall p_{in_i} : B_{in_i})(\forall p_{j1} : B_{j1}) \ldots (\forall p_{jn_j} : B_{jn_j})\neg(\theta_i(\bar{p}_i) =_{\Theta(\bar{A})} \theta_j(\bar{p}_j))$$

Negation is not a primitive of the theory; $\neg A$ is defined as $A \to false$. In general to prove an uniqueness property we assume $(\theta_i(\bar{p}_i) =_{\Theta(\bar{A})} \theta_j(\bar{p}_j))$ and derive a contradiction which corresponds to showing that the type *false* is inhabited. Such a proof exhibits a general structure which involves deriving an intermediate equality judgement of the form[3]

$$elim_\Theta(\theta_i(\bar{p}_i), z_1, \ldots, z_k) = elim_\Theta(\theta_j(\bar{p}_j), z_1, \ldots, z_k) : U_1$$

where $elim_\Theta$ is the noncanonical object constructor introduced by the Θ-elimination rule. We take z_i to be the abstraction $[\bar{x}]true$ and we take all the other z's, including in particular z_j (z_i and z_j are the only relevant ones), to be $[\bar{y}]false$. Normalizing both sides of this equality judgement yields the required contradiction $true = false : U_1$.

Closure properties

A universal closure property expresses completely the structure of the canonical objects defined by a type constructor. For instance, the universal closure property for the *List* type may be expressed as

$$(\forall x : List(T))((x =_{List(T)} nil) \vee (\exists h : T)(\exists t : List(T))(x =_{List(T)} h :: t))$$

In general the closure property associated with an arbitrary data type constructor Θ may be expressed by the type[4]

$$(\forall x : \Theta(\bar{A}))P_1(x) \vee \cdots \vee P_k(x)$$

Note that the ith disjunct ($1 \leq i \leq k$) expresses the structure of the canonical constructor θ_i. Proof is by induction on x giving rise to k cases. We assume that θ_i has

---

[1]The equality type $(a =_A b)$ expresses the proposition "a and b are equal objects in the type A".
[2]$\bar{A}$ is an abbreviation for a vector of variables.
[3]U_1 denotes the "type of types", the first in a cumulative hierarchy of universes.
[4]Note that $k = 1$ is a simplification of the general case.

n_i associated introduction variables $u_{i1}, \ldots, u_{in_i}$, where the type of u_{ij} is B_{ij}. Proof of the ith case involves constructing an injection into the type $P_1(\theta_i(\bar{u}_i)) \vee \cdots \vee P_k(\theta_i(\bar{u}_i))$, where $P_i(\theta_i(\bar{u}_i))$ denotes the type

$$(\exists a_{i1} : B_{i1}) \ldots (\exists a_{in_i} : B_{in_i})(\theta_i(u_{i1}, \ldots, u_{in_i}) =_{\Theta(\bar{A})} \theta_i(a_{i1}, \ldots, a_{in_i}))$$

Construction of an object in this type takes place in the context of a list of assumptions C_i which is generated as follows: Firstly, we introduce assumptions of the form

$$u_{ir} : B_{ir}$$

where r ranges over the introduction variables associated with θ_i. Secondly, we introduce assumptions of the form

$$v_{is} : P_1(u_{is}) \vee \cdots \vee P_k(u_{is})$$

where s ranges over the recursive introduction variables associated with θ_i. Recursive introduction variables necessarily have type $\Theta(\bar{A})$, so for each s, B_{is} is $\Theta(\bar{A})$. From this context a judgement is constructed of the form[5]

$$\|[C_i$$
$$\triangleright \ \langle u_{i1}, \ldots \langle u_{in_i}, eq \rangle \ldots \rangle : (\exists a_{i1} : B_{i1}) \ldots (\exists a_{in_i} : B_{in_i})(\theta_i(u_{i1}, \ldots, u_{in_i}) =_{\Theta(\bar{A})} \theta_i(a_{i1}, \ldots, a_{in_i}))$$
$$]\|$$

Denoting the ith injection operator by $inject_i$ then the process described above generates k judgements of the form

$$\|[C_i \triangleright \ inject_i(\langle u_{i1}, \ldots \langle u_{in_i}, eq \rangle \ldots \rangle)) : P_1(\theta_i(\bar{u}_i)) \vee \cdots \vee P_k(\theta_i(\bar{u}_i))]\|$$

By an application of the Θ-elimination rule followed by $\vee$-introduction the closure property is established:

$$\lambda x.closure_\Theta(x) : (\forall x : \Theta(\bar{A}))P_1(x) \vee \cdots \vee P_k(x)$$

Note that $closure_\Theta(x)$ is an abbreviation for the object $elim_\Theta(x, z_1, \ldots, z_k)$ where z_i denotes the abstraction $[\bar{u}_i, \bar{v}_i]inject_i(\langle u_{i1}, \ldots \langle u_{in_i}, eq \rangle \ldots \rangle)$.

Cancellation properties

For two non-empty lists to be equal implies that the first element from each list are also equal. Such a cancellation property may be expressed by the type

$$(\forall a : T)(\forall c : T)(\forall b : List(T))(\forall d : List(T))((a :: b =_{List(T)} c :: d) \rightarrow (a =_T c))$$

In general θ_i has n_i associated cancellation properties expressed by the type

$$(\forall p_{i1} : B_{i1}) \ldots (\forall p_{in_i} : B_{in_i})(\forall q_{i1} : B_{i1}) \ldots (\forall q_{in_i} : B_{in_i})(\theta_i(\bar{p}_i) =_{\Theta(\bar{A})} \theta_i(\bar{q}_i)) \rightarrow (p_{ij} =_{B_{ij}} q_{ij})$$

where j ranges over the introduction variables associated with θ_i. The proof of a cancellation property, like the proof of an uniqueness property, exhibits a general structure.

---

[5]The constant eq is the trivial construction demonstrating equality.

3   A proof procedure for negation

In the context of program synthesis a proof of a negation has no interesting computational content. Formally verified synthesis proofs [Chi87, Ire89] have shown that a significant proportion of the overall proof effort may be taken up with proving negations. Our approach to proving negations is based upon a process of *reduction* and *decomposition* at the level of equalities[6]. If successful this process gives rise to contradiction(s). In Type Theory contradictions arise either at the level of propositions or through the surrounding context. Propositional contradictions are based upon uniqueness properties, whereas contextual contradictions rely on assumptions. Backward propagation of the contradictions yields a proof of the required negation.

3.1   Derived rules for reasoning about equalities

A reduction corresponds to either a *case separation* or an *evaluation* while a decomposition results in the breaking down of data objects into their component parts. Each operation is formalized as a set of derived rules of inference. We present schemata and outline the basis for automating the construction of these rules.

Case separation rules

In order to illustrate case separation, consider the following equality type

$$\alpha(x@y) =_{List(T)} \beta$$

where @ is the list concatenation operator. Note that α, β and y denote arbitrary terms, and x is a variable covered by an assumption $x : List(T)$. Case separation on x yields a disjunction which may be expressed as

$$(\alpha(nil@y) =_{List(T)} \beta) \vee (\exists h : T)(\exists t : List(T))(\alpha(h :: t@y) =_{List(T)} \beta)$$

The general form of the derived case separation rule is:

$$
\begin{array}{ll}
\text{P1} & \|[w : \Theta(\bar{A}) \triangleright (\alpha(w) =_T \beta)\ type]\| \\
\text{P2} & x : \Theta(\bar{A}) \\
\text{P3} & r : (\alpha(x) =_T \beta)
\end{array}
$$

$$\rule{6cm}{0.4pt} \quad \Theta\text{-case}$$

$$case_\Theta(x) : R_1 \vee \ldots \vee R_k$$

P1 is a well-formedness premise while P2 specifies the object on which case separation is to be carried out. P3 is the judgement within which the case separation is to be performed. Establishing the conclusion to the rule, given the premises, corresponds to building a method which constructs an injection into $R_1 \vee \ldots \vee R_k$ from an arbitrary object in $\Theta(\bar{A})$. The forms of $R_1, \ldots, R_k$ will be discussed shortly. Consider the injection into the ith disjunct. The injected value belongs to the type R_i, the structure of which is

---

[6]The approach generalizes by the use of goal transformations which correspond to the subset of DeMorgan's laws for the logicals and quantifiers which are constructively valid.

determined by the introduction rule for θ_i. Assuming that θ_i is a non-nullary constructor with n_i associated introduction variables then R_i will denote the type

$$(\exists a_{i1} : B_{i1}) \ldots (\exists a_{in_i} : B_{in_i})(\alpha(\theta_i(a_{i1} \ldots a_{in_i})) =_T \beta)$$

To construct an object in this type we introduce an assumption of the form

$$y_i : (\exists a_{i1} : B_{i1}) \ldots (\exists a_{in_i} : B_{in_i})(x =_{\Theta(\bar{A})} \theta_i(a_{i1}, \ldots, a_{in_i}))$$

Using the premises the required value of the injection is derived with the use of $\exists$-elimination, substitution and $\exists$-introduction:

$$|[y_i : (\exists a_{i1} : B_{i1}) \ldots (\exists a_{in_i} : B_{in_i})(x =_{\Theta(\bar{A})} \theta_i(a_{i1}, \ldots, a_{in_i}))$$
$$\triangleright \ \langle fst(y_i), \langle \ldots \langle fst(\ldots snd(y_i) \ldots), r \rangle \ldots \rangle \rangle$$
$$: (\exists a_{i1} : B_{i1}) \ldots (\exists a_{in_i} : B_{in_i})(\alpha(\theta_i(a_{i1}, \ldots, a_{in_i})) =_T \beta)$$
$$]|$$

Denoting the type of y_i by $P_i(x)$, then the process described above generates k judgements of the form

$$|[y_i : P_i(x) \triangleright \ inject_i(\langle fst(y_i), \langle \ldots \langle fst(\ldots snd(y_i) \ldots), r \rangle \ldots \rangle \rangle)) : R_1 \vee \ldots \vee R_k]|$$

To combine these k judgements a function is required which yields an injection into $P_1(x) \vee \ldots \vee P_k(x)$, given an arbitrary object x in $\Theta(\bar{A})$. The universal closure property for Θ, as defined in §2, provides such a function. By $\forall$- and $\vee$-elimination the required conclusion is established. Note that in the conclusion to the derived rule $case_\Theta(x)$ is an abbreviation for the object $elim_\vee(closure_\Theta(x), z_1, \ldots, z_k)$ where z_i denotes the abstraction $[y_i]inject_i(\langle fst(y_i), \langle \ldots \langle fst(\ldots snd(y_i) \ldots), r \rangle \ldots \rangle \rangle)$.

Evaluation rules

Evaluation in the context of the equality type

$$\alpha((h :: t)@y) =_{List(T)} \beta$$

yields

$$\alpha(h :: (t@y)) =_{List(T)} \beta$$

The general form of the evaluation rule is:

P1 $|[x : \Theta(\bar{A}); y : D(x) \triangleright \ (\alpha(y) =_T \beta) \ type]|$

P2 $b_{i1} : B_{i1} \ldots b_{in_i} : B_{in_i}$

P3 $|[C_1 \triangleright \ z_1(\bar{u}_1, \bar{v}_1) : D(\theta_1(\bar{u}_1))]|$

         $\vdots$

         $|[C_k \triangleright \ z_k(\bar{u}_k, \bar{v}_k) : D(\theta_k(\bar{u}_k))]|$

P4 $r : (\alpha(elim_\Theta(\theta_i(\bar{b}_i), z_1, \ldots, z_k)) =_T \beta)$

$$\frac{}{eval_{\theta_i} : (\alpha(z_i(\bar{b}_i, \bar{w}_i)) =_T \beta)} \quad \Theta\text{-}eval_{\theta_i}$$

where $\bar{w}_i$ is the vector of expressions corresponding to the step cases in a recursive definition. There is a direct correspondence between $\bar{v}_i$ and $\bar{w}_i$ which is explained in [Bac86]. The premises of the rule are divided into four parts. P1 is a well-formedness premise. P2 and P3 correspond to the major[7] premises of the computation rule for θ_i. The assumption lists $C_1, \ldots, C_k$ are constructed in the manner described in [Bac86] for elimination rules. P4 denotes the equality in which the evaluation is to be performed. The required conclusion is derived as follows: From the premises the evaluation of the subexpression $elim_\Theta(\theta_i(\bar{b}_i), z_1, \ldots, z_k)$ is achieved using the computation rule for θ_i. By substitution the resulting judgement taken together with a reflexive instance of P1 yields the equality judgement

$$(\alpha(elim_\Theta(\theta_i(\bar{b}_i), z_1, \ldots, z_k)) =_T \beta) = (\alpha(z_i(\bar{b}_i, \bar{w}_i)) =_T \beta)$$

This judgement and P4, by an application of the type equality rule, yields the required conclusion.

Decomposition rules

A decomposition is possible when both sides of an equality are non-atomic canonical forms with matching outer structure. For example, consider the following equality type

$$a :: b =_{List(T)} c :: d$$

By decomposition this equality yields a conjunction of the form

$$(a =_T c) \wedge (b =_{List(T)} d)$$

The general form of the decomposition rule is:

$$
\begin{array}{ll}
\text{P1} & b_{i1} : B_{i1} \ldots b_{in_i} : B_{in_i} \\
\text{P2} & d_{i1} : B_{i1} \ldots d_{in_i} : B_{in_i} \\
\text{P3} & r : (\theta_i(\bar{b}_i) =_{\Theta(\bar{A})} \theta_i(\bar{d}_i))
\end{array}
$$
$$\rule{6cm}{0.4pt} \quad \Theta\text{-}decomp_{\theta_i}$$
$$decomp_{\theta_i} : (b_{i1} =_{B_{i1}} d_{i1}) \wedge \cdots \wedge (b_{in_i} =_{B_{in_i}} d_{in_i})$$

The premises are divided into three parts. P1 and P2 correspond to the major premises of the introduction rule for θ_i. P3 denotes the equality in which the decomposition is performed. If θ_i has n_i associated introduction variables, then there exist n_i cancellation properties as described in §2. These cancellation properties, taken together with the premises, give rise to n_i judgements each of which is based upon an equality type of the form $(b_{ij} =_{B_{ij}} d_{ij})$. The required conclusion follows by n_{i-1} applications of $\wedge$-introduction.

3.2 Searching for contradictions

Our proof procedure builds upon the rules derived above for reasoning about equalities. The application of the derived rules is controlled by a procedure called *analyse*.

---

[7] A major premise is any premise which is not a well-formedness premise.

Given a judgement of the form $\|[B \rhd r : (\alpha =_T \beta)]\|$ *analyse* constructs a judgement of the form $\|[B \rhd r' : P]\|$ where $(\alpha =_T \beta) \to P$. This construction process works in outline as follows: If either α or β is noncanonical then a reduction is performed. If a noncanonical expression contains a free variable in its recursive argument position then a case separation is performed. A noncanonical expression is open to evaluation if a canonical expression appears in the recursive argument position. If both α and β are non-atomic canonical forms with matching outer structure, then a decomposition is performed. Note that reductions may introduce choice points into the search space.

The overall search for a proof is controlled by a procedure called *contra-chk*. Assuming we wish to prove $\neg(\alpha =_T \beta)$ in the context of a list of assumptions C, then *contra-chk* first constructs the trivial judgement

$$\|[C; \ r : (\alpha =_T \beta) \rhd r : (\alpha =_T \beta)]\|$$

to which *analyse* is applicable. Assuming that *analyse* constructs the judgement

$$\|[C; \ r : (\alpha =_T \beta) \rhd r' : P]\|$$

then *contra-chk* is recursively applied to P and C. In general P will take the form of a conjunction or a disjunction. Note that in the case of a conjunction only one of the conjuncts needs to be shown to be contradictory. A case separation will usually generate existentially quantified equalities. For instance, consider the equality $(\alpha(x) =_T \beta)$ where the variable x is of type $\Theta(\bar{A})$. Case separation on x will, in general, generate a disjunction with k disjuncts where the ith disjunct takes the form

$$(\exists a_{i1} : B_{i1}) \ldots (\exists a_{in_i} : B_{in_i})(\alpha(\theta_i(a_{i1}, \ldots, a_{in_i})) =_T \beta)$$

Note that *analyse* is not directly applicable to this type because of the proof obligations introduced by the existential quantification. This problem is overcome by a *pre-analysis* step which results in the the initial context being extended with an assumption of the form

$$z : (\exists a_{i1} : B_{i1}) \ldots (\exists a_{in_i} : B_{in_i})(\alpha(\theta_i(a_{i1}, \ldots, a_{in_i})) =_T \beta)$$

thus enabling the search for a contradiction to proceed with the equality

$$\alpha(\theta_i(fst(z), \ldots, fst(\ldots snd(z) \ldots))) =_T \beta$$

As mentioned earlier the process of proving the initial negated equality involves the backward propagation of the contradictions identified by the *contra-chk* procedure. Formalizing this process gives rise to four derived rules similar to the *modus tollens* rule of inference.

3.3 An example

We illustrate the use of our proof procedure through its application to the proof of a negation arising from the synthesis of a table look-up function, the details of which can be found in [Ire89].

Program specification

Our table look-up function is specified by the type

$$(\forall a : A)(\forall l : List(A \times B))Member(a, l, A, B) \vee \neg Member(a, l, A, B) \qquad (1)$$

where A and B denote arbitrary types in U_1. $Member$[8] is defined as

$$Member \equiv [a, l, A, B](\exists h : List(A \times B))(\exists t : List(A \times B))(\exists b : B)$$
$$(h@(\langle a, b \rangle :: t) =_{List(A \times B)} l)$$

Proof of a negation

In the course of satisfying (1) a goal type of the form

$$\neg Member(a, u :: v, A, B) \qquad (2)$$

is generated in a context which includes the following assumptions:

$$x : \neg(a =_A fst(u))$$
$$y : \neg Member(a, v, A, B)$$

By the transformations mentioned earlier (2) may be reduced to

$$\neg(h@(\langle a, b \rangle :: t) =_{List(A \times B)} u :: v) \qquad (3)$$

In addition to the assumptions for h, t and b the context is extended with the following assumption:

$$y' : (\forall h' : List(A \times B))(\forall t' : List(A \times B))(\forall b' : B)\neg(h'@(\langle a, b' \rangle :: t') =_{List(A \times B)} v)$$

(3) is of the required negated equality form and by case separation on h a disjunction is generated giving rise to the following two types:

$$nil@(\langle a, b \rangle :: t) =_{List(A \times B)} u :: v \qquad (4)$$
$$(\exists p : A \times B)(\exists q : List(A \times B))((p :: q)@(\langle a, b \rangle :: t) =_{List(A \times B)} u :: v) \qquad (5)$$

Evaluation reduces (4) to

$$\langle a, b \rangle :: t =_{List(A \times B)} u :: v \qquad (6)$$

and by decomposition (6) is reduced to a conjunction, where the left conjunct

$$\langle a, b \rangle =_{A \times B} u$$

taken together with the assumption denoted by x gives rise to a contradiction. To deal with (5) the existential quantification is first removed introducing the assumption

$$z : (\exists p : A \times B)(\exists q : List(A \times B))((p :: q)@(\langle a, b \rangle :: t) =_{List(A \times B)} u :: v)$$

---

[8]This specification of *Member* would be improved with the use of the subset type. However, the subset type was not supported by the underlying implementation of Type Theory [Pet82] with which our proof procedure was developed.

thus allowing the search for a contradiction to proceed with

$$(fst(z) :: fst(snd(z)))@(\langle a, b\rangle :: t) =_{List(A\times B)} u :: v \tag{7}$$

By evaluation (7) is reduced to

$$fst(z) :: (fst(snd(z))@(\langle a, b\rangle :: t)) =_{List(A\times B)} u :: v \tag{8}$$

(8) decomposes giving rise to a conjunction from which the right conjunct

$$fst(snd(z))@(\langle a, b\rangle :: t) =_{List(A\times B)} v$$

taken together with a specialization of the assumption denoted by y' yields a contradiction. Both branches of the case separation have been shown to give rise to contradictions. Backward propagation gives rise to a proof of (3). The proof of (2) follows by the correctness of the goal transformations.

3.4   Implementation

The proof procedure outlined has been implemented and integrated within a proof assistant[Ham85] which is similar in design to the Nuprl[Con86] interactive proof environment. The goal transformations which generalize the applicability of the proof procedure are implemented using LCF[GMW79] style tactics and tacticals. An implementation of Milner's type check algorithm [Mil78] is used for satisfying well-formedness proof obligations.

4   Related work

An underlying assumption of the work presented here is that the theory can be extended mechanically to incorporate new data type constructors. Backhouse[Bac86] proposes such a scheme for introducing user-defined extensions. This idea has been taken a stage further in the Calculus of Constructions where a mechanism for introducing inductive definitions has been implemented[PM89]. This work strengthens the argument for the basic approach we have adopted in developing our proof procedure.

Proofs of negations are an example of what has been called the *mismatch* between programs and proofs[Bac87]. In Nuprl[Con86] the subset type is used to hide the computationally uninteresting component of an object expression. The need for the subset type is a consequence of the rigid type structure of Martin-Löf's theory. This was a motivation behind the flexible typing adopted by Henson[Hen89] in his constructive set theory TK. In the Calculus of Constructions[Moh89] and PX[HN87] a syntactic notion of *non-informative* propositions is introduced. These mechanisms, however, do not address the problem of satisfying computationally uninteresting proof obligations. In contrast to the approach adopted here Smith[Smi87] argues for the use of nonconstructive methods in dealing with such proof obligations. By adding the law of the excluded middle to Martin-Löf's theory Smith is able to make use of classical logic in reasoning about programs. Whether the use of classical logic simplifies the theorem proving task remains to be seen. Smith admits to not knowing of any programming example where the correctness proof is considerably simplified by the use of classical logic.

5   Conclusions

In this paper we develop a proof procedure for negation based upon general properties of data type constructors. We outline the basis on which these properties can be derived automatically. As a consequence our proof procedure may be extended uniformly to incorporate new data type constructors. The rich type structure of the theory provides an expressive specification language. The price paid for this expressiveness, however, is the loss of decidable type checking. With completeness not an achievable goal, our criteria for evaluating our proof procedure must be based on empirical study. The work presented here represents a starting point; a framework and an algorithm which is both tunable and extendible.

Acknowledgements

I am indebted to Alan Hamilton for numerous discussions during the course of this work and his detailed comments during the preparation of this paper. Paul Chisholm provided useful feedback on an earlier version of this paper for which I am very grateful.

References

[Bac86]   R.C. Backhouse. *On the Meaning and Construction of the Rules in Martin-Löf's Theory of Types*. Computing Science Notes CS 8606, Dept. of Mathematics and Computing Science, University of Groningen, 1986.

[Bac87]   R.C. Backhouse. Overcoming the mismatch between programs and proofs. In P.Dybjer, B. Nordström, K. Petersson, and J.M. Smith, editors, *Proceedings of the Workshop in Programming Logic*, pages 116–122, Marstrand, June 1987.

[BCM89]   R.C. Backhouse, P. Chisholm, and G. Malcolm. Do–it–yourself Type Theory. *Formal Aspects of Computing*, 1:19–84, 1989.

[Chi87]   P. Chisholm. Derivation of a Parsing Algorithm in Martin-Löf's Theory of Types. *Science of Computer Programming*, 8:1–42, 1987.

[Con86]   R.L. Constable *et al. Implementing Mathematics with the Nuprl Proof Development System*. Prentice-Hall, 1986.

[GMW79]   M.J.C. Gordon, R. Milner, and C.P. Wadsworth. *Edinburgh LCF*. Springer-Verlag LNCS 78, 1979.

[Ham85]   A.G. Hamilton. *Program Construction in Martin-Löf Type Theory*. Technical Report, T.R. 24, Dept. of Computing Science, University of Stirling, June 1985.

[Hen89]   M. C. Henson. Program development in the constructive set theory TK. *Formal Aspects of Computing*, 1:173–192, 1989.

[HN87]   S. Hayashi and H. Nakano. *PX, a Computational Logic*. Technical Report, Research Institute for Mathematical Science, Kyoto University, 1987.

[Ire89]   A. Ireland. *Mechanization of Program Construction in Martin-Löf's Theory of Types*. PhD thesis, Dept. of Computing Science, University of Stirling, 1989.

[Mar82]   P. Martin-Löf. Constructive Mathematics and Computer Programming. In L.J. Cohen, J. Łoś, H. Pfeiffer, and K-P. Podewski, editors, *Logic, Methodology and Philosophy of Science VI*, pages 153–175, North-Holland, 1982.

[Mil78]   R. Milner. A Theory of Type Polymorphism in Programming Languages. *Journal of Computer and System Sciences*, 17:348–375, 1978.

[Moh89]   C. Mohring. Extracting F_ω's programs from proofs in the Calculus of Constructions. In *Proceedings of the 16th ACM Symposium of Principles of Programming Languages*, pages 89–104, 1989.

[NPS90]   B. Nordström, K. Petersson, and J. Smith. *Programming in Martin-Löf's Type Theory*. Clarendon Press, Oxford, 1990.

[Pet82]   K. Petersson. *A programming system for type theory*. LPM Memo 21, Department of Computer Science, Chalmers University of Technology, Göteborg, 1982.

[PM89]   F. Pfenning and C. Mohring. Inductively defined types in the Calculus of Constructions. Presented at: *Mathematical foundations of programming language semantics*, 1989.

[Smi87]   J. Smith. On a Nonconstructive Type Theory and Program Derivation. In D.G. Skordev, editor, *Mathematical Logic and its Applications*, pages 331–340, Plenum Publishing Corporation, 1987.

BEING AWARE OF ASSUMPTIONS[1]

Maria R. Cravo and **João P. Martins**
Instituto Superior Técnico
Av. Rovisco Pais
1000 Lisboa, Portugal
351-1-802045-x1265
IST_1416@ptifm.bitnet

Abstract

We present a nonmonotonic logic, SWMC (after Shapiro, Wand, Martins and Cravo) intended to support belief revision systems. SWMC allows the use of default rules and exceptions to default rules. SWMC associates each derived wff with the hypotheses, and assumptions underlying its derivation, and can thus be used to support belief revision systems. SWMC distinguishes three kinds of conclusions that can be drawn from a set of hypotheses: sound conclusions, plausible conclusions, and conceivable conclusions.

1   Introduction

Since the early beginnings of Artificial Intelligence (AI), researchers have been concerned with the development of programs capable of performing commonsense reasoning. One aspect of commonsense reasoning is the ability to jump to conclusions when the available information is not enough to draw these conclusions soundly. Of course, we cannot just jump to any conclusion we need, but only to plausible conclusions. To decide which conclusions are plausible, we use *default rules*—rules which are not universally true, rules with exceptions. Since default rules are not universal rules, conclusions suggested by default rules are *defeasible*: additional information can lead us to abandon some conclusions based on default rules.

The field of nonmonotonic reasoning studies techniques to deal with defeasible conclusions. Over the last ten years, this field has evolved in two different directions:

1. Development of nonmonotonic logics, which concerns the formal study of logics which allow the use of default rules.

2. Development of computational systems called truth maintenance systems, reason maintenance systems, or belief revision systems, henceforth designated by BRS. The main task of these systems is to manage a set of beliefs in such a way that:

---

[1]This work was partially supported by Junta Nacional de Investigação Científica e Tecnológica (JNICT), under Grant 87-107.

1) no belief is held without a reason; 2) no contradictory beliefs are held simultaneously. To achieve this, the key issue is to keep a record of dependencies between propositions. These systems, however, are not concerned with the representation of default rules, have very limited reasoning capabilities, and just record the dependencies among propositions as told by an outside system, the problem solver (an exception to this is the work of [Martins and Shapiro 83, 88] in which the dependencies are computed inside the system but which does not allow the use of default rules).

The work reported in this paper addresses issues that concern researchers in both of these directions: we present a nonmonotonic logic, SWMC, that provides a way of keeping a track of dependencies among propositions. SWMC is an extension of SWM [Martins and Shapiro 83, 88], a monotonic logic that supports belief revision systems.[2]

SWMC uses a quantifier, the default quantifier, to express default rules, has provisos for raising the assumption that a given default rule is applicable to a particular individual, and for expressing that certain classes of individuals are exceptions to a particular default rule. Whenever propositions are derived they are associated with a set that contains all hypotheses and assumptions that underlie their derivation. These sets correspond to the dependency records that are needed in a BRS and are inspected whenever contradictions are detected.

Besides these aspects, SWMC enables the distinction between three types of conclusions: *sound conclusions* are conclusions that must follow, given a set of premises; sound conclusions are monotonic in the sense that adding new premises can never invalidate sound conclusions; *plausible conclusions* are conclusions that follow from the premises but may be invalidated if the number of premises increases; and *conceivable conclusions* are conclusions that follow from a set of premises if we prefer some default rules to other default rules, but will not follow from the same premises if we change our preference on default rules.

SWMC is not yet another nonmonotonic logic, but rather a logic that, if used by a BRS, would allow that the dependencies among propositions be computed by SWMC itself rather than having to force the user (or an outside system) to do this, as in many existing systems. Another distinguishing feature of SWMC is the distinction made between what follows soundly from what is believed, and what it is only plausible to believe. This is crucial in situations where we cannot afford to act based upon less than certain conclusions, for the risks involved are too high, should the conclusion be proved wrong after all.

2 The Language of SWMC

To allow for the support of belief revision systems, SWMC deals with supported wffs. A *supported wff* is of the form $<A, \tau, \alpha>$, where A is a wff, τ an origin tag and α an

---

[2]SWM is monotonic in the sense that any proposition derivable from a given set of propositions will still be derivable from any consistent superset of this set.

origin set. In the supported wff $<A, \tau, \alpha>$, the pair (τ, α) is called the *support* of the wff A, and corresponds to a particular derivation of the wff A: the origin tag indicates how the supported wff was generated and the origin set indicates the dependencies of this supported wff on other wffs. The *origin tag* is an element of the set $\{hyp, asp, der\}$: *hyp* identifies hypotheses, *asp* identifies assumptions, and *der* identifies derived wffs. It is important to make a clear distinction between hypotheses and assumptions. Hypotheses represent the available information, from which we want to draw conclusions. Assumptions, on the other hand, *do not* represent any kind of information. Assumptions are used in the recording of dependencies, when we draw a defeasible conclusion by applying a default rule to a particular individual; assumptions are used to record the fact that the defeasible conclusion depends, among other things, on the *assumption* or *supposition* that the default rule is applicable to that particular individual. Finally, the *origin set* is a set of hypotheses and/or assumptions and contains those hypotheses and assumptions that were used in that particular derivation of the wff.

The full description of SWMC's wffs formation rules can be found in [Cravo and Martins 90a]; for the purpose of this paper it is enough to say that the language of SWMC, $\mathcal{L}$, is the union of three sets: (1) The set of *standard wffs*, $\mathcal{L}_{FOL}$, which corresponds to the language of First Order Logic; (2) The set of *default rules*, $\mathcal{L}_D$, which are of the form $\bigtriangledown(x)\ A(x) \rightarrow B(x)$, where $A(x)$ and $B(x)$, are standard wffs; For example, $\bigtriangledown(x)Bird(x) \rightarrow Flies(x)$ is a default rule, whose intended meaning is *By default birds fly*, or *If I know that something is a bird, then it is plausible to conclude that it flies*; and (3) the set of *extended wffs*, $\mathcal{L}_E$, which contains two types of wffs: (a) *Assumptions*, which are of the form $Applicable(D, c)$ where D is a default rule and "c" is an individual symbol. This wff is intended to represent the assumption that the default rule D is applicable to the particular individual c; (b) Extended wffs of the form $\forall(x)\ A(x) \rightarrow \neg Applicable\ (D, x)$, where D is a default rule, are used to express exceptions to default rules.

In summary, the set of all wffs in SWMC is the union of three disjoint sets: (1) The set of wffs of classical logic, $\mathcal{L}_{FOL}$; (2) The set of default rules, $\mathcal{L}_D$; (3) The set of extended wffs, $\mathcal{L}_E$.

A BRS using SWMC only considers as beliefs the wffs belonging to $\mathcal{L}_{FOL}$. The use of the other wffs is to allow the BRS to do default reasoning, but these wffs are never considered as beliefs of the system. Given a default rule $\bigtriangledown(x)\ A(x) \rightarrow B(x)$, the BRS will neither believe it nor disbelieve it, but rather try, whenever possible, to follow the line of reasoning it suggests, i.e., whenever the system believes that something is an A, it will also believe that it is a B, unless some other of its beliefs contradict this conclusion. A default rule is seen as a suggestion of how a BRS should extend its set of beliefs when faced with incomplete information. This way of looking at a default rule agrees the one followed by [Poole 88].

3 Rules of inference

We now present some of the rules of inference of SWMC. The set of all supported wffs that can be generated by the rules of inference of SWMC is denoted by $\overline{\Sigma}$.

Given a set of wffs α and a wff A, we say that A is *derivable* from α, written $\alpha \vdash_{SWMC} A$, iff there is a supported wff $\mathcal{A} \in \overline{\Sigma}$ whose wff is A and whose origin set is contained in α. This notion of derivability is monotonic: if $\alpha \vdash_{SWMC} A$, and $\alpha \subset \beta$, then $\beta \vdash_{SWMC} A$. The nonmonotonic character of SWMC will become apparent later on, when we define the notion of consequence.

SWMC is a natural deduction system. It has two distinct sets of inference rules: (1) *Standard rules*, which include a rule of hypothesis, and basically two rules for each connective ($\wedge$, $\vee$, $\rightarrow$, $\neg$) and each quantifier ($\forall$, $\exists$); these rules are a modification of the rules of SWM [Martins and Shapiro 83, 88]; (2) *Extended rules*, which deal with default rules. Due to space constraints we only present the extended rules of inference; the standard rules can be found in [Cravo and Martins 90a].

Assumption (Asp). From $<D, hyp, \{D\}>$, $<A(c), \tau, \alpha>$ (where $D = \bigtriangledown(x) A(x) \rightarrow B(x)$, and "$c$" is an individual symbol), and $Applicable(D, c) \notin \alpha$, infer $<Applicable(D, c), asp, \{Applicable(D, c)\} \cup \{D\} \cup \alpha >$.
Assumptions are necessary to record the fact that when $B(c)$ is inferred from $\bigtriangledown(x) A(x) \rightarrow B(x)$, and $A(c)$, the inferred wff depends not only on these two wffs, but also on the *assumption* that this particular default rule is applicable to the particular individual c, i.e., $Applicable(\bigtriangledown(x) A(x) \rightarrow B(x), c)$.

Default Elimination ($\bigtriangledown$E). From $<D, hyp, \{D\}>$, $<A(c), \tau, \alpha>$ (where $D = \bigtriangledown(x) A(x) \rightarrow B(x)$, and "$c$" is an individual symbol), and $<Applicable(D, c), asp, \{Applicable(D, c)\} \cup \{D\} \cup \alpha >$, infer $<B(c), der, \{Applicable(D, c)\} \cup \{D\} \cup \alpha >$.

4 The notion of consequence

SWMC's notion of derivability is not enough for a BRS using SWMC, to know what wffs it should believe, given a set of wffs: Suppose that a BRS believes that *Tweety is a bird*, and is given the default rule *By default birds fly*. How do we express the fact that the BRS should believe that *Tweety flies*? Using the notion of derivability we defined, the best we can do is to write $\{Bird(Tweety), \bigtriangledown(x) Bird(x) \rightarrow Flies(x), Applicable(\bigtriangledown(x) Bird(x) \rightarrow Flies(x), Tweety)\} \vdash_{SWMC} Flies(Tweety)$. Furthermore, if the BRS were now told that *Tweety doesn't fly*, we could still write $\{Bird(Tweety), \bigtriangledown(x) Bird(x) \rightarrow Flies(x), Applicable(\bigtriangledown(x) Bird(x) \rightarrow Flies(x), Tweety), \neg Flies(Tweety)\} \vdash_{SWMC} Flies(Tweety)$.

Two inconveniences arise if we use $\vdash_{SWMC}$ to express what a BRS should believe: (1) We would like to express the fact that the BRS should believe that $Flies(Tweety)$, if it just believes that $Bird(Tweety)$, and is given the rule $\bigtriangledown(x) Bird(x) \rightarrow Flies(x)$, without having to mention the assumption that must be raised in order to draw that conclusion; (2) Given that the BRS believes that $\neg Flies(Tweety)$, it should not believe that $Flies(Tweety)$. In this case, the logic should provide the BRS with the information that it cannot believe that $Flies(Tweety)$, even though it believes that $Bird(Tweety)$, and is given the suggestion to conclude that anything that is a bird flies, unless some other of its beliefs contradict this conclusion, as is the case.

We need a notion of consequence that, given the information available to a BRS, tells it what it should believe. Consequence will be based on two concepts, context and belief space determined by a context. A *context* is any set of hypotheses, $\beta \subset \mathcal{L}$.[3] Given a consistent context,[4] a *belief space* determined by this context is a consistent set of wffs in $\mathcal{L}_{FOL}$, which are derivable from the hypotheses in the context, and eventually some assumptions. If we think of a context as representing the information available to a BRS, a belief space defined by this context will correspond to an acceptable set of beliefs of the BRS.

Determining the belief spaces defined by a context β is not a single step process. Rather it involves the construction of three intermediate sets of supported wffs: (1) The extended context of β, (2) the primitive cores of β, and (3) the cores of β. We now define each of these concepts.

Given a consistent context β, the *extended context* determined by this context, $EC(\beta)$, is a set of *supported wffs* whose origin tags are either *hyp* or *asp*: The hypotheses are all the hypotheses in the context, and the assumptions correspond to the assumptions which can consistently be added to the context. Before formally defining extended context we need another definition:

Definition 4.1 *Given a context β, a default rule $D \in \beta$, and an individual symbol c, we define*

$$Implicit(D, c, \beta) = \{\neg F(c) : \forall(x)F(x) \rightarrow \neg Applicable(D, x) \in \beta\}$$

When we apply a default rule D to an individual c, the set $Implicit(D, c)$ can be seen as the set of implicit assumptions we are making. For instance, when we assume that *Tweety flies*, based on the information that *Tweety is a bird, By default birds fly, Penguins and ostriches are an exception to this rule*, and the assumption that *The default rule is applicable to Tweety*, we are also implicitly assuming that *Tweety is not a penguin* and *Tweety is not an ostrich*. For this reason, the set $Implicit(D, c)$ is called *the set of implicit assumptions* of assumption $Applicable(D, c)$. We use the expression $Implicit(\alpha, \beta)$, where α is a set of wffs, to represent the union of the sets of implicit assumptions of all the assumptions in α.

Given a consistent context, β, the extended context it determines, represented by $EC(\beta)$, is defined as:

$$
\begin{aligned}
EC(\beta) = \{\mathcal{A} \in \overline{\Sigma} : \ & (ot(\mathcal{A}) = hyp \ and \ wff(\mathcal{A}) \in \beta) \ or \\
& (ot(\mathcal{A}) = asp, \ and \ hyps(os(\mathcal{A})) \subset \beta \\
& and \ os(\mathcal{A}) \cup \beta \cup Implicit(os(\mathcal{A}), \beta) \ is \ consistent)\}
\end{aligned}
$$

---

[3] A hypothesis is any wff A in a supported wff of the form $<A, hyp, \{A\}>$. The rule of Hypothesis restricts the possible hypotheses to the union of the sets $\mathcal{L}_{FOL}$, $\mathcal{L}_D$, and the set of extended wffs of the form $\forall(x) A(x) \rightarrow \neg Applicable(D, x)$.

[4] An *inconsistent* set of wffs γ is a set of wffs such that a contradiction is derivable from γ, i.e., $\gamma \vdash_{SWMC} (A \wedge \neg A)$. A *consistent* set of wffs is a set of wffs which is not inconsistent.

where the function *hyps* takes as argument a set of wffs and selects from them those that correspond to hypotheses:

$$hyps(\alpha) = \{A \in \alpha : (\exists \mathcal{A} \in \overline{\Sigma} : ot(\mathcal{A}) = hyp \text{ and } wff(\mathcal{A}) = A)\}.$$

Since the extended context may contain assumptions which are mutually incompatible, or whose implicit assumptions are mutually incompatible, the next step is to split the extended context into maximal subsets, that only contain assumptions which are mutually compatible, and so are their implicit assumptions. These maximal subsets of the extended context of a context β are called the primitive cores of context β. Each of these primitive cores will be a potential basis for constructing an acceptable state of beliefs.

Definition 4.2 *Given a consistent context β, the primitive cores it determines are defined to be the maximal subsets Σ of the extended context that satisfy the following conditions:*

- $\beta \subset wffs(\Sigma)$

- $\forall \mathcal{A} \in \Sigma : os(\mathcal{A}) \subset wffs(\Sigma)$

- $wffs(\Sigma) \cup Implicit(wffs(\Sigma), \beta)$ *is consistent*

where the function $wffs$ takes as argument a set of supported wffs, and returns a set of wffs, and is defined as follows:

$$wffs(\Phi) = \{A : (\exists \mathcal{A} \in \Phi : wff(\mathcal{A}) = A)\}.$$

The set of all primitive cores determined by a context β is denoted $Pcores(\beta)$.

Each of the primitive cores is a potential basis for constructing an acceptable set of beliefs, or belief space. Although the definition of a belief space from each of the primitive cores will produce reasonable belief spaces in many cases, there are some situations in which the belief spaces corresponding to some of the primitive cores cannot be considered acceptable sets of beliefs. Such situations occur when one primitive core Σ does not contain an assumption $\mathcal{A}$ that belongs to the extended context, simply because the presence of $\mathcal{A}$ in Σ (or, which is the same, the presence of the conclusion,[5] $B(c)$, of that assumption in Σ) would contradict the implicit assumptions of the assumptions in Σ (the example at the end of this section illustrates this situation).

So, the next step is to discard those primitive cores that would correspond to unacceptable belief spaces. The remaining are called the cores of the context, and each of them will define an acceptable set of beliefs.

Definition 4.3 *Given a primitive core Σ of a consistent context β, we say that Σ is a core of β, written $\Sigma \in Cores(\beta)$, iff for every assumption $Applicable(D, c)$ $(D = \bigtriangledown(x)$ $A(x) \to B(x))$ that belongs to the wffs of some primitive core of β, and does not belong to the wffs of Σ, one of the following conditions is verified:*

---

[5] Given an assumption $Applicable(\bigtriangledown(x) A(x) \to B(x), c)$, its conclusion is the wff $B(c)$.

- $wffs(\Sigma) \not\vdash_{SWMC} A(c)$.

- $wffs(\Sigma) \cup \{B(c)\} \cup Implicit(wffs(\Sigma), \beta)$ *is consistent.*

- $wffs(\Sigma) \cup \{B(c)\} \cup Implicit(D, c, \beta)$ *is inconsistent.*

It is interesting to note that there is a similarity between our definition of cores from primitive cores and 1) The definition of extension base from maximal consistent assumption set in [Junker 89]; 2) The definition of priority-preserving extensions (corresponding to belief spaces in SWMC) from CDL-extensions (where CDL stands for Cumulative Default Logic) in [Brewka 90].

Finally, we can define the belief spaces determined by a context β. There will be one belief space for each core Σ determined by β. That belief space consists of all the *standard wffs* derivable from $wffs(\Sigma)$. Given $\Sigma \in Cores(\beta)$, the corresponding belief space is defined by:

$$BS(\Sigma) = \{A \in \mathcal{L}_{FOL} : wffs(\Sigma) \vdash_{SWMC} A\}$$

In summary, given a context β, i.e., a set of hypotheses, the goal is to compute the belief spaces it determines. However, to go from a context β to the belief spaces it determines, we need to go through several intermediate steps, namely the construction of the extended context of β, the primitive cores of β, and the cores of β.

Having defined belief space we can now define the notion of consequence, between a context and a wff in $\mathcal{L}_{FOL}$.[6] In SWMC, when we say that a wff $A \in \mathcal{L}_{FOL}$ is a consequence of a set of wffs β, we may mean one of three things: (1) Only the hypotheses in β were used in the derivation of A. In this case, the wff A will be in every belief space determined by β, and will be in every belief space determined by any consistent superset of β. In this case we say that A is a *sound consequence* of β and write $\beta \vdash A$; (2) The wff A was derived using not only the hypotheses in β, but also possibly some assumptions that belong to every core determined by β. In this case, the wff A will also belong to every belief space determined by β. Yet, in this case, there may be consistent supersets of β such that A is no longer in all, or even in any, of the belief spaces they determine. In this case we say that A is a *plausible consequence* of β and write $\beta \vdash_P A$; (3) Finally, we may just mean that there is at least one belief space determined by β that contains A. In this case we say that A is a *conceivable consequence* of β and write $\beta \vdash_C A$.

Intuitively, these notions correspond to: Given β then A *must* follow; Given β *there are reasons to suppose* A, and *no reasons against it*; Given β, *there are reasons to suppose* A, *but there are also reasons against supposing* A. The notion of sound consequence is monotonic, i.e., if $\alpha \vdash A$, and $\alpha \subset \beta$, then $\beta \vdash A$, for any consistent contexts α and β. The nonmonotonicity of the logic is reflected in the notions of plausible and conceivable consequence.

We think that the distinction between the different kinds of conclusions that can be drawn from a set of hypotheses is very important: on one hand, when faced with

---

[6]We are only interested in wffs from $\mathcal{L}_{FOL}$ because only these will correspond to beliefs of a BRS using SWMC.

incomplete information the BRS using SWMC should be able to extend its set of beliefs with the conclusions suggested by the default rules; but in some situations, it is crucial to know whether a given conclusion is a sound one, or just a plausible or conceivable one.

To illustrate the concepts presented in this section we present an example taken from [Junker 89]: "On workdays, Peter must normally go to work. This is not true if he has an excuse. If he is ill he normally has an excuse. However, his employer does not accept this if Peter has only caught a cold." Suppose, furthermore, that today is a workday, and that Peter is ill today. What can we conclude?

Let $D_1 = \triangledown(x)Workday(x) \rightarrow Work(Peter, x)$ and $D_2 = \triangledown(x)Ill(Peter, x) \rightarrow HasExcuse(Peter, x)$. We can translate the information available in the example by:

$$\beta = \{ \triangledown(x)Workday(x) \rightarrow Works(Peter, x),$$
$$\forall(x)HasExcuse(Peter, x) \rightarrow \neg Applicable(D_1, x),$$
$$\triangledown(x)Ill(Peter, x) \rightarrow HasExcuse(Peter, x),$$
$$\forall(x)HasCold(Peter, x) \rightarrow \neg Applicable(D_2, x),$$
$$\forall(x)HasCold(Peter, x) \rightarrow Ill(Peter, x),$$
$$Workday(today), Ill(Peter, today)\}$$

From the hypotheses in β it is possible to raise two assumptions:

$$\mathcal{A}_1 = <Applicable(D_1, today), asp, \{Applicable(D_1, today), D_1, Workday(today)\} >$$

and

$$\mathcal{A}_2 = <Applicable(D_2, today), asp, \{Applicable(D_2, today), D_2, Ill(Peter, today)\} > .$$

The conclusions of these assumptions are, respectively:

$$\mathcal{C}_1 = <Works(Peter, today), der, \{Applicable(D_1, today), D_1, Workday(today)\} >$$

and

$$\mathcal{C}_2 = <HasExcuse(Peter, today), der, \{Applicable(D_2, today), D_2, Ill(Peter, today)\} > .$$

By Definition 4.1, we have:

$$Implicit(D_1, today, \beta) = \{\neg HasExcuse(Peter, today)\}$$
$$Implicit(D_2, today, \beta) = \{\neg HasCold(Peter, today)\}$$

Since

$$\beta \cup os(\mathcal{A}_1) \cup Implicit(D_1, today, \beta) \ is \ consistent, \ and$$
$$\beta \cup os(\mathcal{A}_2) \cup Implicit(D_2, today, \beta) \ is \ consistent,$$

both $\mathcal{A}_1$ and $\mathcal{A}_2$ belong to $EC(\beta)$. But these assumptions cannot belong to the same primitive core, because the conclusion of $\mathcal{A}_2$ ($HasExcuse(Peter, today)$) contradicts the implicit assumption of $\mathcal{A}_1$ ($\neg HasExcuse(Peter, today)$). So, we have two primitive cores of β, Σ_1 containing $\mathcal{A}_1$, and Σ_2 containing $\mathcal{A}_2$. Both primitive cores contain, by definition, all the hypotheses in β.

Now let's check if both Σ_1 and Σ_2 are cores of β. Starting with Σ_1, we have that Σ_1 does not contain $\mathcal{A}_2$ which belongs to Σ_2, and:

- $wffs(\Sigma_1) \vdash_{SWMC} Ill(Peter, today)$,

- $wffs(\Sigma_1) \cup \{HasExcuse(Peter, today)\} \cup \{\neg HasExcuse(Peter, today)\}$ is *not* consistent, and

- $wffs(\Sigma_1) \cup \{HasExcuse(Peter, today)\} \cup \{\neg HasCold(Peter, today)\}$ is *not* inconsistent.

Then, by Definition 4.3, Σ_1 is not a core of β.

Now, let's check if Σ_2 is a core of β. Σ_2 does not contain $\mathcal{A}_1$ which belongs to Σ_1, but $wffs(\Sigma_2) \cup \{Works(Peter, today)\} \cup \{\neg HasCold(Peter, today)\}$ is consistent, so, by Definition 4.3, Σ_2 is a core of β.

Then context β determines one belief space containing $HasExcuse(Peter, today)$. We have:

$$\beta \vdash \{Workday(today), Ill(Peter, today)\}$$

$$\beta \vdash_P HasExcuse(Peter, today)$$

5 Comparison of SWMC with Default Logic

A detailed comparison of SWMC with Reiter's Default Logic (DL) [Reiter 80] is under study.

Although no formal results have been proved yet, the work done suggests that the main outcome of this comparison is as follows.

First, we have to define a way of translating a context in SWMC's language to a default theory in DL.

Definition 5.1 *Given a context β, the corresponding default theory, $\Delta = (D, W)$ is defined by:*

$$W = \beta \cap \mathcal{L}_{FOL}$$
$$D = \{\frac{A(x) \; : \; B(x), \neg F_1(x), ..., \neg F_n(x)}{B(x)} : \{\triangledown(x)A(x) \rightarrow B(x),$$
$$\forall(x)F_1(x) \rightarrow \neg Applicable(\triangledown(x)A(x) \rightarrow B(x), x), ...,$$
$$\forall(x)F_n(x) \rightarrow \neg Applicable(\triangledown(x)A(x) \rightarrow B(x), x)\} \subset \beta\}$$

As to the comparison between the belief spaces of SWMC and the extensions of DL, we have:

Theorem 5.2 *Let $\Delta = (D, W)$ be the default theory corresponding to a consistent context β. Let E be an extension of Δ. Then, there is a belief space γ defined by β, such that $E = \gamma$, iff*

$$JUSTIFICATIONS(GD(E, \Delta)) \cup E \; is \; consistent$$

where

$$GD(E, \Delta) = \{\frac{A \; : \; B, \neg F_1, \ldots, \neg F_n}{B} \in D \; : \; A \in E \text{ and } \neg B, F_1, \ldots, F_n \notin E\}$$

and, for any set of defaults D'

$$JUSTIFICATIONS(D') = \{F_i : \frac{A \; : \; F_1, \ldots, F_n}{B} \in D'\}$$

6 Concluding remarks

We presented SWMC, a nonmonotonic logic that allows for default reasoning. SWMC is suitable for supporting BRS in the sense that it associates with each proposition the reasons that lead to its derivation. The logic allows the distinction between what must follow from a set of premisses, what is a plausible conclusion and what is a conceivable conclusion.

A semantics has been developed for SWMC, based on the notion of classical model, and on an ordering of sets of models [Cravo and Martins 90b].

Work is under way towards defining a practical BRS (practical in the sense that it can be implemented) which uses SWMC as the underlying logic.

7 References

Brewka G., "Cumulative Default Logic: In Defense of Nonmonotonic Inference Rules", Proc. DRUMS (ESPRIT Basic Research Action 3085), Workshop RP1, Marseille, France, 1990.

Cravo M.R. and Martins J.P., "Defaults and Belief Revision: A Syntactical Approach", Technical Report GIA 90/02, Lisbon, Portugal: Instituto Superior Tecnico, Technical University of Lisbon, 1990a.

Cravo M.R. and Martins J.P., "A Semantics for SWMC", Technical Report GIA 90/03, Lisbon, Portugal: Instituto Superior Tecnico, Technical University of Lisbon, 1990b.

Junker U., "A Correct Non-Monotonic ATMS", *Proc. IJCAI-89*, pp.1049-1054, 1989.

Martins J.P. and Shapiro S.C., "Reasoning in Multiple Belief Spaces", *Proc. IJCAI-83*, pp.370-373, 1983.

Martins J.P. and Shapiro S.C., "A Model for Belief Revision", *Artificial Intelligence 35*, pp.25-79, 1988.

Poole D., "A Logical Framework for Default Reasoning", *Artificial Intelligence 36*, No. 1, pp.27-47, 1988.

Reiter R., "A Logic for Default Reasoning", *Artificial Intelligence 13*, No. 1-2, pp.81-132, 1980.

A Mathematical Formulation of Dempster-Shafer's Belief Functions

Chun-Hung Tzeng*
Computer Science Department
Ball State University
Muncie, IN 47306

Abstract. This paper introduces a unified mathematical formulation for both Bayesian approach and Dempster-Shafer's approach in handling uncertainty in artificial intelligence. Each body of uncertain information in this formulation is an information quadruplet, consisting of a code space, a message space, an interpretation function, and an evidence space. Each information quadruplet contains prior information as well as possible new evidence which may appear later. Bayes rule is used to update the prior information. This paper also introduces an idea of independent information and its combination, in which a combination formula is derived. A conventional Bayesian prior probability measure is the prior information of a special information quadruplet; Bayesian conditioning is the combination of special independent information. A Dempster's belief function is the belief function of a different information quadruplet; the Dempster combination rule is the combination rule of such independent quadruplets. This paper shows that both the conventional Bayesian approach and Dempster-Shafer's approach originate from the same mathematical theory.

1 Introduction

In handling uncertainty in artificial intelligence, Bayesian and Dempster-Shafer's approaches are usually viewed as two basically different theories (Pearl 1988). Dempster-Shafer's evidence is introduced as an extension of probability (Dempster 1968; Shafer 1976). Let T represent the set of all possible answers to a question. Then a proposition is represented as "The answer is in A," where A is a subset of T. The set T is the frame of discernment, and the power set of T, 2^T, is the set of propositions. A given probability assignment m over 2^T (i.e., Dempster *basic probability assignment*) represents a body of evidence for the answer. The quantity $m(A)$ is designed to measure the belief that one commits exactly to A. The belief function $\mathrm{Bel}(A)$ is the total belief committed to A:

$$\mathrm{Bel}(A) = \sum_{B \subseteq A} m(B).$$

---

*This work was supported in part by the National Science Foundation under grant number IRI-8505735 and a summer research grant of Ball State University.

In Dempster-Shafer's formulation, the measures of T may be affected by a related question (Shafer 1987). Suppose S is a set of possible answers to a distinct but related question. Let $s \in S$ and $t \in T$. We use sCt to represent the fact that the answers s and t are compatible. Then given a probability measure P over S, we may define a basic probability measure over 2^T and express the belief function on subsets of T as follows:

$$\mathrm{Bel}(A) = P\{s \mid \text{if } sCt, \text{ then } t \in A\}, \ A \subseteq T.$$

Consider an example from Shafer (Shafer 1987). Let the first question be "Are streets outside slippery?" Let T denote the set of possible answers to this question: $T = \{\text{yes, no}\}$. Consider the second question: Is Fred going to speak truthfully, or is he going to speak carelessly? Let S denote the set of possible answers to this question: $S = \{\text{truthful, careless}\}$. Suppose we have a probability measure P over S: $P(\text{truthful}) = .8$ and $P(\text{careless}) = .2$. Suppose we also have Fred's announcement, "The streets outside are slippery." Therefore, "truthful" is compatible with "yes" but not with "no," while "careless" is compatible with both "yes" and "no." Therefore, we have the following belief function:

$$\mathrm{Bel}(\{\text{yes}\}) = .8 \ \text{ and } \ \mathrm{Bel}(\{\text{no}\}) = .0.$$

For the same problem, a Bayesian argument would need two additional probability measures. The first one is a prior probability, say p, for the proposition that the streets are slippery, and the second one is a conditional probability, say q, that Fred's announcement will be accurate even though it is careless. Using Bayesian conditioning, we can obtain the posterior probability that Fred's announcement that the streets are slippery is true:

$$\frac{.8p + .2qp}{.8p + .2qp + .2(1-q)(1-p)}.$$

This paper introduces a unified mathematical formulation of both approaches. Let T be the set of all possible answers to a specific question. We assume that the uncertainty is probabilistic, but its probability measure is not necessarily given. Each piece of information about the answer is represented by a 4-tuple $(S, M, i, \mathbf{E})$, called an *information quadruplet*. Both S and M are given probability spaces: S is the *code space*; M the *message space*. Each element $a \in M$ is interpreted by the proposition: $i(a)$, a subset of T, where i is a function from M to 2^T. Finally, $\mathbf{E}$, the *evidence space*, is a set of functions from S to M, each function representing an encoded message.

The information quadruplet contains prior information as well as possible new evidence which may appear later. Based on the prior information, we define a basic probability and a belief function over subsets of T. Given new evidence (i.e., an element of $\mathbf{E}$), we use Bayes rule to update the prior information. After we introduce a concept of independence between information quadruplets and define their combination, we can derive a combination rule for the basic probabilities.

A conventional Bayesian prior probability measure is the belief function of a special information quadruplet; Bayesian conditioning is the independent combination of two special information quadruplets. A conventional Dempster-Shafer's belief function is the belief function of a different special information quadruplet; the Dempster-Shafer combination rule is the combination rule for independent information quadruplets. Therefore, both the conventional Bayesian approach and Dempster-Shafer's approach originate from the same mathematical theory.

2 Evidence Model

Let T be the set of all possible answers to a specific question; t the random variable representing the right answer. We assume that t is probabilistic, but its probability is not necessarily known. For convenience, we assume that all of probability spaces discussed in this paper are discrete.

Message Space and Code Space. Let M be a probability space with a function $i : M \rightarrow 2^T$. Let $A \in M$ and $i(A) = X \in 2^T$. Then A is interpreted by the proposition: t is in X, or $t \in X$. We assume that the occurrence of a message depends on t in the sense that an occurring message A always implies "$t \in i(A)$." We also suppose that the probability measure P_M over M is previously given.

We call such a pair (M, i) a *message model* of T, in which M is the *message space* and i is the *interpretation function*. Since each message A means that "$t \in i(A)$," it is necessary that $i(A) \neq \emptyset$ if $P_M(A) > 0$.

Evidence Function and Evidence Model. Let S be a space, called *code space*, with a given probability measure P_S. We call any partial function from S to M an *evidence function*. We consider a special space of evidence functions:

Definition 1. A nonempty set $\mathbf{E}$ of evidence functions is an *evidence space* if the following two conditions are true:

1. For any $E_1, E_2 \in \mathbf{E}$, if $E_1(s) = E_2(s)$ for an $s \in S$, then $E_1 = E_2$.

2. For any $A \in M$, if $P_M(A) > 0$, then there is at least an $E \in \mathbf{E}$ such that $E(s) = A$ for some $s \in S$ with $P_S(s) > 0$.

Given an evidence space $\mathbf{E}$, an encoder encodes an occurring message as follows. Suppose that a message $A \in M$ has occurred. After the encoder independently choses a code $s \in S$ according to P_S, it finds an evidence function $E \in \mathbf{E}$ such that $E(s) = A$. If such an evidence function does not exist, a code will be repeatedly and independently chosen until a suitable one is found. Suppose that E ($\in \mathbf{E}$) is a given evidence function. Then we say that the evidence E supports A at s ($\in S$) if $E(s) = A$.

The first condition of $\mathbf{E}$ guarantees that the evidence function sent is uniquely determined by the occurring message and the chosen code. The second condition guarantees that any possible message A (i.e., $P_M(A) > 0$) can be encoded into an evidence function.

Finally, we define an information quadruplet of t as follows.

Definition 2. An *information quadruplet* is a 4-tuple $(S, M, i, \mathbf{E})$ of a code space S, a message space M, an interpretation function i, and an evidence space $\mathbf{E}$.

Figure 1 is an information quadruplet, in which M consists of four different messages, S three different codes, and $\mathbf{E}$ two different evidence functions.

Prior Information. The prior information about t in an information quadruplet $(S, M, i, \mathbf{E})$ is the probability measure P_M. Using this information, we define *basic probability* m and *belief function* Bel about t as follows

$$m(X) = \sum_{A \in M; i(A) = X} P_M(A); \quad \text{Bel}(X) = \sum_{Y \subseteq X} m(Y),$$

where X is a subset of T. The basic probability m forms a probability measure over 2^T: $\sum_{X \in 2^T} m(X) = 1$ and $m(\emptyset) = 0$.

Posterior Information. Given an evidence function in $\mathbf{E}$ we update the information quadruplet as follows.

First, consider some relevant sets. For an $A \in M$ and an $E \in \mathbf{E}$, let $S_{A,E} = \{s : s \in S, E(s) = A\}$, which is empty if E does not support A at all. Note that, from the first property of $\mathbf{E}$, $S_{A,E} \cap S_{A,E'} = \emptyset$ if $E \neq E'$. All of $S_{A,E}$'s for a fixed A , therefore, form a partition of S_A: $S_A = \bigcup_{E \in \mathbf{E}} S_{A,E}$. From the second property of $\mathbf{E}$, $S_A \neq \emptyset$ if $P_M(A) > 0$. For each E, consider $S_E = \{s : s \in S; E(s) \text{ is defined}\}$, the domain of E. Then all of $S_{A,E}$'s with a fixed E form a partition of S_E: $S_E = \bigcup_{A \in M} S_{A,E}$.

Suppose that $A \in M$ has occurred. Then it is necessary that $P_M(A) > 0$ and $S_A \neq \emptyset$. An evidence function appears if and only if an $s \in S_A$ is chosen. Therefore, given A, the conditional probability of an $s \in S_A$ being chosen is

$$
\begin{aligned}
P(s|A) &= P_S(s) + (1 - P_S(S_A))P_S(s) + (1 - P_S(S_A))^2 P_S(s) + \cdots \\
&= \frac{P_S(s)}{P_S(S_A)} = P_S(s|S_A).
\end{aligned}
$$

Furthermore, a specific evidence function E appears if and only if an $s \in S_{A,E}$ is chosen. Therefore, given A, the conditional probability of E is

$$
P(E|A) = \sum_{s \in S_{A,E}} P(s|A) = \sum_{s \in S_{A,E}} P_S(s|S_A) = P_S(S_{A,E}|S_A) = \frac{P_S(S_{A,E})}{P_S(S_A)}.
$$

Hence, the probability of E is

$$
P(E) = \sum_{A \in M} P(E|A)P_M(A) = \sum_{A \in M} \frac{P_S(S_{A,E})}{P_S(S_A)} P_M(A).
$$

Now, consider the posterior probability of A, given an evidence function E. Let $A \in M$ have a positive prior probability. Using Bayes rule, we have the posterior probability of A, given the evidence E, as follows:

$$
P(A|E) = \frac{P(E|A)P_M(A)}{P(E)} = \frac{\frac{P_S(S_{A,E})}{P_S(S_A)} P_M(A)}{\sum_{A \in M} \frac{P_S(S_{A,E})}{P_S(S_A)} P_M(A)} \tag{1}
$$

Given an evidence function E, consider a new information quadruplet $(S, M, i, \{E\})$, where the probability over M is updated by the posterior probability $P(\cdot|E)$, and E is the only possible evidence function. We call this new information quadruplet the *posterior information quadruplet*, given E. We have the basic probability and the belief function of the posterior information quadruplet as follows:

$$
m(X|E) = \sum_{i(A)=X} P(A|E); \quad \mathrm{Bel}(X|E) = \sum_{Y \subseteq X} m(Y|E), \quad X \subseteq T.
$$

We call $m(X|E)$ and $\mathrm{Bel}(X|E)$ the *posterior basic probability* and the *posterior belief function* (given E), respectively.

Note that, if **E** consists of only one evidence function, the evidence function does not provide any new information about t and the posterior information is identical with the prior information.

Shafer's Example.

Consider Fred's announcement in Shafer's example. Here $T = \{\text{yes, no}\}$, the set of answers to the question "Are streets outside slippery?"

First, suppose that we only know the probability of Fred's being truthful or careless. Then, we have the following information quadruplet. The code space $S = \{\text{truthful, careless}\}$; the message space $M = 2^T$ with the following probabilities:

$$P(\{\text{yes}\}) = .8; \ P(\{\text{yes, no}\}) = .2; \ P(\{\text{no}\}) = 0.$$

The evidence space consists of only one evidence function E_0:

$$E_0(\text{truthful}) = \{\text{yes}\}; \ E_0(\text{careless}) = \{\text{yes, no}\}.$$

The belief function of this information quadruplet is Shafer's original belief function:

$$\text{Bel}(\{\text{yes}\}) = .8; \ \text{Bel}(\{\text{no}\}) = .0.$$

Second, suppose we also know both the prior probability p for the proposition that the streets are slippery and the prior conditional probability q that Fred's announcement will be accurate even though it is careless. This prior information is represented by the following information quadruplet. The code space $S = \{t, c_a, c_i\}$ (t means truthful; c_a careless but accurate; c_i careless and inaccurate) with the probabilities:

$$P(t) = .8; \ P(c_a) = .2q; \ P(c_i) = .2(1-q).$$

The message space $M = T$, with the prior probabilities and the interpretation function i:

$$P(\text{yes}) = p \quad ; \quad P(\text{no}) = 1 - p;$$
$$i(\text{yes}) = \{\text{yes}\} \quad ; \quad i(\text{no}) = \{\text{no}\}.$$

Representing Fred's two possible announcements, the evidence space consists of two functions, E_1 (The Streets outside are slippery) and E_2 (The Streets outside are not slippery):

$$E_1(t) = \{\text{yes}\}; \ E_1(c_a) = \{\text{yes}\}; \ E_1(c_i) = \{\text{no}\};$$
$$E_2(t) = \{\text{no}\}; \ E_2(c_a) = \{\text{no}\}; \ E_2(c_i) = \{\text{yes}\}.$$

The belief function of this information quadruplet is the prior probability measure over T.

Fred's announcement (i.e., "The streets outside are slippery.") corresponds to the evidence function E_1. Given E_1, we have from the equation (1) the posterior probability of the message space T:

$$P(\text{yes}|E_1) = \frac{(.8 + .2q)p}{(.8 + .2q)p + .2(1-q)(1-p)};$$
$$P(\text{no}|E_1) = \frac{.2(1-q)(1-p)}{(.8 + .2q)p + .2(1-q)(1-p)}.$$

That is, we have the same results as in the Bayesian argument. This example shows that both Dempster-Shafer's belief function and Bayesian posterior probabilities can be derived from our formulation.

3   Special Models

In the following, we show that some familiar models are special cases in our formulation.

Probability Measure over T.   We represent any probability measure P over T by an information quadruplet $(S_0, M_P, i_p, \mathbf{E}_T)$ (depicted in Figure 2) as follows. Let $M_P = T$ with the given P. The interpretation function $i_p : T \to 2^T$ is defined as $i_p(x) = \{x\}$ for $x \in T$. Let $S_0 = \{s_0\}$, consisting of only one element; $\mathbf{E}_T = \{E_x : x \in T\}$, where $E_x(s_0) = x$ for each $x \in T$.

The basic probability m is the given probability assignment and the belief function Bel is the given probability measure: $m(x) = P(x)$ for $x \in T$ and $\mathrm{Bel}(X) = P(X)$ for $X \subseteq T$.

Suppose that an evidence function E_x appears. Then it is certain that $t = x$. That is, any new evidence in $(S_0, M_P, i_p, \mathbf{E}_T)$ provides complete information about t.

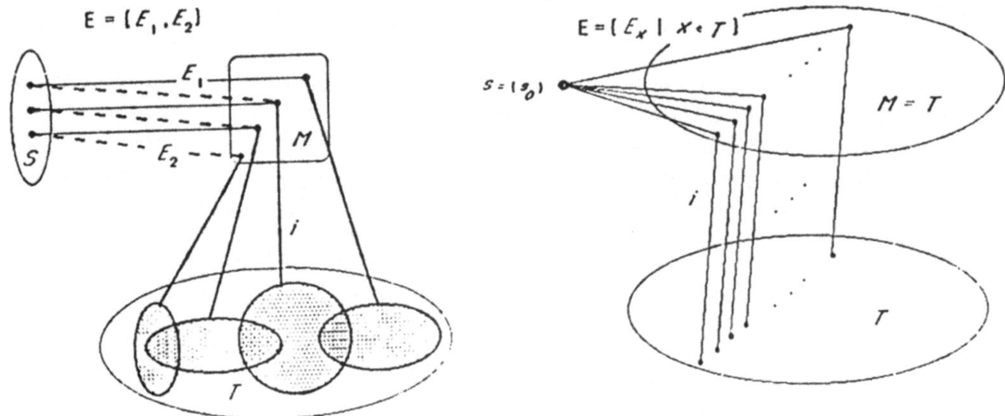

Figure 1. A general evidence model.   Figure 2. A probability distribution of T.

The Information $t \in X$. Consider the information "$t \in X$" for a subset $X \subseteq T$. Let $M_0 = \{m_0\}$, consisting of only one element; i_X the interpretation function, defined as $i_X(m_0) = X$; $\mathbf{E}_0 = \{E_0\}$, consisting of only one function from S_0 to M_0: $E_0(s_0) = m_0$. Then the information quadruplet $(S_0, M_0, i_X, \mathbf{E}_0)$ (depicted in Figure 3) represents the information "$t \in X$."

In this information, the basic probability and the belief function satisfy

$$m(X) = 1 \; ; \quad m(Y) = 0 \text{ if } Y \neq X;$$
$$\mathrm{Bel}(Y) = 1 \;\text{ if } X \subseteq Y; \quad \mathrm{Bel}(Y) = 0 \;\text{ otherwise.}$$

Since $\mathbf{E}_0$ consists of only one evidence function, this information quadruplet does not contain any other non-trivial new evidence which may appear later.

Dempster's Evidence. A piece of Dempster's evidence (Dempster 1967) is a function E from a given probability space S to 2^T. Suppose that $X \subseteq T$. Let $S_{X,E} = \{s : E(s) = X\}$ and $S_E = \{s : E(s) \text{ is defined}\}$. Then Dempster's basic probability, m_D, and Dempster's belief function, Bel_D, are defined as follows:

$$m_D(X) = P(S_{X,E}|S_E) = \frac{P(S_{X,E})}{P(S_E)}; \quad \text{Bel}_D(X) = \sum_{Y \subseteq X} m_D(Y).$$

Let $M = 2^T$. Let P_M be Dempster's basic probability M_D; id the identity function: $id(X) = X$ for $X \in 2^T$. Then $(S, M, id, \{E\})$ (depicted in Figure 4) forms an information quadruplet. In this information quadruplet, $m(X) = m_D(X)$ and $\text{Bel}(X) = \text{Bel}_D(X)$ for each $X \subseteq T$.

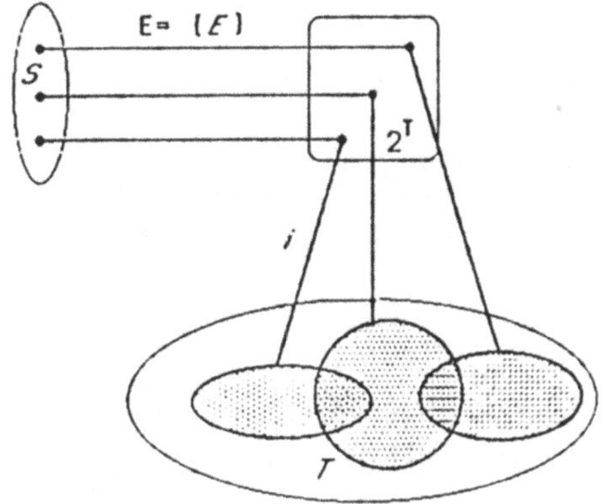

Figure 4. A piece of Dempster's evidence.

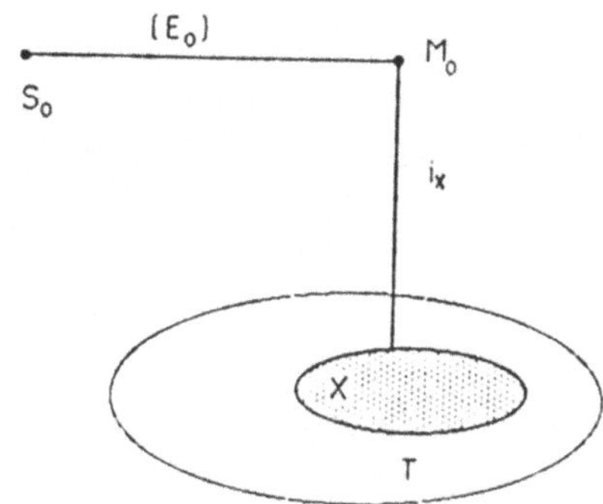

Figure 3. The information $t \in X$.

4   Independent Combination

This section introduces an idea of independent information and its combination. **Independent Model.** Suppose that $(S_1, M_1, i_1, \mathbf{E}_1)$ and $(S_2, M_2, i_2, \mathbf{E}_2)$ are two information quadruplets. Let P_{M_1} and P_{M_2} be the respective probability measures over M_1 and M_2; P_{S_1} and P_{S_2} the respective probability measures over S_1 and S_2. Let $M = M_1 \times M_2$, the product space with $P = P_{M_1} \times P_{M_2}$; $S = S_1 \times S_2$, the product space with $P_S = P_{S_1} \times P_{S_2}$.

Suppose that a_1 and a_2 are the random variables representing the occurring messages from M_1 and M_2, respectively. Consider the random vector $a = <a_1, a_2>$. If $a_1 = A_1$ and $a_2 = A_2$ (i.e., $a = <A_1, A_2>$), we call the pair $<A_1, A_2>$ a *message pair*. Since the messages A_1 and A_2 together mean that t is in both $i_1(A_1)$ and $i_2(A_2)$, $i_1(A_1) \cap i_2(A_2) \neq \emptyset$. Therefore, if both a_1 and a_2 are defined simultaneously, then there is at least a pair $<A_1, A_2> \in M_1 \times M_2$ such that $P_{M_1}(A_1) > 0$, $P_{M_2}(A_2) > 0$, and $i_1(A_1) \cap i_2(A_2) \neq \emptyset$.

Let M_T be the following subset of $M_1 \times M_2$:

$$M_T = \{<A_1, A_2> : A_1 \in M_1, A_2 \in M_2, i_1(A_1) \cap i_2(A_2) \neq \emptyset\}.$$

Then M_T contains all possible message pairs. We use M_T to define independence as follows:

Definition 3. Two information quadruplets $(S_1, M_1, i_1, \mathbf{E}_1)$ and $(S_2, M_2, i_2, \mathbf{E}_2)$ are *independent* if the following conditions are true:

1. It is possible that both a_1 and a_2 are defined simultaneously.

2. The two codes of the two information quadruplets are to be chosen independently.

3. The condition for $<A_1, A_2>$ being a possible message pair is that $<A_1, A_2> \in M_T$; that is, the probability that $a = <A_1, A_2>$ is equal to the conditional probability $P(a = <A_1, A_2> \mid a \in M_T)$, where $P = P_{M_1} \times P_{M_2}$.

Independent Combination. Suppose that $(S_1, M_1, i_1, \mathbf{E}_1)$ and $(S_2, M_2, i_2, \mathbf{E}_2)$ are independent. Consider $M_1 \times M_2$ with the function i defined by $i(<A_1, A_2>) = i_1(A_1) \cap i_2(A_2) \subseteq T$. Let P_{M_T} be the probability measure:

$$
\begin{aligned}
P_{M_T}(<A_1, A_2>) &= P(<A_1, A_2> \mid <A_1, A_2> \in M_T) \\
&= \frac{P_{M_1}(A_1) P_{M_2}(A_2)}{1 - \sum_{i_1(A_1) \cap i_2(A_2) = \emptyset} P_{M_1}(A_1) P_{M_2}(A_2)}.
\end{aligned}
\tag{2}
$$

Note that the first condition of independence guarantees that M_T is not empty and $P(M_T) > 0$. Then $(M_1 \times M_2, i)$ with P_{M_T} becomes a message model, which is called the *independent product* of (M_1, i_1) and (M_2, i_2).

Consider any two evidence functions E_1 and E_2, $E_1 \in \mathbf{E}_1$ and $E_2 \in \mathbf{E}_2$. Let $E_1 * E_2$ be a partial function from $S_1 \times S_2$ to $M_1 \times M_2$ defined as follows: $E_1 * E_2(<s, u>) = <E_1(s), E_2(u)>$ if both $E_1(s)$ and $E_2(u)$ are defined; $E_1 * E_2$ is not defined for other cases. $E_1 * E_2$ is called the *independently combined evidence function* (of E_1 and E_2) if it is defined for at least a pair $<s, u>$ ($\in S_1 \times S_2$). Let $\mathbf{E}_1 * \mathbf{E}_2$ be the set of all independently combined evidence functions. It can be shown that $\mathbf{E}_1 * \mathbf{E}_2$ is an evidence space with respect to the message model $(M_1 \times M_2, i)$ and the code space $S_1 \times S_2$. Then $(S_1 \times S_2, M_1 \times M_2, i, \mathbf{E}_1 * \mathbf{E}_2)$ becomes an information quadruplet.

Definition 4. The *independent combination* of $(S_1, M_1, i_1, \mathbf{E}_1)$ and $(S_2, M_2, i_2, \mathbf{E}_2)$ is the information quadruplet $(S_1 \times S_2, M_1 \times M_2, i, \mathbf{E}_1 * \mathbf{E}_2)$.

Consider the basic probability of the independent combination. For each $X \subseteq T$ we can derive from Equation (2) that

$$
m(X) = \frac{\sum_{X_1 \cap X_2 = X} m_1(X_1) m_2(X_2)}{1 - \sum_{X_1 \cap X_2 = \emptyset} m_1(X_1) m_2(X_2)}.
\tag{3}
$$

where m_1 and m_2 are the basic probabilities of $(S_1, M_1, i_1, \mathbf{E}_1)$ and $(S_2, M_2, i_2, \mathbf{E}_2)$, respectively. Equation (3) is the Dempster combination rule.

Given an independently combined evidence function $E_1 * E_2$, consider the posterior basic probability of the independent combination. Since the two respective codes are chosen independently, we have for each possible message pair $<A_1, A_2>$

$$
P(E_1 * E_2 \mid <A_1, A_2>) = P(E_1 \mid A_1) P(E_1 \mid A_1).
$$

Therefore,

$$P(\langle A_1, A_2\rangle \mid E_1 * E_2) = \frac{P(E_1 * E_2 \mid \langle A_1, A_2\rangle) P_{M_T}(\langle A_1, A_2\rangle)}{P(E_1 * E_2)}$$

$$= \frac{P(E_1 \mid A_1) P(E_1 \mid A_1) P_{M_T}(\langle A_1, A_2\rangle)}{P(E_1 * E_2)}.$$

Hence, for each $X \subseteq T$, we have

$$m(X \mid E_1 * E_2) = c_1 \sum_{i_1(A_1) \cap i_2(A_2) = X} P(E_1 \mid A_1) P(E_2 \mid A_2) P_{M_T}(\langle A_1, A_2\rangle)$$

$$= c_2 \sum_{i_1(A_1) \cap i_2(A_2) = X} P(E_1 \mid A_1) P(E_2 \mid A_2) P_{M_1}(A_1) P_{M_2}(A_2)$$

$$= c_3 \sum_{X_1 \cap X_2 = X} m_1(X_1 \mid E_1) m_2(X_2 \mid E_2),$$

where c_1, c_2, and c_3 are normalizing factors. Finally, we have a formula for the posterior basic probability:

$$m(X \mid E_1 * E_2) = \frac{\sum_{X_1 \cap X_2 = X} m_1(X_1 \mid E_1) m_2(X_2 \mid E_2)}{1 - \sum_{X_1 \cap X_2 = \emptyset} m_1(X_1 \mid E_1) m_2(X_2 \mid E_2)}. \tag{4}$$

Therefore, we have the following theorem.

Theorem 1. If two information quadruplets are independent, then the prior probabilities and the posterior basic probabilities can be combined by the Dempster combination rule (i.e., Equations (3) and (4)).

Bayesian Conditioning. Consider the conventional Bayesian approach. Let P be the prior probability measure over T. Given the information $t \in X$ ($X \subseteq T$), the posterior probability measure is the conditional probability $P(\cdot \mid X)$.

As in Section 3, let the prior probability P be represented by $(S_0, M_P, i_p, \mathbf{E}_T)$; the information $t \in X$ by $(S_0, M_0, i_X, \mathbf{E}_0)$. Consider their independent combination $(S_0 \times S_0, M_P \times M_0, i, \mathbf{E}_T * \mathbf{E}_0)$. Then the basic probability and belief function satisfy

$$m(x) = P(x \mid X), \quad x \in T;$$
$$\mathrm{Bel}(Y) = P(Y \mid X), \quad X \subseteq T.$$

Therefore, we have the following theorem.

Theorem 2. The Bayesian conditional probability $P(\cdot \mid X)$ is the belief function of the independent combination of the prior probability and the information $t \in X$.

5 Conclusions

The uncertainty model introduced in this papaer is based upon probability theory and Bayes rule. The Dempster combination rule is a method to combine independent information. The concept of a belief function in our formulation is more general than that of

156

a conventional probability distribution. Since both the conventional Bayesian approach and Dempster-Shafer's approach are special cases of this formulation, this mathematical formulation may provide a unified theory of probabilistic uncertainty in artificial intelligence.

References

[1] Dempster, A P (1967) Upper and lower probabilities induced by a multivalued mapping, *Annals of Mathematical Statistics* (38) 325-339

[2] Dempster, A P (1968) A generalization of Bayesian inference, *Journal of the Royal Statistical Society* (38) 205-247

[3] Hummel, R A and Landy, M S (1988) A Statistical Viewpoint on the Theory of Evidence, *IEEE Transactions on Pattern Analysis and Machine Intelligence* **10**, no. 2, 235-247

[4] Kyburg, H E Jr (1987) Bayesian and non-Bayesian evidential updating, *Artificial Intelligence* **31**, 271-293

[5] Laskey, K B (1987) Belief in belief functions: an examination of Shafer's canonical examples, in *Uncertainty in Artificial Intelligence, Third Workshop on Uncertainty in Artificial Intelligence*, Seattle, Washington, 39-46

[6] Pear, J (1988) *Probabilistic Reasoning in Intelligent System: Networks of Plausible Inference*, Morgan Kaufmann Publisher, San Mateo, California.

[7] Ruspini, E H (1987) Epistemic logics, probability, and the calculus of evidence, in *Proceedings of IJCAI-87*, 924-931

[8] Shafer, G (1976) *A mathematical theory of evidence*, Princeton University Press, Princeton, New Jersey

[9] Shafer, G (1981) Constructive probability, *Synthese* **48**, 1–60

[10] Shafer, G (1987) Probability Judgment in Artificial Intelligence and Expert Systems, *Statistical Science* **2** No. 1, 3–44

[11] Tzeng, CH (1988a) *A Theory of Heuristic Information in Game-Tree Search*, Springer-Verlag, Berlin

[12] Tzeng, CH (1988b) A Study of Dempster-Shafer's Theory through Shafer's Canonical Examples, *Proceedings of International Computer Science Conference '88, Artificial Intelligence: Theory and Applications*, Hong Kong, December 19-21, 1988, 69-76

[13] Tzeng, CH (1990) A Mathematical Formulation of Uncertain Information, to appear in *Annals of Mathematics and Artificial Intelligence.*

[14] William, P M (1982) Discussion of "belief functions and parametric models" by Glenn Shafer, *Journal of the Royal Statistical Society*, Ser. B, 44(3), 341–343

Qualitative Spatial Reasoning with Cardinal Directions[1]

Andrew U. Frank
National Center for Geographic Information
  and Analysis (NCGIA) and
Department of Surveying Engineering
University of Maine
Orono, ME 04469 USA
FRANK@MECAN1.bitnet
(207) 581-2174, FAX (207) 581-2206

and

Technical University Vienna
Gusshausstrasse 27-29
A-1040 Wien
Austria

Abstract

Following reviews of previous approaches to spatial reasoning, a completely qualitative
method for reasoning about cardinal directions, without recourse to analytical procedures, is
introduced and a method is presented for a formal comparison with quantitative formulae. We
use an algebraic method to formalize the meaning of cardinal directions. The standard
directional symbols (N, S, E,W) are extended with a symbol 0 to denote an undecided case,
which greatly increases the power of inference. Two examples of systems to determine and
reason with cardinal directions are discussed in some detail and results from a prototype are
given. The deduction rules for the coordination of directional symbols are formalized as
equations; for inclusion in an expert system they can be coded as a look-up table (given in the
text). The conclusions offer some direction for future work.

1.   Introduction

Qualitative spatial reasoning is widely used by humans to understand, analyze, and conclude
about the spatial environment when the information is qualitative; for example, received
through a verbal channel. A formalization and computer implementation for qualitative spatial
reasoning is necessary to understand spatial information expressed in natural language, is
generally useful for user interfaces to spatial information systems (e.g. Geographic
Information Systems), and is useful for optimization of spatial queries and for inclusion in
expert systems.

Most methods of spatial reasoning translate the given problem from the quantitative to the
qualitative realm and use analytical geometry to find a solution. This is not always a workable
solution. The treatment of the inherent uncertainty in qualitative spatial descriptions creates
problems. The construction of expert systems that deal with space and spatial problems has
been recognized as difficult (Bobrow, et al. 1986). Here, a strictly qualitative approach is
proposed and algebraic methods are used towards a formalization. The major step is the

[1] Funding from NSF for the NCGIA under grant SES 88-10917, from Intergraph Corporation and Digital
Equipment Corporation is gratefully acknowledged.

introduction of an identity symbol 0, that allows for a definition of rules which yield answers for all input values.

This paper is restricted to the specific problem of reasoning with cardinal directions. The problem addressed, described in practical terms, is the following: given the information that San Francisco is west of St. Louis, Chicago is north of St. Louis, and Baltimore is east of St. Louis, one can deduce the direction from San Francisco to Baltimore by the chain of deductions as follows:

1. Use 'San Francisco is west of St. Louis' and 'Baltimore is east of St. Louis', to establish a sequence of directions San Francisco - St. Louis - Baltimore .
2. Deduce 'St. Louis is west of Baltimore' from 'Baltimore is east of St. Louis'
3. Use the concept of transitivity: 'San Francisco is west of St. Louis' and 'St. Louis is west of Baltimore', thus conclude 'San Francisco is west of Baltimore' .

This paper formalizes such rules and makes them available for inclusion in an expert system.

The description of directional relationships between points in the plane can be formulated as propositions 'A is north of B' or 'north (A, B)'. Given a set of propositions one can then deduce other relative positions as the induced set of spatial constraints (Dutta 1990). Following an algebraic concept, one does not concentrate on directional relations between points but rather finds rules for the manipulation of the directional symbols themselves, when combined by operators. An algebra is defined by a set of symbols that are manipulated (here the directional symbols), a set of operations and axioms that define the outcome of the operations.

The two operations considered here are *'inversion'* and *'combination'* of paths. Directional symbols with the operations defined have properties very similar to the properties of algebraic groups, if one introduces an additional symbol for 0 (identity), such that a ∞ 0 = a. This symbol can be interpreted as 'two points are so close that one cannot determine a direction'.

Cardinal directions are similar to the four directions 'front', 'back', 'left', and 'right', which are regularly used in spatial references (Herskovits 1986, Retz-Schmidt 1987). Cardinal directions are easier to analyze because the frame of reference is fixed in space. However, the solution reported here is directly applicable for treating reference frames once a qualitative operation to integrate frames of different orientation is devised.

This work is part of a larger effort to understand how we describe and reason about space and spatial situations. In particular, within the research initiative 2, 'Languages of Spatial Relations' of the National Center for Geographic Information and Analysis (NCGIA 1989) a need for multiple formal descriptions of spatial reasoning—both quantitative-analytical and qualitative—became evident (Mark, et al. 1989, Mark and Frank 1990, Frank and Mark 1991, Frank 1990, Frank 1991).

The structure of this paper is as follows: the next section discusses previous work. Then the two basic operations on direction symbols and their properties are formalized, using geometric intuition; we also define what 'exact qualitative spatial reasoning' means. Two examples of systems of cardinal directions are constructed and then compared. The paper concludes with some research questions for future work.

2. Related work

A standard approach to spatial reasoning is to translate the problem posed into analytical geometry and to use quantitative methods for its solution. Many problems can be conveniently reformulated as optimization with a set of constraints, e.g. location of a resource or shortest path question. A similar approach has been applied to understand spatial references in natural language text (Herskovits 1986, Nirenburg and Raskin 1987, Retz-Schmidt 1987). A special problem is posed by the inherent uncertainties in these descriptions and their translation into an analytical format. (McDermott and Davis 1984) introduced a method using 'fuzz' and in (Dutta 1988, Dutta 1990, Retz-Schmidt 1987) fuzzy logic (Zadeh 1974) is used to combine such approximately metric data.

An entirely qualitative approach was utilized in the work on symbolic projections (Chang, et al. 1990). They translate exact metric information, primarily about objects in pictures, into a qualitative form Segments in pictures are projected vertically and horizontally, and their order of appearance is encoded in two strings. Spatial reasoning, especially spatial queries, are executed as fast substring searches (Chang, et al. 1987).

One is tempted to apply first-order predicate calculus to spatial reasoning with directions:

> "The direction relation NORTH. From the transitive property of NORTH one can conclude that if A is NORTH of B and B is NORTH of C then A must be NORTH of C as well (Mark, et al. 1989)"

This leads to complex rules of inference, stating conditions for points and the directional relations between them. Hernández combines directional and topological relations and gives rules for the deduction of spatial relations based on multiple, perspective observations (Hernández 1990).

Our concern is different from (Peuquet and Zhan 1987), where 'an algorithm to determine the directional relationship between arbitrarily-shaped polygons in the plane' is given and no inferences from given directional relations are drawn.

3.   An algebra of cardinal directions

The intuitive properties of cardinal directions are described in the form of an algebra with two operations applicable to direction symbols:

- the reversing of the direction of travel (*inverse*), and
- the combination of the direction symbol of two consecutive segments of a path (*combination*).

The operational meaning of cardinal direction is captured in a set of formal axioms. These axioms define the properties of cardinal directions. The rules are, for a part, formally similar to vector algebra. We find that the axioms deduced from geometric intuition are approximating geometrically exact reasoning and as a system logically contradictory.

3.1. Cardinal Directions

Direction is a binary function from two points in the plane (P_1, P_2) that map onto a symbolic direction d. The specific directional symbols available depend on the system of directions used, e.g., $d_4 = \{N, E, S, W\}$ or more extensive $d_8 = \{N, NE, E, SE, S, SW, W, NW\}$.

We avoid the limitation, that direction is only meaningful if the two points are different and introduce a special symbol 0 (for 'zero'), in algebra usually called identity. It means 'two points too close for a direction to be determined'. This simplifies the rules and increases deductive power.

3.2. Reversing direction

Cardinal directions depend on the direction of travel. If a direction is given for a line segment between points P_1 and P_2, the direction from P_2 to P_1 can be deduced (Peuquet and Zhan 1987, Freeman 1975). This operation is called *inverse* (Figure 1), with

$$\text{inv (dir } (P_1, P_2)) = \text{dir } (P_2, P_1) \quad \text{and inv (inv } (d)) = d.$$

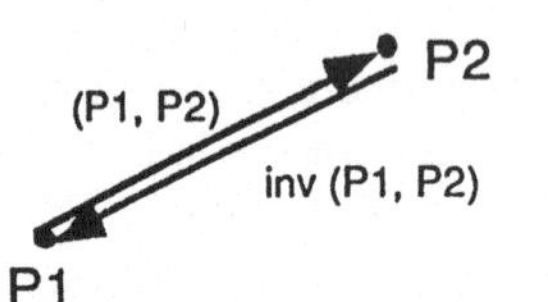

Figure 1: Inverse

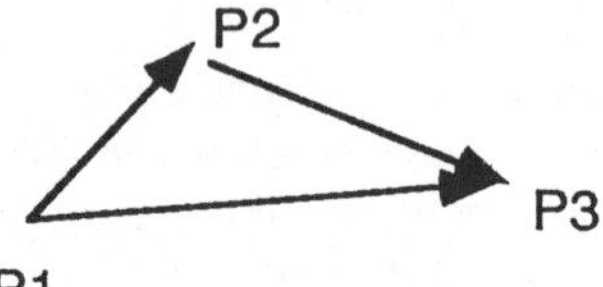

Figure 2: Combination

3.3. Combination

The second operation combines the directions of two contiguous line segments, such that the end point of the first direction is the start point of the second one (Figure 2).

$$d_1 \infty d_2 = d_3 \quad \text{means} \quad \text{dir } (P_1, P_2) \infty \text{dir } (P_2, P_3) = \text{dir } (P_1, P_3)$$

It is not necessary that combination is commutative ($a \infty b \neq b \infty a$), but this is the case for both examples of definitions for cardinal directions studied here, are.

Associativity: Combinations of more than two directions should be independent of the order in which they are combined:

$$a \infty (b \infty c) = (a \infty b) \infty c = a \infty b \infty c \qquad \text{(associative law)}$$

This rule follows immediately from a figure or from the definition of combination in terms of line segments.

Identity: Adding the direction from a point to itself, $\text{dir}(P_1, P_1) = 0$, to any other direction does not change the direction.

Algebraic definition of inverse: In algebra, an inverse to a binary operation is defined such that a value, combined with its inverse, results in the identity value. Geometrically the inverse is the line segment that combines with a given other line segment to lead back to the start (see Figure 3).

$$\text{inv } (d) \infty d = 0 \quad \text{and} \quad d \infty \text{inv } (d) = 0$$

Computing the combination of two directions, where one is the inverse of the other, is in the general case an *approximation* and not Euclidean exact. The degree of error depends on the definition of 0 used and the difference in the distance between the points - if they are the same, the inference rule is exact. This represents a type of reasoning like: New York is east of San Francisco, San Francisco is west of Baltimore, thus New York is too close to Baltimore (in the frame of reference of the continent) to determine the direction. In general one observes that deduction based on directions alone is only applicable if all the distances are of the same order of magnitude.

Figure 3: d ∞ inv (d) = 0

Figure 4: d₁ = d₃ ∞ inv (d₂)

The inverse is also used to compute the completion of one path to another (Figure 4) and one finds that a combined path is piece-wise reversible inv (a ∞ b) = inv (b) ∞ inv (a).

Idempotent: If one combines two line segments with the same direction, one expects that the result maintains the same direction. This is transitivity for a direction relation:

> from d (A,B) and d (B,C) follows d (A,C)

This rule for directional symbols is substantially different from the corresponding rule for vector addition. From an algebraic point of view, all directions are idempotent:

> d ∞ d = d, for any d.

3.4. Definition of Euclidean exact reasoning

The rules for qualitative spatial reasoning given are compared with the quantitative methods using analytical geometry. The following definition gives a precise framework for such a comparison. A qualitative rule is called *Euclidean exact,* if the result of applying the rule is the same as if we had translated the data to analytical geometry and applied the equivalent functions, i.e. if we have a homomorphism. Otherwise it is called *Euclidean approximate.*

> dir(P_1,P_2) ∞ dir (P_2, P_3) = dir ((P_1, P_2) + (P_2, P_3))

3.5. Summary of Properties of Cardinal Directions

The basic rules for cardinal directions and the operations of inverse and combination are:

- The combination operation is associative (1').
- The direction between a point and itself is a special symbol 0, called *identity* (1) (2')
- The direction between a point and another is the *inverse* of the direction between the other point and the first (2) (3').
- The set of directions is closed under inverse and combination.
- Combining two equal directions results in the same direction (*idempotent*, transitivity for direction relation) (3) - an approximate rule
- The combination can be inverted (4).
- Combination is piece-wise invertible (5).

dir (P_1, P_1) = 0	(1)	d ∞ (d ∞ d) = (d ∞ d) ∞ d	(1')
dir (P_1, P_2) = inv (dir (P_2, P_1))	(2)	d ∞ 0 = 0 ∞ d = d	(2')
d ∞ d = d	(3)	d ∞ inv (d) = 0	(3')
for any a, b in D exist unique x in D such that			
a ∞ x = b and x ∞ a = b	(4)		
inv (a ∞ b) = inv (a) ∞ inv (b)	(5)		

Properties of direction	Group properties

Several of the properties of directions are similar to properties of algebraic groups or follow immediately from them. Unfortunately, the approximate cancellation rule (3') d ∞ inv (d) = 0 leads to a contradiction with the remaining postulates. Searching for an inverse x for any d ∞ x = 0, we find x = inv (d) (using (3)) or x = 0 (using 3'). A standard solution is to define a non approximate rule, d ∞ inv (d) = {d, 0, inv (d)}, which reinstates logical consistency. We prefer the plausible reasoning solution and use (3') but give up associativity (1') and uniqueness of the inverse (4).

4.   Two Examples of Systems of Cardinal Directions

Two examples of systems of cardinal directions are studied, both using the same set of eight directional symbols (plus the identity). One is based on cone-shaped (or triangular) areas of acceptance, the other is based on projections. These two semantics for cardinal direction can be related to Jackendoff's principles of centrality, necessity and typicality (Jackendoff 1983) as pointed out by Peuquet (Mark, et al. 1989, p. 24).

4.1.   Directions in 8 or More Cones

Cardinal directions relate the angular direction between a position and a destination to some directions fixed in space. An angular direction is assigned the nearest named direction which results in cone shaped areas for which a symbolic direction is applicable. This model has the property that "the area of acceptance for any given direction increases with distance" (Peuquet and Zhan 1987, p. 66) (with additional references) and is sometimes called 'triangular'.

We use the set of directional symbols

V_9 = {N, NE, E, SE, S, SW, W, NW, 0}.

and define a turn of an eighth anti-clockwise:

e (N) = NE, e (NE) = E, e (E) = SE, ... , e (NW) = N,   e (0) = 0

with 8 eighth turns being the identity function e^8 (d) = d. The inverse is defined as 4 eighth turns inv (d) = e^4 (d). The rules for combination of directions are(2') (3) and the approximative rule (3'). This allows for a deduction of about one third of possible combinations. A set of averaging rules, which allow the combination of directional values which are apart by 1 or 2 eighth turns, is necessary to complete the system. For example N is combined with NE to yield N.

e (e (d)) ∞ d = e (d),   e (d) ∞ d = d,   e (d) ∞ inv (d) = 0,   d ∞ e (d) = d, etc.

In this system, from all the 81 pairs of values (64 for the subset without 0) combinations can be inferred, but most of them only approximately. Written as a table, where lower case denotes Euclidean approximate inferences:

	N	NE	E	SE	S	SW	W	NW	0
N	N	n	ne	o	o	o	nw	nw	N
NE	n	NE	ne	e	o	o	o	n	NE
E	ne	ne	E	e	se	o	o	o	E
SE	o	e	e	SE	se	s	o	o	SE
S	o	o	se	se	S	s	sw	o	S
SW	o	o	o	s	s	SW	sw	w	SW
W	nw	o	o	o	sw	sw	W	w	W
NW	nw	n	o	o	o	w	w	NW	NW
0	N	NE	E	SE	S	SW	W	NW	0

Directions so defined do not fulfill all the requirements, because they violate the associative property (i.e. 328 out of 729 cases); for example (S ∞ N) ∞ E = 0 ∞ E = E but

S ∞ (N ∞ E) = S ∞ NE = 0. The evaluation of a complex expression depends on the order. The differences are minor and are probably a reflection of the inherent vagueness of the concept of directions (Herskovits 1986, p. 192)

4.2. Cardinal Directions Defined by Projections

4.2.1.   Directions in 4 half-planes

One can define four directions such that they are pair-wise opposites (Peuquet and Zhan 1987) and each pair divides the plane into two half-planes. The direction operation assigns for each pair of points a combination of two directions, e.g., South and East for a total of 4 different directions (Figs. 5 and 6).

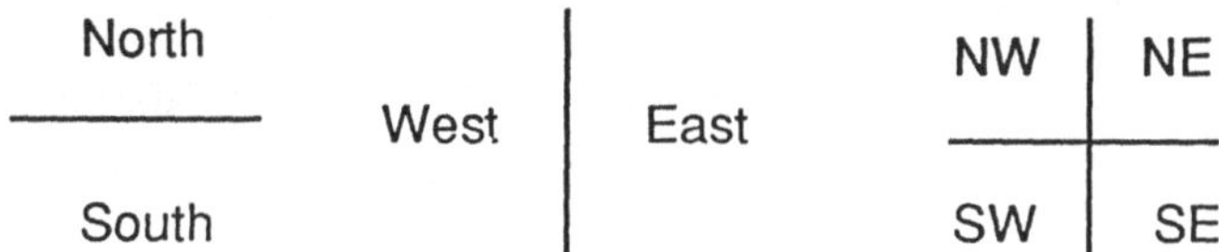

Figure 5: Two sets of half-planes.   Figure 6: Directions defined by half-planes.

Another justification for this definition of cardinal direction is found in the structure that geographic longitude and latitude impose on the globe. Cone directions better represent the direction of 'going toward', whereas the 'half-planes' (or equivalent parts of the globe) better represent the relative position of points on the earth. Frequently, the two coincide.

In this system, the two projections can be dealt with individually. When the two projections in N-S and E-W are combined to form a single system with the directional symbols:

$$V_4 = \{ NE, NW, SE, SW\}$$

only the trivial cases (NE ∞ NE = NE, etc.) can be resolved.

4.2.2.   Projection-Based Directions with Neutral Zone

If points which are near to due north (or west, east, south) are not assigned a second direction, i.e. one does not decide whether or not such a point is more east or west, one divides effectively the plane into 9 regions (Figure 7): a central neutral area, four regions where only one direction applies and 4 regions where two are used. We define for N-S three values for direction d_{ns} {N, P, S} and for the E - W direction the values d_{ew} {E, Q, W}.

NW	N	NE
W	O_c	E
SW	S	SE

Figure 7: Directions with neutral zone

It is important to note that the width of the 'neutral zone' is not defined a priori. Its size is effectively decided when the directional values are assigned and a decision is made that P_2 is north (not north-west or north-east) of P_1. The algebra deals only with the directional symbols, not how they are assigned. The system assumes that these decisions are consistently made in order to determine if a deduction rule is Euclidean exact or not.

Allowing a neutral zone introduces a 'tolerance geometry' point of view. Whenever an identity direction dir $(P_1, P_2) = 0$ is assigned in cases where $P_1 \neq P_2$, the transitivity assumption of equality is violated (Robert 1973, Zeeman 1962).

In one projection, selecting $d_{ns} = \{N, P, S\}$ as the prototype, the inverse operation is defined as inv $(N) = S$, inv $(S) = N$, inv $(P) = P$. For the combination, we require the rules (3), (2') and (3'). These rules together violate associativity. In 200 of the 729 cases, the result depends on the order of evaluation.

The two projections in N-S and E-W are then combined to form a single system, in which for each line segment one of 9 combinations of directions are assigned.

$$V_9 = \{NE, NQ, NW, PE, PW, PQ, SE, SQ, SW\}$$

Adding some syntactic sugar, P and Q are eliminated (replacing PQ by 0)

$$V_9 = \{NE, N, NW, E, W, 0, SE, S, SW\}$$

If any of the results of the two projections is approximate, the total result is considered approximate reasoning.

The inverse operation is combined from the inverse for each projection, written as a table:

d	NE	N	NW	E	W	0	SE	S	SW
inv(d) =	SW	S	SE	W	E	0	NW	N	NE

The combination operation is defined as the combination for each projection. Using the three rules, we can compute the values for each combination. Written as a table (again, lower case indicates approximate reasoning):

$*_d$	N	NE	E	SE	S	SW	W	NW	0
N	N	NE	NE	e	o	w	NW	NW	N
NE	NE	NE	NE	e	e	o	n	n	NE
E	NE	NE	E	SE	SE	s	o	n	E
SE	e	e	SE	SE	SE	s	s	o	SE
S	o	e	SE	SE	S	SW	SW	w	S
SW	w	o	s	s	SW	SW	SW	w	SW
W	NW	n	o	s	SW	SW	W	NW	W
NW	NW	n	n	o	w	w	NW	NW	NW
0	N	NE	E	SE	S	SW	W	NW	0

4.3. Assessment

The power of the 8 direction cone-shaped and the 4 half-plane based directional system are similar. Each system uses 9 directional symbols, 8 cone directions plus identity on one hand, the Cartesian product of 3 values (2 directional symbols and 1 identity symbol) for each projection on the other hand. The same three rules are used to build both systems, but the cone-shaped system had to be completed with a number of 'averaging rules'

Introducing the identity symbol 0 increases the number of deduction in both cases considerably. Only 8 out of 64 combinations could be resolved for cone shaped directions and only trivial cases can be resolved for the half-plane based system. Without the identity symbol the systems with identity allow conclusions for any pair of input values (81 different pairs) at least approximately. The comparison reveals that the cone-shaped directions result in more cases of approximative results than the projection-based system (56 vs. 32) and that it yields more often the value 0 (25 vs. 9). Considering the actual values (other than 0) deduced, we see differences only for results where the 'averaging rules' are used for the cone-shaped directions, and the values differ by one eighth turn only. The two systems produce essentially the same deduction results.

Both systems violate some of the desired properties. One can easily observe that associativity is not guaranteed, but the differences seem not to be very significant.

An implementation of these rules and a comparison of the computed combinations with the exact value was carried out and these results confirm the theoretical findings. Comparing all possible 10^6 combinations in a grid of 10 by 10 points (with a neutral zone of 3 for the projection-based directions) shows that the results for the projection-based directions are correct in 50% of cases and for cone-shaped directions in only 25%. The result 0 is the outcome of 18% of all cases for the projection-based, but 61% for the cone-shaped directions. The direction-based system with an extended neutral zone produces in 2% of all cases, a result that is a quarter turn off. Otherwise, the deviation from the correct result is never more than one eighth of a turn, namely in 13% of all cases for cone-shaped and 26% for projection-based direction systems. In summary, the projection-based system of directions produces in 80% of all cases a result that is within 45° and otherwise the value 0.

5. Conclusions

This paper introduced a system for inference rules for qualitative spatial reasoning with cardinal distances from an algebraic point of view. Two operations, *inverse* and *combination* are applied to direction symbols and their meanings formalized with a set of axioms. Three requirements, that such directions should fulfill, are (1) the direction from a point to itself is a special value, meaning 'too close to determine a direction', (2) every direction has an inverse, namely the direction from the end point to the start point of the line segment, and (3) the combination of two lines segments with the same direction results in a line segment with the same direction.

These rules can be used to identify some systems which are not suitable for cardinal directions, e.g., a system with an uneven number of cardinals. In order to compare the qualitative rules with quantitative calculations, we define the notion of 'Euclidean exact', using a homomorphism. A deduction rule is called 'Euclidean exact' if it produces the same results as those obtained using Euclidean geometry operations.

Two different systems for cardinal directions were discussed in detail, both fulfilling the requirements for directions. One is based on cone-shaped (or triangular) directions, the other deals with directions in two orthogonal projections. The introduction of the identity element 0 simplifies the reasoning rules in both cases and increases the power for both, cone and projection-based directional systems. The half-plane based system of directions is slightly easier to describe and formalize, as we can deal with each projection separately, yielding simpler inference rules.

Both systems yield results for all the 81 different inputs for the combination operation, but the projection-based system does more often yield an Euclidean exact result than the cone-based one (49 vs. 25 cases). It also produces less often the value 0 (9 vs. 25 cases). Another important result is that the two systems do not differ substantially in their conclusions, if definite conclusions can be drawn, i.e. not the value 0. This reduces the potential for testing with human subjects to find out which system they use, observing cases where the conclusion using one or the other line of reasoning would yield different results.

We have implemented these deduction rules and compared the results obtained for all combinations in a regular grid. The projection-based system results in 53% of all cases in exact results and in another 26% in results which are not more than 45° off. In 18% of all cases the application of the rules yields a value of 0. The results for the cone-shaped directions are less accurate. The methods shown here can be used to quickly assess whether the combination of two directions yields a value that falls within some limits, and a more accurate and slower computation should be done.

Acknowledgements

Discussions with Matt McGranaghan and Max Egenhofer helped clarify concepts and presentation. I appreciate their help.

References

D. G. Bobrow, S. Mittal and M. J. Stefik. 1986. Expert Systems: Perils and Promise. *Communications of the ACM* 29 (9) : 880-894.

S.-K. Chang, E. Jungert and Y. Li. 1990. "The Design of Pictorial Databases Based Upon the Theory of Symbolic Projection". In *Design and Implementation of Large Spatial Databases*. Edited by A. Buchmann, O. Günther, T. R. Smith and Y.-F. Wang. 303 - 324. New York NY: Springer Verlag.

S. K. Chang, Q. Y. Shi and C. W. Yan. 1987. Iconic Indexing by 2-D String. *IEEE Transactions on Pattern Analysis and Machine Intelligence* 9 (3) : 413 - 428.

S. Dutta. 1988. "Approximate Spatial Reasoning". In *First International Conference on Industrial and Engineering Applications of Artificial Intelligence and Expert Systems*. 126 - 140. Tullahoma, Tennessee: ACM Press.

S. Dutta. 1990. "Qualitative Spatial Reasoning: A Semi-quantitative Approach Using Fuzzy Logic". In *Design and Implementation of Large Spatial Databases*. Edited by A. Buchmann, O. Günther, T. R. Smith and Y.-F. Wang. 345 - 364. New York NY: Springer Verlag.

A. U. Frank. 1990. "Spatial Concepts, Geometric Data Models and Data Structures". In *GIS Design Models and Functionality*. Edited by D. Maguire. Leicester, UK: Midlands Regional Research Laboratory, University of Leicester.

A. U. Frank. 1991. Qualitative Spatial Reasoning about Cardinal Directions. In *Autocarto 10*. Edited by D. Mark and D. White. 148-167.

A. U. Frank and D. M. Mark. 1991. "Language Issues for Geographical Information Systems". In *Geographic Information Systems: Principles and Applications*. Edited by D. Maguire, D. Rhind and M. Goodchild. London: Longman Co. (in press).

J. Freeman. 1975. The modelling of spatial relations. *Computer Graphics and Image Processing* 4 : 156-171.

D. Hernández. 1990. *Relative Representation of Spatial Knowledge: The 2-D Case*. Report FKI-135-90. Munich FRG: Technische Universität München.

A. Herskovits. 1986. *Language and Spatial Cognition - An Interdisciplinary Study of the Propositions in English*. Stiudies in Natural Language Processing. Cambridge UK: Cambridge University Press.

R. Jackendoff. 1983. *Semantics and Cognition*. Cambridge, Mass.: MIT Press.

D. M. Mark and A. U. Frank. 1990. *Experiential and Formal Representations of Geographic Space and Spatial Relations*. Technical Report (in press). : NCGIA.

D. M. Mark, A. U. Frank, M. J. Egenhofer, S. M. Freundschuh, M. McGranaghan and R. M. White. 1989. *Languages of Spatial Relations: Initiative Two Specialist Meeting Report*. Technical Report 89-2. : National Center for Geographic Information and Analysis.

D. McDermott and E. Davis. 1984. Planning routes through uncertain territory. *Artificial Intelligence* 22 : 107-156.

NCGIA. 1989. The U.S. National Center for Geographic Information and Analysis: An overview of the agenda for research and education. *International Journal of Geographical Information Systems* 2 (3) : 117-136.

S. Nirenburg and V. Raskin. 1987. "Dealing with Space in Natural Language Processing". In *Spatial Reasoning and Multi-Sensor Fusion*. Edited by A. Kak and S.-s. Chen. 361 - 370. Pleasan Run Resort, St. Charles, IL: Morgan Kaufmann Publishers.

D. Peuquet and C.-X. Zhan. 1987. An algorithm to determine the directional relationship between arbitrarily-shaped polygons in a plane. *Pattern Recognition* 20 : 65-74.

G. Retz-Schmidt. 1987. "Deitic and Intrinsic Use of Spatial Propositions: A Multidisciplinary Comparison". In *Spatial Reasoning and Multi-Sensor Fusion*. Edited by A. Kak and S.-s. Chen. 371 -380. Pleasan Run Resort, St. Charles, IL: Morgan Kaufmann Publishers.

F. S. Robert. 1973. Tolerance Geometry. *Notre Dame Journal of Formal Logic* 14 (1) : 68-76.

L. A. Zadeh. 1974. "Fuzzy Logic and Its Application to Approximate Reasoning". In *Information Processing*. : North-Holland Publishing Company.

E. C. Zeeman. 1962. "The Topology of the Brain and Visual Perception". In *The Topology of 3-Manifolds*. Edited by M. K. Fort. 240 -256. Englewood Cliffs, NJ: Prentice Hall.

Model-Based Diagnosis with Constraint Logic Programs

Igor Mozetič*
Austrian Research Institute for Artificial Intelligence
Schottengasse 3, A-1010 Vienna, Austria

Christian Holzbaur
Austrian Research Institute for Artificial Intelligence, and
Department of Medical Cybernetics and Artificial Intelligence
University of Vienna
Freyung 6, A-1010 Vienna, Austria

Abstract

Model-based diagnosis is the activity of locating malfunctioning components of a system solely on the basis of its structure and behavior. In the paper we describe the role of Constraint Logic Programming (CLP) in representing models and the search space of minimal diagnoses. In particular, we concentrate on two instances of the CLP scheme: $CLP(\mathcal{B})$ and $CLP(\mathfrak{R})$. $CLP(\mathcal{B})$ extends the standard computational domain of logic programs by boolean expressions, while $CLP(\mathfrak{R})$ comprises a solver for systems of linear equations and inequalities over real-valued variables.

1 Introduction

There are two fundamentaly different approaches to diagnostic reasoning. In the first, heuristic approach, one encodes diagnostic rules of thumb and experience of human experts in a given domain. In the second, model-based approach, one starts with a model of a real-world system which explicitly represents the structure and components of the system (e.g., Genesereth 1984, Davis 1984, de Kleer & Williams 1987, Reiter 1987). When the system's actual behavior is different from the expected behavior, the diagnostic problem arises. The model is then used to identify faulty components and their internal states which account

---

*Invited talk at the 6th Czechoslovak Annual Conf. on AI, Prague, June 25-27, 1991.

for the observed behavior. One usually requires a parsimonious diagnosis, i.e., a *minimal* set of faulty components.

In our view there are two major obstacles which prevented a wider application of model-based techniques to real-world problems. First, the complexity of algorithms which find all minimal diagnoses is exponential in the number of components. This problem was addressed only recently, either by focusing just to a small number of most probable diagnoses (de Kleer & Williams 1990, Mozetic & Holzbaur 1991b), by interleaving diagnosis and treatment (Friedrich *et al.* 1990), or by introducing abstractions (Gallanti *et al.* 1989, Mozetic 1990). Second, models are usually restricted to qualitative descriptions. GDE (de Kleer & Williams 1987), for example, is unable to solve simultaneous equations, which makes it unpractical for a large class of applications.

In the paper we describe the role of Constraint Logic Programming (CLP, Jaffar *et al.* 1986, Cohen 1990) in representing a larger class of models. CLP are logic programs extended by interpreted functions. A proper implementation of the CLP scheme allows for an easy integration of specialized problem solvers into the logic programming framework. For example, in Metaprolog (an extension of C-Prolog, Holzbaur 1990) specialized solvers communicate with the standard Prolog interpreter via extended semantic unification and are implemented in Prolog themselves. So far, we have implemented three solvers: constraint propagation over finite domains by forward checking, $CLP(\mathcal{B})$ — a solver over boolean expressions, and $CLP(\Re)$ — a solver for systems of linear equations and inequalities over reals[1].

In section 2 we show how to model structure and behavior by logic programs. We clarify the relationship between the behavior of a component and its internal state (normal or malfunctioning). In section 3 we define the concepts of a diagnosis and conflict and show how to compute them by a logic programming system. For compact modeling of discrete systems, e.g., digital circuits, and for representing the search space of minimal diagnoses $CLP(\mathcal{B})$ can be used (section 4). In contrast, to model continuos systems, e.g., analogue circuits, a more expressive formalism is needed. In section 5 we outline the use and operation of $CLP(\Re)$.

2 Modeling structure and behavior

Model-based reasoning about a system requires an explicit representation (a model) of the system's components and their connections. Reasoning is typically based on theorem proving if a model is represented by first-order logic (Genesereth 1984, Reiter 1987), or on constraint propagation coupled with an ATMS (de Kleer & Williams 1987). We represent models by *logic programs* (Lloyd 1987), or by *constraint logic programs* (Jaffar *et al.* 1986).

---

[1]Metaprolog and the three specialized solvers are available on request from the second author.

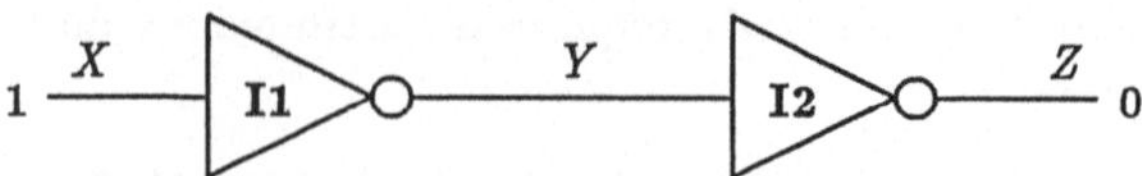

Figure 1: Two inverters, with states I1 and I2, and an observation $\langle 1,0 \rangle$.

Definition. A *model* of a system is a triple $\langle SD, \ COMPS, \ OBS \rangle$ where

1. *SD*, the system description, is a logic program with a distinguished top-level binary predicate *m(COMPS, OBS)*.

2. *COMPS*, states of the system components, is an n-tuple $\langle S_1, \ldots, S_n \rangle$ where n is the number of components, and variables S_i denote states (e.g., normal or abnormal) of components.

3. *OBS*, observations, is an m-tuple $\langle In_1, \ldots, In_i, Out_{i+1}, \ldots, Out_m \rangle$ where *In* and *Out* denote inputs and outputs of the model, respectively.

In a logic program, n-tuples are represented by terms of arity n. Variables start with capitals and are implicitly universally quantified in front of a clause, and constants start with lower-case letters. In *SD* and definitions we refer to a distinguished constant *ok* to denote that the state S_i of the component i is normal. This corresponds to the statement $\neg ab(S_i)$ used in the consistency-based approach.

Example (two inverters, de Kleer *et al.* 1990, Figure 1). *COMPS* is a pair $\langle I1,I2 \rangle$ and *OBS* is a pair $\langle X,Z \rangle$. *SD* consists of the following clause which specifies the structure of the device, and of additional clauses which define behavior of an inverter:

```
m( ⟨I1,I2⟩, ⟨X,Z⟩ )  ←
    inv( I1, X, Y ),
    inv( I2, Y, Z ).
```

Connections between components are represented by shared variables. Specification of the behavior depends on the available knowledge about possible faults. We distinguish between three types of fault models: weak, exoneration, or strong.

A **weak** fault model defines just normal behavior of components (state *ok*), abnormal behavior (state *ab*) is unconstrained:

```
inv( ok, 0, 1 ).
inv( ok, 1, 0 ).
inv( ab, _, _ ).
```

An **exoneration** model (Raiman 1989) is a special case of a strong fault model and specifies as abnormal any behavior different than normal:

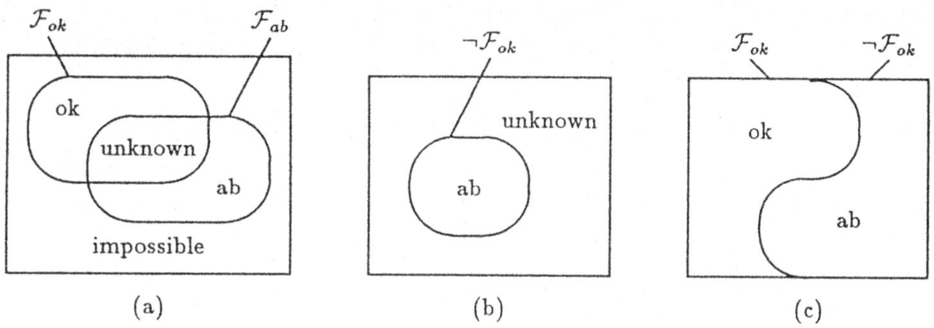

Figure 2: General relation (a) between the behavior ($\mathcal{F}_{ok}$, $\mathcal{F}_{ab}$) and the state (ok, ab, unknown) of a component. Two special cases are a weak fault model (b), and an exoneration model (c).

$\mathcal{F}_{ok}$	$\mathcal{F}_{ab}$	S	Meaning
0	0	fail	impossible
0	1	1	ab
1	0	0	ok
1	1	W	unknown

Table 1: A decision table encoding the state S of a component as a function of normal ($\mathcal{F}_{ok}$) and abnormal ($\mathcal{F}_{ab}$) behavior. $\mathcal{F} = 1$ denotes that the behavior is achieved, while $\mathcal{F} = 0$ denotes that the behavior is not achieved.

inv(ok, 0, 1).
inv(ok, 1, 0).
inv(ab, X, X).

A **strong** fault model (Struss & Dressler 1989) specifies all the possible ways in which a component can fail. In general, a component may have several failure states (e.g., stuck-at-0 or stuck-at-1), but in our example we allow just for one:

inv(ok, 0, 1).
inv(ok, 1, 0).
inv(ab, _, 0).   *% stuck-at-0*

General relation between the behavior and the state of a component is depicted in Figure 2. Instead of using essentially extensional descriptions of the weak, exoneration, and strong fault models we can formulate them in terms of boolean algebra expressions. In the following $\mathcal{F}_{ok}$ denotes a normal, and $\mathcal{F}_{ab}$ an abnormal behavior of a component. If we encode the normal state as 0 (zero) instead of *ok*, and the faulty state as 1 instead of *ab* then the following expression computes the state from the behavior (Table 1):

$$S \equiv (\neg\mathcal{F}_{ok} \vee \mathcal{F}_{ab} \wedge W) \leftarrow \mathcal{F}_{ok} \vee \mathcal{F}_{ab}.$$

In a special case of a weak fault model (where $\mathcal{F}_{ab}$ is unconstrained) the state S is computed as $S \equiv (\neg\mathcal{F}_{ok} \vee W)$. If a normal behavior is not achieved we conclude that the component is faulty. Otherwise we cannot conclude anything (an unbound variable W).

In a special case of an exoneration model (where $\mathcal{F}_{ab} \equiv \neg\mathcal{F}_{ok}$) the state is simply $S \equiv \neg\mathcal{F}_{ok}$. If a normal behavior is not achieved we conclude that the component is faulty. Otherwise we conclude it functions correctly.

For the inverter example, the normal behavior is defined as $\mathcal{F}_{ok}$: $\neg X \equiv Y$. The following three clauses specify the weak, exoneration, and strong fault model, respectively, and $\oplus$ is the *xor* operator:

$$inv(\ (\neg X \oplus Y) \vee W,\ X,\ Y\ ).$$
$$inv(\ \neg X \oplus Y,\ X,\ Y\ ).$$
$$inv(\ (\neg X \oplus Y) \vee (\neg Y \wedge W),\ X,\ Y\ ) \leftarrow ((\neg X \equiv Y) \vee \neg Y) = 1.$$

3 Computing diagnoses and conflicts

In order to define the concepts of a diagnosis and a conflict, we assume that an observation, a ground instance of *OBS*, is given. In the following definitions $\forall F$ denotes universal closure, i.e., all free variables in the formula F are universally quantified.

Definition. An *ok-instance* of a term is an instance where some variables are replaced by the constant *ok*. A *ground instance* is an instance where all the variables are replaced by constants.

Definition. A *diagnosis D* for $\langle SD, COMPS, OBS \rangle$ is an instance of *COMPS* such that $SD \models \forall m(D, OBS)$.

Definition. A *conflict C* for $\langle SD, COMPS, OBS \rangle$ is an *ok-instance* of *COMPS* such that $SD \models \forall \neg m(C, OBS)$.

This characterization of a diagnosis subsumes most of the previous ones. In the consistency-based approach (Reiter 1987) a diagnosis[2] is a set of abnormal ($\neq ok$) components such that *SD* and *OBS* are consistent with all other components being *ok*. De Kleer & Williams (1989) extended the definition to include a behavioral mode (state) for each component. In both cases a diagnosis is essentially a ground instance of *COMPS*. Poole (1989) observed that a diagnosis need not commit a state to each component when the state is 'don't care'. This led to the definition of a partial diagnosis (de Kleer *et al.*

---

[2]Reiter's definition of a diagnosis actually includes the minimality criterion and corresponds to our definition of a minimal diagnosis.

1990) which corresponds to a non-ground instance of *COMPS* but, on the other hand, does not include states of components. The definition of a conflict is standard, i.e., a set of components which cannot be simultaneously *ok*, and can be easily extended to a minimal conflict.

Apart from being simple, our definitions are also operational since diagnoses and conflicts can easily be computed by a logic programming system. The search for a logical consequence of *SD* is realized by the search for an answer substitution Θ such that $SD \cup \{\neg m(A\Theta,\ OBS)\}$ is unsatisfiable. We just have to make sure that A is an ok-instance of *COMPS*. If such a substitution exists we can conclude $D = A\Theta$ is a diagnosis. If not, and regarding *SD* as implicitly completed (Lloyd 1987), we can conclude that $C = A$ is a conflict. Like in consistency-based diagnosis, A can be interpreted as an assumption that some components are not abnormal, i.e., are *ok*.

Example. Take the two inverters example, the boolean specification of the fault models, and the observation $OBS = \langle 1,0 \rangle$. In the case of the strong fault model we get the following diagnosis:

$\leftarrow\ m(\ \langle I1,I2 \rangle,\ \langle 1,0 \rangle).$
$I1 = W$
$I2 = 1$

This means that $I2$ is certainly faulty, while $I1$ might or might not be *ok*. With the exoneration model we get:

$\leftarrow\ m(\ \langle I1,I2 \rangle,\ \langle 1,0 \rangle).$
$I1 = Y$
$I2 = 1 \oplus Y$

This is equivalent to $I1 = \neg I2$, i.e., either $I1$ or $I2$ is faulty, but not both. The weak fault model yields:

$\leftarrow\ m(\ \langle I1,I2 \rangle,\ \langle 1,0 \rangle).$
$I1 = Y \oplus Y \wedge W1 \oplus W1$
$I2 = 1 \oplus Y \oplus Y \wedge W2$

which is equivalent to $I1 \vee I2 = 1$. The observation can be explained by each individual inverter being faulty, or by both inverters being faulty. In such cases one seeks a parsimonious diagnosis, i.e., a *minimal* number of faulty components which are still consistent with observations.

In order to compute minimal diagnoses it is convenient to represent the search space of diagnoses and conflicts as a subset-superset lattice (de Kleer & Williams 1987). The top element of the lattice corresponds to a tuple where all components are $\neq ok$, and the bottom element to the tuple where all components are *ok*. Reiter's algorithm (1987), for example, searches the lattice bottom-up (from conflicts to diagnoses), in a breadth-first fashion (diagnoses of smaller cardinality are found first) and relies on the underlying ATMS-like theorem prover. In contrast, our algorithm (Mozetic & Holzbaur 1991b) better fits into the logic programming environment, and implements a top-down, depth-first search through the lattice. In diagnosing real systems, the search lattice is large and minimal diagnoses are usually near the bottom of the lattice. Depth-first search, coupled with non-ground model calls, allows for deep 'dives' into the lattice and in the average case at least a few diagnoses are found quickly. Further, by computing minimal diagnoses incrementaly, we can ensure that the worst case complexity of the algorithm remains polynomial.

4   Boolean domains — using CLP($\mathcal{B}$)

In this section we show how a richer computational domain than the Herbrand universe interacts with a model and the diagnostic algorithm. We stay in the context of logic programming but extend syntactic unification by solving equations over interpreted terms (Jaffar *et al.* 1986) — boolean expressions in this particular case. The resulting constraint logic programming language CLP($\mathcal{B}$) was realized in the general Metaprolog framework (Holzbaur 1990), where the implementation reduces to the *Prolog* formulation of a specialized unification algorithm. There exist several boolean unification algorithms (Crone-Rawe 1989). We chose the one published by (Büttner & Simonis 1987); the origin of the method goes back to (Boole 1947). The algorithm computes the *most general boolean ring unifier* θ of two terms t_1 and t_2. It operates on a deterministic disjunctive minimal normal form (Martin & Nipkov 1986) for terms in the boolean ring $\langle V, \oplus, \wedge, 0, 1\rangle$, i.e., all boolean functions are expressed in terms of $\oplus$ and $\wedge$.

Example.
$\neg X \rightarrow 1 \oplus X$
$X \vee Y \rightarrow X \oplus Y \oplus X \wedge Y$

The use of CLP($\mathcal{B}$) is limited to discrete devices which compute some boolean function. However, it allows for a compact representation of the search lattice, since a minimal diagnosis can be computed deterministically, without any backtracking.

Example (binary adder, Genesereth 1984, Figure 3). The top-level binary predicate m is *adder*, *COMPS* is a five-tuple $\langle X1, X2, A1, A2, O1\rangle$, *OBS* is a five-tuple $\langle A, B, C, D, E\rangle$, and *SD* consists of the following logic program:

$adder(\ \langle X1, X2, A1, A2, O1\rangle,\ \langle A, B, C,\ D, E\rangle)\ \leftarrow$
$\qquad xorg(\ X1,\ A,\ B,\ X\ ),$
$\qquad xorg(\ X2,\ C,\ X,\ D\ ),$
$\qquad andg(\ A1,\ A,\ B,\ Y\ ),$
$\qquad andg(\ A2,\ C,\ X,\ Z\ ),$
$\qquad org(\ O1,\ Y,\ Z,\ E\ ).$

$xorg(\ (X \oplus Y \oplus Z) \vee W,\ X,\ Y,\ Z\ ).$

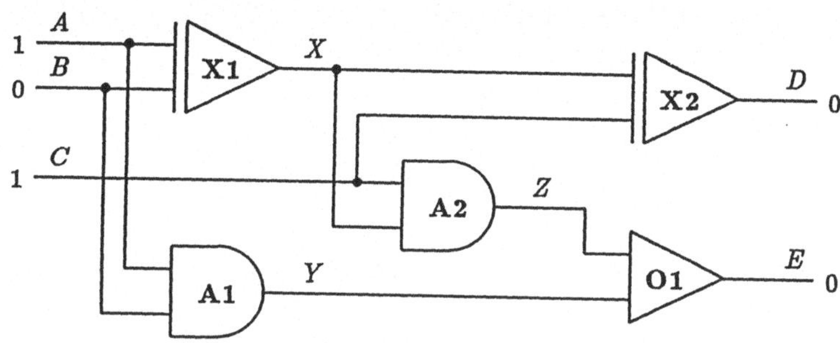

Figure 3: A binary adder consisting of two EXCLUSIVE-OR gates (X1, X2), two AND gates (A1, A2) and an OR gate (O1). The output $E = 0$ is faulty.

$andg(\ ((X \wedge Y) \oplus Z) \vee W, X, Y, Z\ ).$
$org(\ ((X \vee Y) \oplus Z) \vee W, X, Y, Z\ ).$

Given the observation $\langle 1,0,1,\ 0,0\rangle$ and the above weak fault model of the adder, CLP($\mathcal{B}$) returns the following answer substitutions which constitute a solved system of boolean equations in the normal form:

$\leftarrow\ adder(\ \langle X1,X2,A1,A2,O1\rangle,\ \langle 1,0,1,\ 0,0\rangle).$
$X1 = 1 \oplus X \oplus X\wedge W1$
$X2 = 1 \oplus X \oplus X\wedge W2$
$A1 = Y \oplus Y\wedge W3 \oplus W3$
$A2 = X \oplus X\wedge W4 \oplus Z \oplus Z\wedge W4 \oplus W4$
$O1 = Y \oplus Y\wedge Z \oplus Y\wedge Z\wedge W5 \oplus Y\wedge W5 \oplus Z \oplus Z\wedge W5 \oplus W5$

Note that this answer substitution captures *all* diagnoses, i.e., the whole lattice above the boundary between the diagnoses and conflicts. A minimal diagnosis is computed by setting a maximum number of state variables to *ok* (0).

Example. Assume that we already succeeded setting $X1, X2, A1$ to 0, which is logically equivalent to the model call:

$\leftarrow\ adder(\ \langle 0,0,0,A2,O1\rangle,\ \langle 1,0,1,\ 0,0\rangle).$
$A2 = 1 \oplus Z \oplus Z\wedge W4$
$O1 = Z \oplus Z\wedge W5 \oplus W5$

Next, $A2$ is set to 0, forcing Z to 1 and $O1$ to 1, thus yielding the first minimal singleton diagnosis $\langle 0,0,0,0,1\rangle$, i.e., the or gate $O1$ is faulty. An alternative diagnosis is computed from a disjoint label $\langle X1,X2,A1,A2,0\rangle$, which yields the second minimal diagnosis $\langle 0,0,0,1,0\rangle$. In both cases we know that the diagnoses are minimal — there is no need to even consider the label $\langle 0,0,0,0,0\rangle$.

After the discovery of the two single faults the label $\langle X1,X2,A1,0,0 \rangle$ leads to the model call with the following answer substitutions:

$\leftarrow$ adder($\langle X1,X2,A1,0,0 \rangle$, $\langle 1,0,1, 0,0 \rangle$).
$X1 = 1$
$X2 = 1$
$A1 = W3$

This corresponds to the minimal diagnosis $\langle 1,1,0,0,0 \rangle$ — no need to check $\langle 1,0,0,0,0 \rangle$ or $\langle 0,1,0,0,0 \rangle$. In addition, under the assumption that both $A2$ and $O1$ are *ok* we known that neither $X1$ nor $X2$ can possibly be *ok*. This yields the two conflicts $\langle X1,0,A1,0,0 \rangle$ and $\langle 0,X2,A1,0,0 \rangle$. Therefore, from three calls to the model we got the three minimal diagnoses and even the two conflicts, which in total covers the search lattice.

5 Real-valued domains — using CLP($\Re$)

There are domains where pure logic programs or ATMS-like systems have insufficient expressive power to reason about the system under consideration. In particular, modeling real-valued system parameters with tolerances requires some degree of numerical processing, and feedback loops in general cannot be resolved by local constraint propagation methods. Examples of such systems are analogue circuits, such as amplifiers or filters (Dague *et al.* 1990).

Here we illustrate the modeling of a simple amplifier (taken from Wakeling & McKeon 1989) by CLP($\Re$). The description of a transistor we use is from Heinze *et al.* (1987). We assume that any transistor or resistor in the circuit can be faulty.

Example (an amplifier, Wakeling & McKeon 1989, Figure 4). The top-level binary predicate m is *amplifier*, *COMPS* is an eleven-tuple $\langle Q1,Q2,Q3,R1,\ldots,R8 \rangle$, *OBS* is a four-tuple $\langle Vcc,Vee,Vin,Vout \rangle$, and *SD* consists of the following logic program:

```
amplifier( ⟨Q1,Q2,Q3,R1,R2,R3,R4,R5,R6,R7,R8⟩, ⟨Vcc,Vee,Vin,Vout⟩ )  ←
        transistor( npn, Q1, V1, V3, V2, Ib1, Ic1, Ie1 ),
        transistor( npn, Q2, V6, V4, V2, Ib2, Ic2, Ie2 ),
        transistor( pnp, Q3, V4, Vout, V5, Ib3, Ic3, Ie3 ),
        resistor( R1, 10000, Vin, V1, I1 ),
        resistor( R2, 10000, Vout, V1, I2 ),
        resistor( R3, 6800, Vcc, V3, Ic1 ),
        resistor( R4, 6800, Vcc, V4, I4 ),
        resistor( R5, 560, Vcc, V5, Ie3 ),
        resistor( R6, 560, 0, V6, Ib2 ),
        resistor( R7, 15000, V2, Vee, I7 ),
        resistor( R8, 3300, Vout, Vee, I8 ),
```

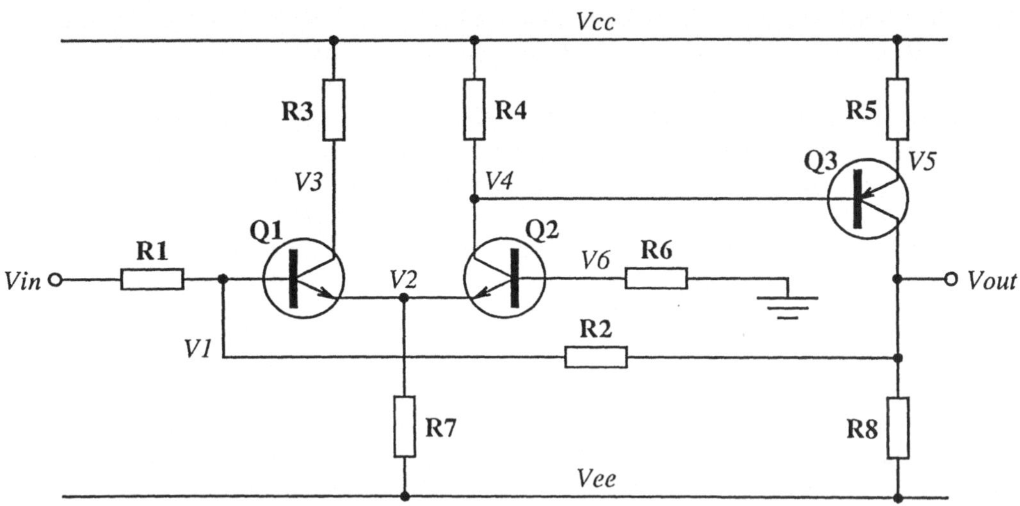

Figure 4: An amplifier consisting of transistors (Q1, Q2, Q3) and resistors (R1, ..., R8).

$$Ib1 = I1 + I2, \quad I7 = Ie1 + Ie2, \quad Ic2 = I4 + Ib3, \quad Ic3 = I2 + I8.$$

resistor(ok, R, V1, V2, I) ← *V1−V2=I*R.*
resistor(ab, _, _, _, _).

transistor(npn, cutoff, Vb, Vc, Ve, Ib, Ic, Ie) ←
    Vb< Ve+0.7, Ib=0, Ic=0, Ie=0.
transistor(npn, active, Vb, Vc, Ve, Ib, Ic, Ie) ←
    *Vb=Ve+0.7, Vc≥Vb, Ib≥0, Ic=100*Ib, Ie=Ic+Ib.*
transistor(npn, saturated, Vb, Vc, Ve, Ib, Ic, Ie) ←
    Vb=Ve+0.7, Vc=Ve+0.3, Ib≥0, Ic≥0, Ie=Ic+Ib.
transistor(_, ab, _, _, _, _, _, _).

In CLP($\Re$) linear equations are kept in *solved form*. Variables appearing in the equations are split into two disjoint sets: *dependent* variables and *independent* variables. Dependent variables are expressed through terms containing independent variables. When a new equation is to be combined with a system of equations in solved form, all its dependent variables are replaced by their definitions which results in an expression over independent variables. An independent variable is selected then, and the expression is solved for it. After the resulting definition has been back-substituted into the equation system, the isolated variable can be added as a new dependent variable, and the equation system is in solved form again. Inequalities are expressed in terms of independent variables.

One traditional method for deciding linear inequalities is the simplex method. The simplex method works by turning inequalities into equations through the introduction of so-called 'slack variables'. This leads to a 'contamination' of the equation system with artificial variables from the user's point of view In our experience, the amount of code that is needed to compute a human readable form of the (in)equation system is unproportionally high in comparison to the code that does the actual job. Therefore, we rather selected the Shostak's 'Loop Residue' method (Shostak 1981). Besides being better suited for small inequalities, this method operates with a 'direct' representation of inequalities. For each set of inequalities a graph is constructed whose vertices correspond to the variables and edges to the inequalities. Kraemer (1989) proves the equivalence between a satisfiable set of inequalities and the corresponding closed graph without any infeasible loop.

Our Metaprolog implementation of CLP($\Re$) is preferred over other existing implementations of CLP($\Re$) (Heintze *et al.* 1987, Jaffar 1990) since it allows for the simultaneous use of solvers for different domains in a consistent framework. In this respect Metaprolog is very well suited for the computational demands that arise in the context of hierarchical abstractions (Mozetic 1990, Mozetic & Holzbaur 1991a). The numerical level of the model can be formulated with CLP($\Re$) for example, and successive qualitative abstractions thereof typically utilize constraint propagation over finite domains where forward checking or CLP($\mathcal{B}$) can be used.

6   Conclusion

The paper outlines the potential applicability of Constraint Logic Programs to model-based diagnosis. For the CLP($\mathcal{B}$) case we show how the diagnostic algorithm can actively benefit from an increased expressiveness in the language. Another solver, CLP($\Re$), is able to solve systems of simultaneous linear equations over $\Re$eals. This is beyond the capabilities of the local constraint propagation methods used by de Kleer & Williams (1987). In our framework the simultaneous application of several specific solvers is truly operational due to their realization in the uniform Constraint Logic Programming scheme.

Acknowledgements

This work was supported by the Austrian Federal Ministry of Science and Research. Thanks to Robert Trappl for creating an enjoyable working environment.

References

Boole, G. (1947). *The Mathematical Analysis of Logic.* Macmillan.

Büttner, W., Simonis, H. (1987). Embedding Boolean expressions into logic programming.

Journal of Symbolic Computation 4, pp. 191-205.

Cohen, J. (1990). Constraint logic programming languages. *Communications of the ACM 33 (7)*, pp. 52-68.

Crone-Rawe, B. (1989) Unification algorithms for boolean rings. SEKI Working Paper SWP-89-01, University of Kaiserslautern, Germany.

Dague, P., Deves, P., Luciani, P., Taillibert, P. (1990). Analog systems diagnosis. *Proc. 9th ECAI*, pp. 173-178, Stockholm.

Davis, R. (1984). Diagnostic reasoning based on structure and behaviour. *Artificial Intelligence 24*, pp. 347-410.

de Kleer, J., Mackworth, A.K., Reiter, R. (1990). Characterizing diagnoses. *Proc. 8th AAAI*, pp. 324-330, Boston, MIT Press.

de Kleer, J., Williams, B.C. (1987). Diagnosing multiple faults. *Artificial Intelligence 32*, pp. 97-130.

de Kleer, J., Williams, B.C. (1989). Diagnosis with behavioral modes. *Proc. 11th IJCAI*, pp. 1324-1330, Detroit, Morgan Kaufmann.

de Kleer, J., Williams, B.C. (1990). Focusing the diagnosis engine. Unpublished draft, presented at the *First Intl. Workshop on Principles of Diagnosis*, Stanford University.

Friedrich, G., Gottlob, G., Nejdl, W. (1990). Hypothesis classification, abductive diagnosis and therapy. *Proc. First Intl. Workshop on Principles of Diagnosis*, pp. 124-128, Stanford University.

Gallanti, M., Roncato, M., Stefanini, A., Tornielli, G. (1989). A diagnostic algorithm based on models at different level of abstraction. *Proc. 11th IJCAI*, pp. 1350-1355, Detroit, Morgan Kaufmann.

Genesereth, M.R. (1984). The use of design descriptions in automated diagnosis. *Artificial Intelligence 24*, pp. 411-436.

Heintze, N., Jaffar, J., Michaylov, S., Stuckey, P., Yap, R. (1987). The CLP($\Re$) programmer's manual. Dept. of Computer Science, Monash University, Australia.

Heintze, N., Michaylov, S., Stuckey, P. (1987). CLP($\Re$) and some electrical engineering problems. *Proc. 4th Intl. Conference on Logic Programming*, pp. 675-703, Melbourne, Australia, The MIT Press.

Holzbaur, C. (1990). Specification of constraint based inference mechanisms through extended unification. Ph.D. Thesis, Vienna University of Technology, Austria.

Jaffar, J. (1990). CLP($\Re$) version 1.0 reference manual. IBM Research Division, T.J. Watson Research Center, Yorktown Heights, NY.

Jaffar, J., Lassez, J.-L., Mahler, J. (1986). A logic programming language scheme. In D. de Groot, G. Linstrom (eds.), *Logic Programming: Functions, Relations, and Equations*, Prentice-Hall, Englewood Cliffs, NJ.

Kraemer, F.-J. (1989). A decision procedure for Presburger arithmetic with functions and equality. SEKI working paper SWP-89-4, FB Informatik, University of Kaiserslautern, Germany.

Lloyd, J.W. (1987). *Foundations of Logic Programming* (Second edition). Springer-Verlag, Berlin.

Martin, U., Nipkov, T. (1986). Unification in boolean rings. *Proc. 8th Intl. Conference on Automated Deduction*, pp. 506-513.

Mozetic, I. (1990). Reduction of diagnostic complexity through model abstractions. Report TR-90-10, Austrian Research Institute for Artificial Intelligence, Vienna. *Proc. First Intl. Workshop on Principles of Diagnosis*, pp. 102-111, Stanford University, Palo Alto.

Mozetic, I., Holzbaur, C. (1991a). Integrating qualitative and numerical models within Constraint Logic Programming. Report TR-91-2, Austrian Research Institute for Artificial Intelligence, Vienna, Austria. *Proc. 1st European Workshop on Qualitative Reasoning about Physical Systems*, Genova, Italy.

Mozetic, I., Holzbaur, C. (1991b). Controlling the complexity in model-based diagnosis. Report TR-91-3, Austrian Research Institute for Artificial Intelligence, Vienna, Austria.

Poole, D. (1989). Normality and faults in logic-based diagnosis. *Proc. 11th IJCAI*, pp. 1304-1310, Detroit, Morgan Kaufmann.

Raiman, O. (1989). Diagnosis as a trial: the alibi principle. IBM Scientific Center, Paris.

Reiter, R. (1987). A theory of diagnosis from first principles. *Artificial Intelligence 32*, pp. 57-95.

Shostak, R. (1981). Deciding linear inequalities by computing loop residues. *Journal of the ACM 28 (4)*, pp. 769-779.

Struss, P., Dressler, O., (1989). "Physical negation" — integrating fault models into the general diagnostic engine. *Proc. 11th IJCAI*, pp. 1318-1323, Detroit, Morgan Kaufmann.

Wakeling, A., McKeon A. (1989). On automatic fault finding in analogue circuits. *Electronic Engineering*, pp. 95-101, Nov. 1989.

Band 240: D. Tavangarian, Flagorientierte Assoziativspeicher und -prozessoren. XII. 193 Seiten. 1990.

Band 241: A. Schill, Migrationssteuerung und Konfigurationsverwaltung für verteilte objektorientierte Anwendungen. IX, 174 Seiten. 1990.

Band 242: D. Wybranietz, Multicast-Kommunikation in verteilten Systemen. VIII, 191 Seiten. 1990.

Band 243: U. Hahn, Lexikalisch verteiltes Text-Parsing. X, 263 Seiten. 1990.

Band 244: B. R. Kämmerer, Sprecherunabhängigkeit und Sprecheradaption. VIII, 110 Seiten. 1990.

Band 245: C. Freksa, C. Habel (Hrsg.), Repräsentation und Verarbeitung räumlichen Wissens. VIII, 353 Seiten. 1990.

Band 246: Th. Bräunl, Massiv parallele Programmierung mit dem Parallaxis–Modell. XII, 168 Seiten. 1990

Band 247: H. Krumm, Funktionelle Analyse von Kommunikationsprotokollen. IX, 122 Seiten. 1990.

Band 248: G. Moerkotte, Inkonsistenzen in deduktiven Datenbanken. VIII, 141 Seiten. 1990.

Band 249: P. A. Gloor, N. A. Streitz (Hrsg.), Hypertext und Hypermedia. IX, 302 Seiten. 1990.

Band 250: H. W. Meuer (Hrsg.), SUPERCOMPUTER '90. Mannheim, Juni 1990. Proceedings. VIII, 209 Seiten. 1990.

Band 251: H. Marburger (Hrsg.), GWAI-90. 14th German Workshop on Artificial Intelligence. Eringerfeld, September 1990. Proceedings. X, 333 Seiten. 1990.

Band 252: G. Dorffner (Hrsg.), Konnektionismus in Artificial Intelligence und Kognitionsforschung. 6. Österreichische Artificial-Intelligence-Tagung (KONNAI), Salzburg, September 1990. Proceedings. VIII, 246 Seiten. 1990.

Band 253: W. Ameling (Hrsg.), ASST '90. 7. Aachener Symposium für Signaltheorie. Aachen, September 1990. Proceedings. XI, 332 Seiten. 1990.

Band 254: R. E. Großkopf (Hrsg.), Mustererkennung 1990. 12. DAGM-Symposium, Oberkochen-Aalen, September 1990. Proceedings. XXI, 686 Seiten. 1990.

Band 255: B. Reusch, (Hrsg.), Rechnergestützter Entwurf und Architektur mikroelektronischer Systeme. GME/GI/ITG-Fachtagung, Dortmund, Oktober 1990. Proceedings. X, 298 Seiten. 1990.

Band 256: W. Pillmann, A. Jaeschke (Hrsg.), Informatik für den Umweltschutz. 5. Symposium, Wien, September 1990. Proceedings. XV, 864 Seiten. 1990.

Band 257: A. Reuter (Hrsg.), GI–20. Jahrestagung I. Stuttgart, Oktober 1990. Proceedings. XVIII, 602 Seiten. 1990.

Band 258: A. Reuter (Hrsg.), GI–20. Jahrestagung II. Stuttgart, Oktober 1990. Proceedings. XVIII, 602 Seiten. 1990.

Band 259: H.-J. Friemel, G. Müller-Schönberger, A. Schütt (Hrsg.), Forum '90 Wissenschaft und Technik. Trier, Oktober 1990. Proceedings. XI, 532 Seiten. 1990.

Band 260: B. J. Frommherz, Ein Roboteraktionsplanungssystem. XI, 134 Seiten. 1990.

Band 261: W. Zimmermann, Automatische Komplexitätsanalyse funktionaler Programme. VII, 194 Seiten. 1990.

Band 262: W. Gerth, P. Baacke (Hrsg.), PEARL 90 - Workshop über Realzeitsysteme. 11. Fachtagung, Boppard, November 1990. Proceedings. X, 187 Seiten. 1990.

Band 263: H. Eckhardt, Entwurfstransaktionen für modulare Objektsysteme. VIII, 144 Seiten. 1990.

Band 264: T. Härder, H. Wedekind, G. Zimmermann (Hrsg.), Entwurf und Betrieb verteilter Systeme. Fachtagung, Dagstuhl, September 1990. Proceedings. XII, 283 Seiten. 1990.

Band 265: U. Herrmann, Mehrbenutzerkontrolle in Nicht-Standard-Datenbanksystemen. VIII, 183 Seiten. 1991.

Band 266: R. Cunis, A. Günter, H. Strecker (Hrsg.), Das PLAKON-Buch. VIII, 279 Seiten. 1991

Band 267: W. Effelsberg, H. W. Meuer, G. Müller (Hrsg.), Kommunikation in verteilten Systemen. GI/ITG-Fachtagung, Mannheim, Februar 1991. Proceedings. X, 589 Seiten. 1991.

Band 268: J. Raczkowsky, Multisensordatenverarbeitung in der Robotik. X, 168 Seiten. 1991.

Band 269: G. Hommel (Hrsg.), Prozeßrechensysteme '91. Berlin, Februar 1991. Proceedings. XIV, 449 Seiten. 1991.

Band 270: H.-J. Appelrath (Hrsg.), Datenbanksysteme in Büro, Technik und Wissenschaft. GI-Fachtagung, Kaiserslautern, März 1991. Proceedings. XIII, 507 Seiten. 1991.

Band 271: A. Pfitzmann, E. Raubold (Hrsg.), VIS '91, Verläßliche Informationssysteme. GI-Fachtagung, Darmstadt, März 1991. Proceedings. VIII, 355 Seiten. 1991.

Band 272: R. Grebe, C. Ziemann, Parallele Datenverarbeitung mit dem Transputer. Aachen, September 1990. Proceedings. X, 300 Seiten 1991.

Band 273: M. Timm (Hrsg.), Requirements Engineering '91. VIII, 208 Seiten. 1991.

Band 274: R. Denzer, H. Hagen, K.-H. Kutschke (Hrsg.), Visualisierung von Umweltdaten. Workshop, Rostock, November 1990. Proceedings. VII, 97 Seiten. 1991.

Band 276: H. Maurer (Hrsg.), Hypertext / Hypermedia '91. Tagung der GI, SI und OCG, Graz, Mai 1991. Proceedings. VIII, 299 Seiten. 1991.

Band 277: U. Borgolte, Flexible, realzeitfähige Kollisionsvermeidung in Mehrroboter-Systemen. XIII, 105 Seiten. 1991.

Band 278: H. W. Meuer (Hrsg.), SUPERCOMPUTER '91. Proceedings. VIII, 266 Seiten. 1991.

Band 279: G. Schwichtenberg (Hrsg.), Organisation und Betrieb von Informationssystemen. 9. GI — Fachgespräch über Rechenzentren, Dortmund, März 1991. Proceedings. IX, 337 Seiten. 1991.

Band 280: B. Westfechtel, Revisions- und Konsistenzkontrolle in einer integrierten Softwareentwicklungsumgebung. X, 321 Seiten. 1991.

Band 281: W. Emde, Modellbildung, Wissensrevision und Wissensrepräsentation im Maschinellen Lernen. XI, 204 Seiten. 1991.

Band 282: P. Buchholz, Die strukturierte Analyse Markovscher Modelle. VII, 192 Seiten 1991.

Band 283: M. Dal Cin, W. Hohl (Hrsg.), Fault-Tolerant Computing Systems. 5th International GI/ITG/GMA Conference, Nürnberg, September 1991. Proceedings. XII, 425 Seiten. 1991.

Band 284: R. Stadler, Ausführbare Spezifikation von Directory-Systemen in einer logischen Sprache. X, 142 Seiten. 1991.

Band 285: T. Christaller (Hrsg.), GWAI-91. 15. Fachtagung für Künstliche Intelligenz, Bonn, September 1991. IX, 273 Seiten. 1991.

Band 286: A. Lehmann, F. Lehmann (Hrsg.), Messung, Modellierung und Bewertung von Rechensystemen. 6. GI/ITG-Fachtagung, Neubiberg, September 1991. Proceedings. VIII, 338 Seiten. 1991.

Band 287: H. Kaindl (Hrsg.), 7. Österreichische Artificial-Intelligence-Tagung, Wien, September 1991. Proceedings. VIII, 180 Seiten. 1991.